A WANT OF INHABITANTS

First published by Eastwood Books, 2021
Dublin, Ireland
www.eastwoodbooks.com
@eastwoodbooks
First Edition

Eastwood Books is an imprint of The Wordwell Group

Eastwood Books
The Wordwell Group
Unit 9, 78 Furze Road
Sandyford
Dublin, Ireland

© Geraldine Powell, 2021

ISBN:978-1-8380416-4-9 (Paperback)
ISBN: 978-1-913934-09-5 (mobi)
ISBN 978-1-913934-10-1 (epub)

The right of Geraldine Powell to be identified as the author of this work has been asserted in accordance with the Copyright and Related Rights Act, 2000. All rights reserved. No part of this book may be reprinted or reproduced or utilised in any form or by any electronic, mechanical or other means, now known or hereafter invented, including photocopying and recording, or in any information storage or retrieval system, without the permission in writing of the publishers.

British Library Cataloguing in Publication Data.
A catalogue record for this book is available from the British Library.

A WANT OF INHABITANTS

The Famine in Bantry Union

GERALDINE POWELL

Eastwood

CONTENTS

Acknowledgements	vii
Abbreviations	ix
Notes on currency and measurement	xi
Introduction	xiii
1. Setting the scene	1
2. Evolution of a crisis, 1843–46	27
3. Death by mismanagement, 1846–47	59
4. Battling for survival, 1847–48	89
5. From bad to worse, 1848–49	121
Conclusion	155
Appendices	165
Bibliography	183
Endnotes	201

DEDICATION

To the people of Bantry,
those who died,
those who survived
and those who emigrated.

ACKNOWLEDGEMENTS

I would like to acknowledge the generous help of the staff of the following: The Boole Library (UCC), especially the staff in Special Collections; Steven Skeldon and Brian McGee of Cork City and County Archives; Kieran Wyse of the Cork County Library; Noel O'Mahony and the other staff in the Bantry County Library; the History Department of UCC; the National Archives of Ireland; the National Library of Ireland; and the Royal Irish Academy.

I want to thank the following people individually: Mary Lombard of Special Collections in UCC, who took me under her wing and smoothed the way for me; Pat Crowley, an inimitable collector of West Cork and Durrus local history; Professor Cormac Ó Gráda, who selflessly read and critiqued my work; Katie Cuddihy, who read and reread my words, insisting on clarity; John Murphy, for encouragement and many loaned journals and books in the long winter months; Hazel Vickery, for showing me local landmarks and organising visits to private sites; Colum Hourihane (and his brother Kevin), for interesting analysis and bearing with my many questions; Richard Harrison, for meeting me for coffee in Cork city to discuss his years of writing and research on local history in West Cork; Frank O'Mahony (now deceased), who lit a fire for me in his library and let me loose in it; Noel McCarthy of Kilcrohane, the late Jim Daly of Knockroe and Jerry O'Mahony of Ahakista;

Jane Chambers, for her quiet, insightful remarks; Liz McManus, for photographing the plan of the fever hospital; and my husband, Kim Masters, for his unfailing support.

Thank you for the myriad of ways in which you all, and others not individually mentioned, gave me encouragement and advice.

ABBREVIATIONS

British Relief Association   BRA

Justice of the Peace   JP

Office of Public Works   OPW

Ordnance Survey   OS

Poor Law Commissioners   PLC

Royal Navy   RN

NOTES ON CURRENCY AND MEASUREMENT

Money: £50 in 1845 is equivalent to a relative value today of £4,983 but an income value today of £61,420 (the initial salary for a workhouse doctor).

Weight: 7lb of meal is equivalent to about 3.2kg (the weekly ration for one person for outdoor relief in early 1849).

Volume: 180 imperial gallons equals about 818 litres (a rough capacity of bigger soup pots). 8 imperial fluid ounces equals about 0.237 litres (one helping of soup).

Length: 1 Irish mile equalled about 1.27 statute miles.

INTRODUCTION

The little poverty-stricken town nestling between the sides of a valley of unsurpassable grandeur [...] the princely mansion of Lord Berehaven; the Abbey filled with the dead [...] the exquisite bay with its deep green emerald waters.

Limerick and Clare Examiner, 12 June 1847

In this idyllic setting in Bantry Union (created under the Poor Relief [Ireland] Act, 1838) thousands of destitute inhabitants starved to death in the 1840s. Little is known about the famine in the union and how the tragedy unfolded. Many people living in West Cork today think the ravages were less severe in Bantry than in neighbouring Skibbereen Union. Not even the geographical extent of the union is clearly known because of confusion between the boundary declared in 1840 and the later boundary established in 1849.

Instead of individual famine memories, one anecdote was retold so often to this author that it seemed to represent a collective community memory.[1] It concerned a kind family who regularly supplied milk to starving neighbours until the day none of the family were left alive to retrieve the jug. This story might be a 'screen memory' for the famine years – a relatively harmless memory that masks a more traumatic one.

A WANT OF INHABITANTS: THE FAMINE IN BANTRY UNION

Local people varied in their responses when I enquired about stories passed down by word of mouth in their families. Most denied knowing anything about the famine. Several minimised the disaster, saying it had been more severe in other areas. A few pointed out ruins of famine houses. A few were aware of some soup kitchens and of some outdoor relief locations, but many of these remained unclear. A few random and relevant comments are noted in the text. One person wondered if a type of survivor guilt was responsible for the silence from the past.[2] A story that Bantry had refused to sell fish to Skibbereen during the famine could not be verified. No one responded to an advertisement I placed in a West Cork newspaper seeking missing Bantry workhouse minutes. A local postman told me, 'Don't bother asking. It's a closed shop.'

It was difficult to reconcile this lack of knowledge with the enormity of the devastating loss of life revealed in the 1851 census results. Why had Bantry not embraced its history as Skibbereen had done with its heritage centre and numerous publications? Even at the time of the famine in West Cork, the flood of information focused on Skibbereen and the Mizen peninsula. That flood stopped at Caheragh, on the Skibbereen to Bantry road, the site of the well-known sketch in *The Illustrated London News* of a starving boy and girl scrounging for potatoes.[3] The same magazine produced no drawings of emaciated people in Bantry Union. This helped to perpetuate the myth that the famine there was less severe.

Preliminary reading on the famine in Bantry Union in the few available texts revealed a confusing and fragmentary narrative.[4] By chance, my interest was sparked by a randomly discovered newspaper clipping detailing an instance of callous neglect in 1847 Bantry. The piece involved a gentleman in a position of trust; he was charged with such indifference to the welfare of the poor that the newspaper accused him of murder. This discovery intensified my resolve to break through the fog that had settled over the past. I began to see the task

INTRODUCTION

ahead in terms of finding out who had been in charge and what they had done. I hoped that I could identify the real people who managed the union in the 1840s. I wondered about their personalities and whether any of them had stood out in any way.

As a research stratagem, I made a list of areas to investigate: the extent and boundaries of the union; the economic and physical aspects of the union; the figures in authority; the Poor Law Act and the issues of ratepayers and the poor rate; the dates of the building and occupation of the workhouse; the workhouse Board of Guardians; their replacement by vice-guardians; the soup kitchens; the clergy; and the extent of outdoor relief in the union. The answers, it turned out, were waiting to be uncovered in the newspaper and manuscript archives of the period.

As material began to accrue, it became obvious that certain sections of the population were underrepresented. Of the almost 50,000 poor people in the union, only a few were quoted verbatim. Since a majority of those most vulnerable in the union were illiterate and did not speak English fluently, there is frustratingly little record of them. We are left to rely on remarks about them from witnesses among landlords, foreign travellers and the clergy. In some other unions, letters from emigrants during and after the famine give more information, but almost none were found from Bantry Union emigrants.

The actions of groups of the poor were noted occasionally in contemporary records but often only when their intentions were seen as hostile. Some of the traders who supplied the workhouse were named, but seldom was there any comment on their attitudes or even their existence except when they sued the guardians for non-payment or they themselves became pauperised. The other large underrepresented group was the middling-to-better-off farmers. They were almost absent on the Beara peninsula, but on Sheep's Head they did exist, and some survived, as evidenced by the Durrus rent rolls immediately after the famine.[5] They must have kept a low profile, as they were not mentioned in the newspapers of the time except when some were reported to be emigrating and deserting their lands. There may still be letters in existence that remain to be discovered. These could provide additional information.

On the other hand, primary sources do provide information about the workhouse guardians; the large landowners and magistrates; government officials, who came from Dublin and the Office of Public Works (OPW); and army and navy officers. A small collection of private correspondence was also discovered that threw additional light on some important and not-so-important personages in the union.

In his book *Writing the Irish Famine*, Professor Christopher Morash said that 'like all past events, the Famine is primarily a retrospective textual creation', meaning, I believe, that people during the famine years were not aware they were living through the period known later as the Great Irish Famine.[6] In Bantry Union an acute consciousness existed of the disaster. Virtually all the material in this narrative is drawn from contemporary newspapers and manuscripts, from which it is clear that people knew they were living in extraordinary times.

It is hoped that this narrative succeeds in recreating the reality of the 1840s. That reality, from the perspective of a survivor in the decade from 1845 to 1855, was of tortuous worry. No one knew if shortages would end or if worse was yet to come. There was no reason for anyone in Bantry Union to believe that things would normalise in a few years. This insecurity must have informed much of their thinking, both at the time and for years after the worst was over. It must be taken into account when evaluating their actions.

Some famine histories revolve around the 'Big House', with its estate and tenants. This account does not. The owners of the 'Big House' in Bantry played a minor role during the famine, despite the fact that the Earl of Bantry and his son Viscount Berehaven held and controlled most of the town of Bantry, along with large estates on the Beara peninsula.

INTRODUCTION

One of the challenges in writing this narrative lay in maintaining a balance between local events and the outside world of Dublin Castle and Westminster, not to mention being aware of upheavals and agitation occurring in other unions, the turmoil surrounding Repeal (of the 1800 Act of Union) and the Young Irelanders, and the excitement of local investment in the railways. These external factors are considered as they relate to the conditions of Bantry Union during the period of this narrative.

Besides general famine literature, and in particular those accounts dealing with the south of Ireland and West Cork, many local histories of the famine in different unions were examined in order to develop a sense of perspective and an appreciation of how different approaches can influence a reader's experience. It became apparent that a chronological analysis would provide a more global perspective than a thematic one and a clearer exposition of a complex topic.

One might ask, what is the point in writing yet another famine history? We know what happened. There was no happy ending. To misquote Tolstoy: while effective organisations share key features in common, dysfunctional ones are defective each in their own way.[7] It is important to probe the factors that led to Bantry Union's careening ride off the cliff edge in the 1840s. If we can see what led to disaster, maybe we can to some extent prevent a similar outcome in the future.

The purpose of this history is to bring to life the famine years in Bantry Union and, as far as possible, to reconstruct the situation where a few people held the power of life and death over the many. It is an attempt to resurrect a story that has been forgotten and misperceived.

1.
SETTING THE SCENE

A PLAN TO MANAGE POVERTY IN IRELAND

To grasp what happened in Bantry Union during the 1840s, one needs to be aware of how in the previous decade the government in Westminster drew up and implemented a nationwide plan to deal with poverty in Ireland. As the limits of Ireland's voluntary system of care (charitable organisations)[8] became apparent, a royal commission was launched to investigate and make recommendations on improving conditions for the Irish poor. Richard Whately, the Church of Ireland Archbishop of Dublin and a supporter of both Catholic and Jewish emancipation, was chairman. He published reports between 1835 and 1836 stating that the English Poor Law and workhouse system would be too expensive and impracticable for Ireland. Among other suggestions, he recommended a plan of economic growth for the country. His commission reported the Irish as eager for work but found that employment was unavailable. Such a glut of Irish labourers existed that the average Irish agricultural worker earned only 2s–2s 6d per week compared with 8s–10s per week for the English equivalent.[9]

Whately's plan involving investment in Ireland was anathema to the Westminster politicians of the day, all of whom, whether adhering to ideas of utilitarianism, laissez-faire policies or individualism, opposed what they regarded as public charity on economic and moral grounds. In 1836 the Whig government under Lord Melbourne, with a slim majority in parliament, exhibited no interest in pursuing it. Instead, they looked to the English system, where if poor people were unable to find work, their only recourse was the workhouse. As a deterrent to the 'idle', the living conditions of these workhouses were ordered to be made worse than those of the poorest paid worker outside.

In 1836, George Nicholls, a Cornishman who had given advice on workhouses to the first (English) Poor Law Commissioners, was sent by the government on a six-week tour around Ireland in order to develop reports more congruent with their thinking. Nicholls stated that workhouse space would be needed for only 80,000 people instead of the two million that Whately had predicted. He did mention that 'the occurrence of a famine, if general, seems to be a contingency altogether above the powers of a Poor Law to provide for.'[10] The Nicholls reports became the rationale for the introduction of the Poor Law to Ireland.

The Irish clergy was generally in favour of the Poor Law, but opposition was expressed in parliament by Daniel O'Connell, who said in 1838, 'I totally disapprove of this Bill the object of which is to erect a hundred workhouses, in which 80,000 persons are to be boxed-up and imprisoned for the benefit of their health and the improvement of their morals.'[11] He also accurately foretold that Ireland was 'too poor to support able-bodied relief' – in other words, relief for able workers who could not find employment.[12]

From a modern perspective, one expert identified a main target of the Irish Poor Law as the absentee and neglectful landlord: by forcing landlords to carry the burden of the poor, the result would be the growing social equality of the peasant class.[13] However, most writers today are sceptical about any idealistic intent of the Poor Law.[14]

The Poor Law Act for Ireland was passed in 1838.[15] Its essential points were as follows:

- Ireland would be divided into unions, each of which was to have a workhouse for paupers.

- The unions would be divided into electoral divisions for the purpose of paying poor rates and electing a board of guardians.

- The guardians would levy compulsory poor rates on the ratepayers of each division to finance the building of the workhouses and the administration of the Poor Law.

- The guardians would be answerable to the Poor Law Commissioners (PLC) in Dublin.

- Relief would be granted only to those accommodated in the workhouse (indoor relief). No relief was to be given to people living outside the workhouse (outdoor relief).

Besides the Poor Law Act, a commission was set up in 1843 by Prime Minister Sir Robert Peel to investigate unfair land leasing practices in Ireland. This represented a positive step but was not in time to mitigate the famine. It was informally known as the Devon Commission. Testimony relevant to conditions in Bantry Union was given to this commission in 1844 and was helpful in clarifying some aspects of conditions in the pre-famine period.[16]

FORMING THE BANTRY POOR LAW UNION

A critical first meeting to begin the process of implementing the new Poor Law took place in Bantry courthouse on 6 September 1839, when the PLC in Dublin Castle sent their representative, Assistant Poor

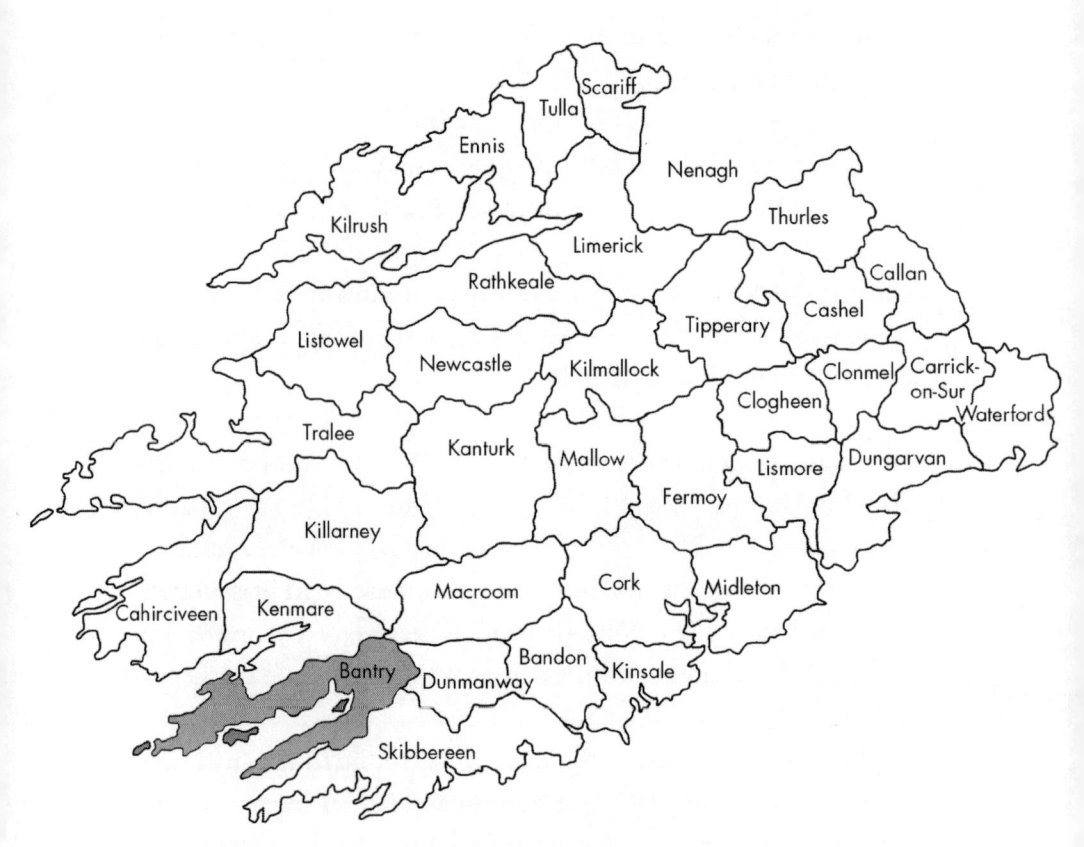

Fig. 1. Munster Poor Law unions, 1842–49 (Bantry Union filled in black). Map reproduced courtesy Trinity College Dublin.

SETTING THE SCENE

Law Commissioner William Voules, to the town. As the newspapers of the day reported, Lord Richard Viscount Berehaven was 'called to the chair'. His father, Lord Bantry, at that time was in his early seventies and in the process of retiring from public life to his lodge in Glengarriff. It therefore fell to Viscount Berehaven, as the 'nobleman' in Bantry House, to chair this important meeting. Lord Berehaven was 39 years old and possessed substantial wealth through his wife, whom he had married three years earlier. He did not speak Irish and did not have the close relationship with the estate tenants that his Irish-speaking father, the first earl, enjoyed. The newspapers did not report on how he travelled the three-quarter-mile distance from Bantry House to the courthouse. It seems unlikely that he walked, because of the town's ill-reputed muddy streets. He probably went on horseback but may have taken his carriage because of the importance of the occasion.

Those listed in attendance at the meeting were local gentry, landlords, clergy and a few prosperous merchants. One can imagine the scene: groups of dignitaries of different denominations and social class waiting, perhaps apprehensively, perhaps complacently. They may have formed in small like-minded clusters both inside and outside the stone courthouse, from whose doors they could see far out over Bantry Bay. The start of the meeting was delayed because Voules arrived late, but just before 1.30 p.m. these local luminaries filed into the dim courthouse to interact directly with a Poor Law commissioner for the first time.

The meeting was cordial and ran smoothly. Viscount Berehaven introduced Commissioner Voules, who explained the process of forming Bantry Union and dividing it into electoral divisions. He clarified how the ratepayers would tax themselves to relieve the poor and maintain a workhouse by paying poor rates into a union fund. A first experience of coerced charity in Bantry, it would force an amalgamation of 'wild' settlements on the Beara and Sheep's Head peninsulas under a town-based authority. This would require Catholics and Protestants to make common cause in administering the new system. Such co-operation would clearly demand extraordinary change, but newspaper reports convey the impression that good manners were prioritised over common-sense queries. Voules responded to only two complaints, one from a Mr Richard Young (a fish merchant) and one from Rev. Henry Sadleir (the Rector of Bantry in 1839), both about the amount of poor land in the union. Rev. Sadleir added that 'some fertile portions [of land] ought to have been attached to Bantry instead of having nineteen wealthy parishes in Skibbereen Union.' Nobody else added their support to these challenges.

Voules said he had 'struck out the Union as best he could [...] any inequities could be remedied in the future.' He described the structure of the Board of Guardians of the union: two-thirds to be elected by ratepayers and one-third appointed *ex-officio* members (e.g. local magistrates). The meeting provoked no questions about the criteria for measuring the success of the Poor Law or the collection of rates, or how to deal with difficulties in collection. This omission, stemming perhaps from intimidation, ignorance or lack of concern, was an opportunity missed, because at that point the Poor Law Commission in Dublin was still at a formative stage. More capable local officials might have negotiated concessions for Bantry. It is of particular interest that neither Viscount Berehaven nor Timothy O'Donovan, a prominent Catholic magistrate, made any significant points.

At the same meeting, the boundaries of the electoral divisions were agreed upon. However, it was not until September 1840 that Bantry Union was officially declared and divided into nine electoral divisions (Fig. 2).[17]

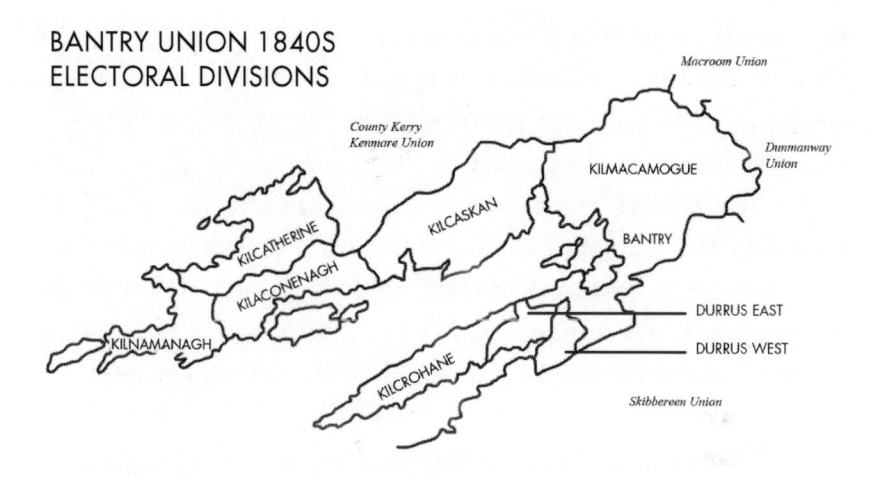

Fig. 2. Map showing the nine electoral divisions in Bantry Union as it was declared in September 1840. Courtesy of Cork City and County Archives.

ELECTING THE UNION GUARDIANS

After the union was declared, preparations were made to elect the Board of Guardians. From the start, Bantry guardians shunned publicity. This was in contrast to Cork Union, whose guardians fought the PLC to allow the presence of reporters.[18] However, in October 1840, nominations for Bantry guardians were advertised.[19] The qualification for guardian required a property worth at least £10. Also eligible was any 'male person of full age liable to county cess of 10s'. (Cess was a local tax, collected to pay officials and to mend roads.) Clergy were excluded. All ratepayers (less than one-third of the local population, see page 40) could vote, but since a system of multiple votes gave more weight to large property owners, the election was not in any way representative of the population.[20]

Because the election results were not published, only the names of the three senior officials of the first Board of Guardians survive:

Lord Bantry (chairman), Viscount Berehaven (vice-chairman) and Timothy O'Donovan, justice of the peace (JP) of O'Donovan's Cove, Sheep's Head (deputy vice-chairman).[21]

Lord Bantry was represented on the board by John Warren Payne (c.1818–1902), his agent, who was then about 22 years old. He replaced his older brother Augustus, who died in 1844. Payne's life and times run closely with the story of both the famine and most of the political intrigues in Bantry until he left in around 1889. Son of Rev. Somers Payne (the Deputy Grand Chaplain of the Cork Orange Order), he was connected to some of the most influential families in Munster through his mother, Charlotte Warren. He was also, on his paternal grandmother's side, a great-nephew of the Sheares brothers, United Irishmen who were executed in 1798. By the end of 1846, by virtue of his own effort, Payne represented the Earl of Bantry and also Viscount Berehaven in almost every capacity in the union. This was the moment the curtain rose on his long and controversial career.[22]

Subsequent board elections were held in 1842–43 and annually thereafter, with occasional supplemental elections.[23] Lists of guardians, which differ from each other and have no source acknowledgements or dates, have been given by three authors.[24] In all, eighteen guardians were elected and six appointed *ex-officio*, making a total of twenty-four. The guardian position was unpaid but was sought for reasons of power and patronage at least as much as altruism. The first notice of the new Bantry Board of Guardians (in December 1840) advertised a meeting in early January 1841 to elect valuators for all rateable property in the union. It was signed by Henry B. Spencer, clerk to the guardians.[25] No minute book has survived of the guardians' weekly Tuesday meetings[26] from December 1840 to August 1846. Minute books from August 1846 to the end of the famine are available, with gaps. At one point in 1849, a guardian quotes from minutes written in 1843, suggesting that the books were kept in the workhouse boardroom. No reliable lists of elected guardians are available from 1840 to mid-1846. However, from 1846 onward, names of guardians who attended the meetings were noted (Appendix I). No registers of individual indoor or outdoor relief recipients, or of Bantry workhouse inmates, were found.[27]

There exists a complete lack of information as to the activities of the Bantry Union guardians from their election at the end of 1840 until they are heard from again in early 1843, when the protests against the Poor Law began. We do not know if the guardians met regularly, where they met, or if they transacted any business at all. Information from a Bantry man who briefly possessed the now-missing workhouse minute book from the early 1840s suggests that the guardians attempted to annex some of the Mizen peninsula into Bantry Union but were prevented in this effort by the PLC.[28]

A SUMMARY SKETCH OF PRE-FAMINE BANTRY UNION

Bantry Union, formed as a result of the Poor Law Act, was number 122 out of 130 unions.[29] Shaped like an irregular horseshoe, it stretched from Dursey Island on the end of the Beara peninsula, around Bantry Bay, to Tooreen on the tip of Sheep's Head peninsula. This was far removed from the original concept of the Poor Law Commission, who intended that the market town at the centre of a union would be within a 10-mile radius of its population. Dursey Island was 44 miles and Tooreen 22 miles from Bantry town. The lack of roads passable by coach on the Beara peninsula and from Durrus to the end of Sheep's Head peninsula added to the difficulties.

The union population, which had soared to 51,000 by 1841, lived mainly in dense rural pockets separated by mountains and bog. A characteristic feature of both peninsulas was a system of farming called 'rundale'. Small groups of houses where tenants held land in common were clustered together. These clusters were called 'clachans' and were an important source of the cultural life in rural districts far from towns.[30] Of the two towns in the union, Bantry had a population of 4,082 and Castletown Berehaven (Castletown) a population of 881.[31] The majority of the union population was extremely poor, with fewer better-off farmers, members of the middle class and resident landowners in Bantry Union than in the remainder of Munster.

Of the three large landowners in the union, only one family, that of Lord Bantry, was resident. Three people owned 1,000–3,000 acres, six people owned 500–1,000 acres, while 66 per cent owned less than 20 acres. The percentage of the population with holdings valued at £4 or below (75 per cent) was higher (meaning worse off) than in any other Cork union. Mallow was next at 71 per cent, while Skibbereen was 58 per cent.[32] Another probable difference was likely a smaller percentage of arable land in Bantry Union, but no definite figures for this are available. [33]

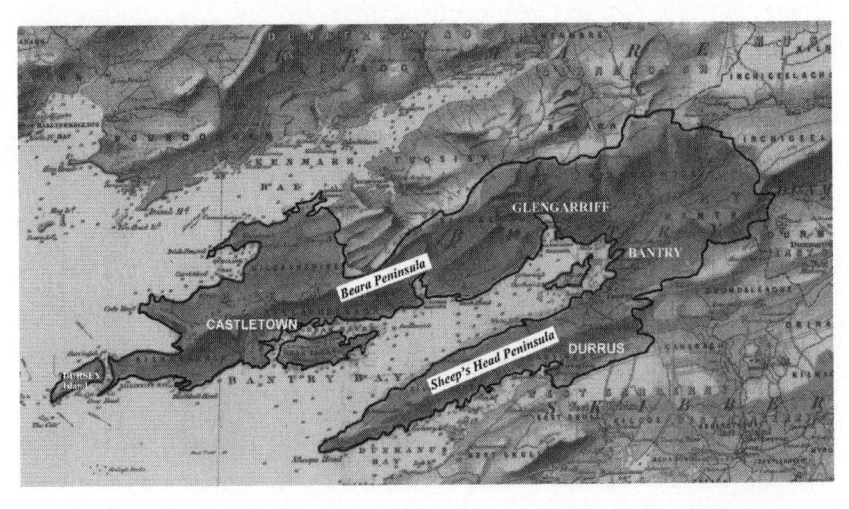

Fig. 3. 1847 map of Beara and Sheep's Head peninsulas. The rugged terrain of Bantry Union is outlined. Map reproduced courtesy Trinity College Dublin.

SETTING THE SCENE

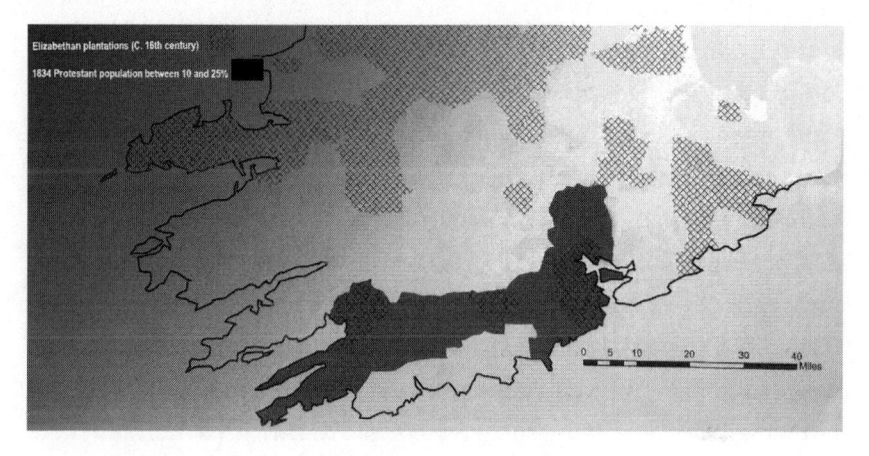

Fig. 4. Map showing Protestant population in Munster in 1834. Notice less than 10 per cent of Protestants lived on the Beara peninsula. Redrawn by author. Courtesy of Indiana University Press.

The proprietors in the union were mostly Protestant. The majority lived in the area between Glengarriff and Durrus, making up 10–25 per cent of the population there. Some were descended from Elizabethan plantation settlers, others were more recent arrivals. In 1852, a traveller was told that one-third of the shopkeepers in Bantry town were Protestant.[34] The Protestants controlled most of the land and tenants and were the most powerful group in the union.

DIVIDED COMMUNITY

A unified response to any adversity affecting the union was made difficult by the divisions in the community. The Protestants, in their enclaves around the established church, did not identify with the union as a whole but with the Crown and with their local and county network of fellow Protestants. They socialised and married within this network and had a generally accepted code of behaviour and manner that to Catholics appeared as an unwarranted and humiliating imposition of authority. In contrast to the Protestants, educated Catholics in the union had a less well-developed social network and almost no supports of any kind other than the impoverished priests and some tenuous friendships with Protestants. Possibly the only Catholics whom the Protestants regarded as equals were Timothy O'Donovan of O'Donovan's Cove and perhaps John Shea Lawlor of Gurteenroe House. Of course, Lord Kenmare was a Catholic, but he was non-resident. Some affluent Catholics like John O'Connell, both a landowner and a merchant, were snubbed by the Protestant gentry. When Catholics made a local showing for a nationalist cause such as Repeal, Protestants were frightened, making for a continued state of strained relations.

UNSOPHISTICATED SOCIAL SKILLS, ADMINISTRATIVE INEXPERIENCE

From a reading of contemporary newspaper accounts of meetings at Bantry courthouse, it is evident that disagreements were taken personally. Compromise was rare, and conflict resolution was primitive. Duels were still a way of dealing with differences of opinion.[35] At many meetings, only doctors or clergy asked realistic questions. Naivety and ignorance were often on display, as at an 1843 meeting when little awareness was in evidence of serious problems ahead. Many of the gentry did not understand the need to plan in order to manage their resources and increase employment in the area.

MONOPOLY OF INFLUENCE

The union was unusual in the consolidation of power in the hands of a tiny number of people. The few large landlords had heavily mortgaged properties. Some, like the Bantry Estate, were engaged in interminable legal battles over disputed lands and contracts.[36] The Earl of Bantry and Viscount Berehaven were acknowledged by the authorities in Dublin as the leading citizens of the entire district. However, they delegated their authority on Beara peninsula to middlemen and elsewhere to their agent John Warren Payne, who became the most powerful man in the union. (In the much-reviled middleman system, the middleman became an intermediate landlord between the owner of the property and multiple sub-tenants.)[37]

In terms of influence, the Beara peninsula was a special case, as almost all of the poor families, technically tenants of Lord Bantry and his relatives, were, with the tacit consent of Bantry House, governed by the O'Sullivan clan (the hereditary chieftains). The degree of their hegemony was unusual and contributed to the misery on that peninsula. (For a fictional perspective on the feuds and the mines on Beara, see Daphne Du Maurier's novel, *Hungry Hill*.)[38]

CONTRASTING CONDITIONS ON THE PENINSULAS

Tenant living conditions differed markedly on each peninsula. The more northerly Beara peninsula was predominantly Catholic. It was managed by Catholic middlemen, mainly the O'Sullivan clan. One of the most notorious middlemen in the 1840s was 'Big' Patrick O'Sullivan from Mill Cove, north of Castletown. He was accused of corruption involving cess tax, regularly abused his tenants, and behaved like a thug on Beara. All this was reported by a Dublin land agent and lawyer, Patrick Prendergast, in a pamphlet published in 1854.[39] Big Pat's ill-fame was so widespread that he was also mentioned in a collection of essays published in 1913, in which it was said of him that 'Local tradition has it that he used to blow his bugle outside the Church after Sunday Mass to summon his tenants to draw hay or turf or whatever other task he designated.'[40] O'Sullivan was also responsible for transporting voters to Cork in 1841 to vote as Lord Bantry desired, an event that led to a public enquiry by the County Cork Board of Elections. Besides Big Pat, other serious problems on Beara included lower literacy rates, greater poverty and more sectarian infighting than on Sheep's Head.

On the Sheep's Head peninsula, the landlords were more numerous and mostly absentee. The majority of the tenants paid their rent to Protestant middlemen whose treatment of them was less harsh than that of the Catholic middlemen in other parts of the union. During his deposition to the Devon Commission in 1844, John O'Connell, a prosperous Catholic corn merchant[41] who was subsequently the principal supplier of meal to the workhouse and to the indigent throughout the famine, made the following statement about a Protestant middleman from Durrus on Sheep's Head, 'We have as kind middlemen in the district as any living, or as there are in the land. I mention as one, the Rev. Mr. Allen Evanson, a clergyman of the established church.'[42]

The Catholic landlord Timothy O'Donovan, JP of O'Donovan's Cove, west of Durrus, who leased large acreage from Lord Riversdale, apparently tried to use his influence to enfranchise some of his tenants.[43] Nevertheless, problems did exist. Patrick Tobin of Gurtavallig, near Kilcrohane on the Sheep's Head peninsula, gave evidence at the 1844 Devon hearings of the necessity of bribing agents and of the existence of multiple middlemen, 'There are no gentlemen there hardly. They hold under third and fourth middlemen.'[44]

CONDITIONS IN BANTRY TOWN AND THE SURROUNDING AREA

In the central area of the union, from Glengarriff to Bantry town, the two largest landlords were Lord Bantry and the Earl of Kenmare, an absentee Catholic landlord. Lord Kenmare drew the ire of Rev. Christopher Freeman (a Bantry curate) at the Devon hearings in 1844. Freeman gave evidence indicating that, since 1840, more than 200 people in Bantry Union who had been paying rent regularly to Lord Kenmare were summarily evicted, and some of them were reduced to beggary and death.[45] On the other hand, Lord Bantry was seen as treating his tenants in this part of the union with benign neglect.

Again, at the Devon Commission hearings, Rev. Thomas Barry, the parish priest of Bantry of twenty-one years' standing, speaking of Lord Bantry said, 'It is only justice to his character to state, that he would be incapable of any act of oppression.'[46] Freeman added, 'The rents are high, but are not rigidly exacted [...] the people have confidence in him. Many of the unfortunate people evicted by Lord Kenmare have taken refuge on Lord Bantry's property.'[47]

This confidence came from the relief Lord Bantry had given to tenants when famine threatened in 1784. He had also encouraged flax production on the Linen Board in the 1820s and had supported the construction of a bridewell and market house in Bantry.[48] However, as Lord Bantry aged (he was 78 years old in 1845), he retreated to his lodge in Glengarriff and was much less active on behalf of his tenants. He and his son Viscount Berehaven were not considered improving landlords.[49] Another smaller landlord in an area to the east of Bantry was Richard White of Inchiclough, a nephew of Lord Bantry. He was praised by Rev. Barry for improving the land and for granting his tenants leases. Rev. Barry said, 'If they [the tenants] are not comfortable, it is their own fault.' He emphasised that White was an exception and that most of the remaining impoverished parishioners had no security because of 'the want of leases'.[50]

ECONOMIC ACTIVITY IN BANTRY UNION

General commercial activity was centred in Bantry, the market town of the union. Its amenities included the port, the market, a post office, Protestant and Catholic churches, a Wesleyan chapel and a sixteen-bedroom hotel (The Bantry Arms owned by a Mr Godson) with a coach house and stabling for twenty horses.[51] A new stone courthouse stood on the main square close by the constabulary station and bridewell. The town had a dispensary and two main schoolhouses, one for Protestants and one for Catholics. Adjacent to the town, looking out to Bantry Bay and the Beara peninsula, lay Bantry House and Bantry demesne, occupied by Viscount Berehaven. Overlooking the town was the union workhouse, completed in 1843 but unoccupied until 1845. Kingston's Mills, in the centre of town, was the main manufacturer in Bantry, producing 12,000 bags of flour annually.[52]

North of Bantry, in Donemark, Michael Murphy, brother of the Protestant Rector of Bantry, owned flour and corn mills and a small brewery. His mills were active before the famine but were idle by 1847.[53] He was married to Jane Besnard, some of whose letters to their daughter Charlotte have survived in the National Archives.

Bantry town also had a small porter brewery,[54] and a tannery was shown on the first Ordnance Survey (OS) map from around 1845 (Fig. 5a and 5b).[55] Slater's Directory mentions the 'extensive corn stores of Mr John O'Connell' on the quay.[56] The linen industry in Bantry had exploded in the early 1820s, growing from 2,000 yards sold in 1822 to 22,890 yards in 1823.[57] Nevertheless, removal of protective tariffs and other factors had caused the £4,000 per year enterprise to become 'almost extinct' by 1844.[58] This was a severe blow to the local economy and to all West Cork. In a letter written in 1826 from Castle Freke, Co. Cork (in the Skibbereen Union) requesting government help, Baron Carbery stated, 'Those who could have earned nearly 2s per day on their looms are now toiling on road works for six penny's worth of meal to feed a family for a day.'[59]

According to John Windele, a Cork historian and antiquarian, a large quantity of butter was brought to Bantry from the countryside and usually was shipped to Cork.[60] Even today, older local people recount how women walked long distances to sell their butter in Bantry town. Corn raised in neighbouring parishes was brought to Bantry. In 1835, 10,000 barrels of wheat and 3,000 barrels of oats were exported to England[61] at an estimated value of £6,212. Imports of tobacco, spirits, sugar, iron, salt and timber amounted to over

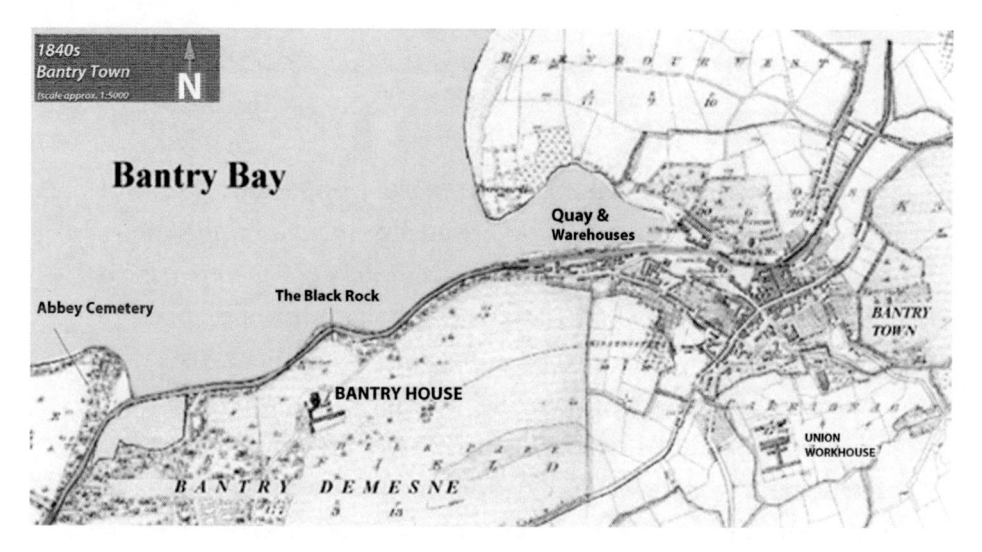

Fig. 5a. Bantry area in the 1840s, adapted from first OS map, showing the Abbey cemetery, Bantry House and Demesne and, to the east, Bantry town and the union workhouse.

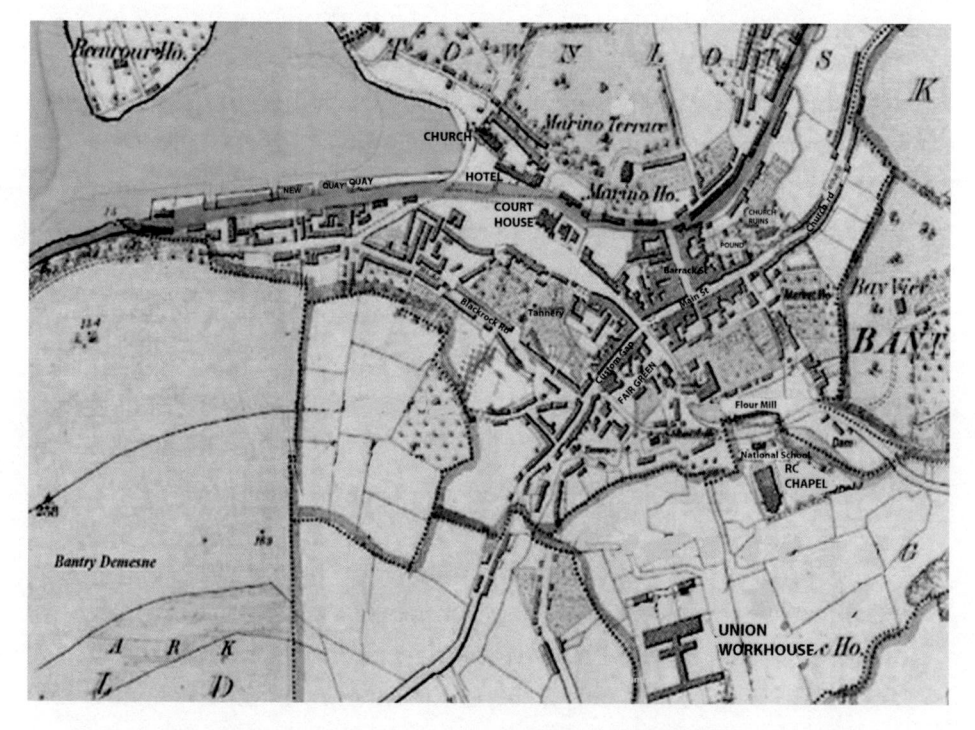

Fig. 5b. Enlarged view of Bantry town in the 1840s, adapted from the OS map, showing the court house, flour mill, market, quay, workhouse and churches.

£17,000. Coral sand dredged locally was an important source of employment worth £4,000–£5,000 annually. It was used as fertiliser and carted inland extensively.[62] The *Parliamentary Gazetteer* remarked that although the 'aggregate trade' was less than that of Skibbereen and Berehaven, it was better than in previous years. They agreed with Windele that Bantry was 'improving' in 1844.[63]

Fishing, which had been a lucrative trade in Bantry, suffered a major setback in 1829 when the government abruptly ended grants for fitting out boats and nets.[64] Despite this, hake and herring were found in abundance in the early 1840s. They were cured in Bantry and sold locally. In discussing boats in the Bantry region, the *Gazetteer* included Bantry boats with Berehaven craft, so the Bantry contribution cannot be determined.[65] The 1836 Commission of Inquiry on the state of Irish fisheries reported that 'there has been no productive fishery in Bantry since 1828'. However, 'There are in Bantry ten such seans [seine boats], owned [...] by respectable persons [...] well found and kept up. To each sean there is a large boat and a smaller sized one, called a follower, and fifteen men are employed.'[66] Documentation is lacking about their status at the time of the famine, but James Johnson, a well-travelled physician and writer originally from Northern Ireland who journeyed through Bantry in 1843, made an indirect comment, 'the solitude of the scene – the absence of shipping on such a noble bay – and the paucity of life in every direction are taken together, there is something depressing rather than exhilarating [...] about Bantry.'[67]

Despite Bantry's position as the centre of general market activity, the profits of the Allihies copper mines in the electoral division of Kilnamanagh on the Beara peninsula exceeded those of Bantry. The valuation of Kilnamanagh at £10,746 in 1841 was slightly higher than the £10,081 valuation of Bantry town. The mines were owned by Robert Puxley and had been continually worked since 1813. By 1837 they employed 1,200–1,500 men and were producing 6,000–7,000 tons of ore per year, valued at £9 per ton. Mills at Ballydonegan crushed the ore, which was shipped to Swansea. Many houses and cottages were built near the mines for the workers, along with a new road connecting them to Castletown. The growing community had a dispensary and barracks, and schools and churches for both Protestants and Catholics. Trade mainly consisted of supplying the miners but was limited inland because of bad roads. The anchorage at Berehaven port, adjacent to Castletown, was deep enough for large ships. The *Gazetteer* reported that in 1833 there were '4 decked boats of 20 tons, 12 hookers [and] 51 yawls which employ 400 fishermen'. In 1835 the exports from the port amounted to £77,360, chief of which were £63,450 for copper ore and £9,000 for butter.[68]

Nonetheless, in 1836 the Fishery Commission reported an equally bleak outlook for commercial fishing in Beara as they had in Bantry:

> The general condition of the hookers, as well as of the smaller fishing boats, is bad and defective; the owners are in bad spirits, mostly poor, and unable to procure the necessary outfit. The loss of the bounty on the fish taken, as well as of the loan fund under the late Fishery Board, was of the greatest injury.[69]

The Sheep's Head peninsula, unlike Bantry and a limited part of the Beara peninsula, had few merchants and little organised economic activity. The exceptions were the start-up of the Gortavallig mine in 1845 and the Durrus community of Protestant weavers. Recent research by Pat Crowley indicates that some of the weavers were brought from as far as Co. Armagh.[70] A tucking mill, used for the fulling of cloth to make it thicker, was recorded in Durrus.[71] When the linen trade failed in the 1820s, the weavers began emigrating to Canada and formed a colony there.[72] It appears most of them had left by the 1840s.

From the late 1830s, one of the most promising developments for the economy of the union lay in the building of new roads that would be passable in bad weather and facilitate transportation of heavy goods. A new route from Durrus to Bantry was built around 1843. A road was also built in the early 1840s linking Bantry more directly to Skibbereen. A tourist way from Bantry to Kenmare took years to build, constructed from the late 1830s into the early 1840s. Travel to Cork took over ten hours. Several coaches, including the mail coach, left from Godson's Bantry Arms Hotel almost every morning, starting at 5.00 a.m. and going to Bandon, Clonakilty, Cork and Skibbereen.[73]

HOUSING

This was markedly poor in the union. In 1841 the Census Commissioners grouped houses into four classes, the lowest or fourth class being one-room mud cabins. The third class had two to four rooms, the second class was a good farmhouse or, in a town, a house having five to nine rooms with windows, and the first class, all houses better than these.[74] In the 1841 census, Bantry Union had 8,298 inhabited houses. Of these, 1.1 per cent were first class, 5.8 per cent second class, 18.6 per cent third class and 74.5 per cent fourth class. If we agree with at least one economic historian that 'housing quality may be viewed as a proxy for income', we can estimate the relative poverty of the union's electoral divisions.[75] Using fourth-class housing as the sole criterion, the four most impoverished electoral divisions in 1841 can be seen as: Kilcrohane, Kilnamanagh, Kilaconenagh and Kilcatherine (Appendix II). The best-off were Bantry town and Castletown.

Substandard housing was almost universal in the pre-famine union. Most people lived in one-roomed smoke-filled mud hovels, with the associated health hazards of overcrowding, noise, dispute, lack of privacy and contamination by human and animal waste.

The contagion caused by this type of overcrowding exacerbated the death rate in epidemics. It had done so during the Bantry cholera epidemic in 1832, and it would again be a significant factor in the death rate during the famine years as starving people crowded into Bantry town.

Thomas Campbell Foster, who was commissioned by the *Times* to report on Ireland, and whose letters were published in that newspaper from 1845 until early 1846, left us with his eye-witness account of housing in Bantry town:

> Four-fifths of the inhabitants live in mud hovels such as you see in the country, and which here form the outskirts of town. These consist usually of a single room, a hole for a window with a board in it, the door generally off the hinges, a wicker basket with a hole in the bottom [...] at one corner of the thatch for a chimney, the pig, as a matter of course, inside the cottage, and an extensive manufacture of manure going on the floor.[76]

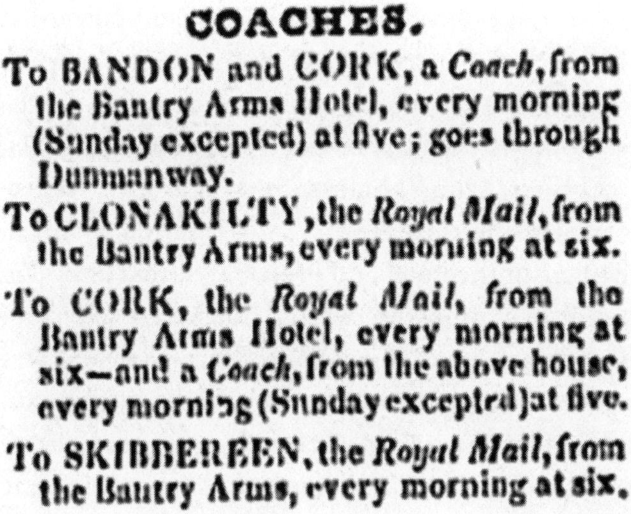

COACHES.

To BANDON and CORK, a *Coach*, from the Bantry Arms Hotel, every morning (Sunday excepted) at five; goes through Dunmanway.

To CLONAKILTY, the *Royal Mail*, from the Bantry Arms, every morning at six.

To CORK, the *Royal Mail*, from the Bantry Arms Hotel, every morning at six—and a *Coach*, from the above house, every morning (Sunday excepted) at five.

To SKIBBEREEN, the *Royal Mail*, from the Bantry Arms, every morning at six.

Fig. 6. Excerpt from Slater's *National Commercial Directory of Ireland* (1846).

OCCUPATIONS

The most important occupation in Bantry Union was agriculture, employing approximately 77–82 per cent of families.[77] For the poor tenant, agriculture meant raising corn, oats and a pig to pay the rent, and growing potatoes to eat. As well as farm work, traditional crafts such as candle making, repairing fishing nets, spinning, growing medicinal herbs, and a certain amount of local brewing and distilling were practised.

Agricultural workers in the union, all of them tenants, came from different economic strata. The most numerous and poorest were landless labourers, followed by smallholders of up to 5 acres, then smallholders of gradually larger acreage who might have a couple of cows, then farmers with cows and horses, and eventually a 'strong farmer' renting around 80 acres. As noted earlier, Bantry Union had the largest percentage of any Cork union of tenants holding land valued at £4 or less (75 per cent). In 1844 that would have represented about 4 arable acres. (For a breakdown of the division between agriculture and trade or manufacturing in specific districts, see Appendix III.)

Foster's letters to the *Times* allow us to view a more detailed picture of employment in Bantry town. Despite the poverty, he describes a busy place in 1845, listing pig jobbers, hide sellers, butchers and slaughter-house attendants; shopkeepers, nailers, doctors, agents, police, cobblers, tailors, blacksmiths, masons, washerwomen, sawyers and labourers. He gives a wry description of broken crockery and dirtiness in the hotel and is dismayed that although Bantry Bay abounds in shrimp and oysters, none are available to buy. He remarks on the lack of vigour in ordinary demand and supply in the local markets and concludes the fault lies in the local landlords' use of the flawed landlord-tenant laws to enrich themselves at the cost of their tenants, leading to a situation where there is neither any supply nor any demand, 'And the very same men, by refusing to give leases, and by equally refusing to refund to a tenant his expenditure in improving the land [...] freeze industry [...] banish labour, and stint the supply.'[78]

NUTRITION

Food availability was insecure throughout the union, with an almost total dependence on potatoes (4–5kg daily per adult male) for at least one-third of the poor and no alternative food source in the case of crop failure.[79] Potatoes were supplemented by scant rations of fish and oat porridge, and small portions of other vegetables. Land was scarce and expensive because of the rapidly increasing population. Green crops were not widely cultivated, as they required significantly more land than the potato crop, where an acre could feed a family of six. There is ample evidence that subsistence farming was the norm for the majority of the people in the union. Poor harvests and epidemics regularly caused severe deprivation, illness and death, particularly of the very young and very old. This situation was little changed by two good pre-famine harvests just prior to 1845.

LITERACY

The literacy rate in the union was low. By amalgamating the 1841 census returns for both 'can read and write' and 'read only', it appears that about one-third of men could read, as opposed to one-fifth of women – except for women on Beara, where the majority were illiterate. In Bantry and Kilmanogue, it was reported that 35 percent of the male population could read, while 20 per cent of the female population could read; in Durrus and Kilcrohane, it was 36 per cent of males and 19 per cent of females; on Beara it was 31 per cent of males and 11 per cent of females.[80]

Low literacy rates translated to poor information stores and impaired communication ability, which would have made negotiation or conflict resolution with landlords or agents virtually impossible. Inability to read English may have prevented people gaining vital information about alternative crops, planned governmental employment strategies and emigration opportunities. Illiteracy effectively disenfranchised thousands of the population just as surely as the lack of suffrage.

HEALTH

Life expectancy in 1830s Ireland was twenty-nine years. Mortality was highest in the youngest.[81] Sir William Wilde, the Dublin medical man and polymath who reported mortality statistics in the 1841 census, concluded that in Ireland 23.38 per cent of children died in the first year of life and 37.79 per cent by five years of age.[82] In 1834, the Bantry dispensary was described as 'a miserable cabin [...] with nevertheless a sufficient supply of medicines'. The dispensary was funded through the Grand Jury (the forerunner of today's county council) and three voluntary subscribers in Bantry, who gave a total of £1 5s annually. The district was so big that some patients had to travel 30 miles to get there.[83] In 1839–40, the dispensary administered to 3,075 patients. Castletown also had a dispensary, which similarly treated 3,540 patients.[84] The many cures and herbal remedies described in the schools' folklore collection (tales from the past written in copybooks by primary students from five thousand schools between 1937 and 1939) for the area give an insight into some alternative treatments employed by the populace.[85] On a positive note, a serious problem that had been reduced before the famine was alcoholism. Father Matthew's famed temperance campaign had succeeded in increasing sobriety, and general health as a result.

In 1842, a young William Makepeace Thackeray visited Bantry and left us this impression:

> A most picturesquely situated town […] the main street […] thronged with squatting blue cloaks, carrying on their eager trade of butter-milk and green apples […] With the exception of this street and the quay with their white-washed and slated houses, it is a town of cabins. The wretchedness of some of them is quite curious […] an ordinary pigsty in England is more comfortable.[86]

At the time of his visit, the union boundaries and its electoral divisions had been determined and the Board of Guardians elected, but so far no poor rates had been collected. Although construction of the workhouse had just begun, all was not as calm as it may have appeared to the future author of *Vanity Fair*. Under the surface, resentment was bubbling among the future ratepayers, and in particular among the larger landowners.

2.

EVOLUTION OF A CRISIS
1843–46

IMPLEMENTING THE POOR LAW

The Bantry guardians appear to have shown their displeasure with the PLC by dragging their feet for the three years following their inception in 1840. Research in the archives and newspapers from 1841 until the end of 1842 found almost nothing relating to Bantry Union. The *Cork Examiner*, the *Constitution* and the *Southern Reporter* published regular notices on the activities of boards of guardians of other unions but not Bantry. Corruption and voter fraud in connection with Lord Bantry's tenants on Beara were reported in the general election of 1841, but as to what the newly elected guardians were doing, we are left in the dark and can only rely on a few scraps of information.

The first step in implementing the Poor Law was the valuation of all rateable property in the union, and we know that process was begun in January 1841. Apart from the initial announcement in the *Southern Reporter*,[87] no further contemporary information was discovered about this important foundation for setting the rate. Except, that is, for an intriguing note in 1849 in the workhouse minutes. According to this note, the final valuation figure caused such dismay among landowners that the guardians, against the wishes of the PLC, reduced it by 20 per cent. This probably happened in 1842.[88]

That the guardians acted with such unanimity and forcefulness against the PLC is striking. It would be interesting to recover the missing minute book that covers these years. It might be speculated that the guardians were aided by Daniel O'Connell, who wrote that the valuation in the neighbourhood of Bantry 'has been enormously overcharged'.[89] It is likely that several unions in the same circumstances wrote to O'Connell for help, as newspapers in other counties also published his remarks on overvaluation. But the reduction was a two-edged sword, as it lowered the amount of rate money available to maintain paupers, as well as making it more difficult for Bantry Union to repay loans from the government.

Another important event in September 1843 was a country-wide change by the Poor Law Commission in the Poor Law that made landlords liable for rates on properties not exceeding £4.[90] This was significant because it removed large numbers of ratepayers eligible to vote in guardian elections and also made evictions a means of indirectly lowering a landlord's tax obligation. This new rule, in combination with the lowering of the union's valuation, worked against the poor. Meanwhile, the PLC forged ahead with their plans for building the Bantry workhouse, where paupers were to be housed and fed. The guardians' task was to set a rate, to hire rate collectors and to manage the funds gathered for the maintenance of the workhouse and its inmates. Nevertheless, the fact that the guardians were not consulted about the size or construction of the workhouse led to resentment.

BUILDING THE WORKHOUSE

The workhouse dominated the Bantry skyline from 1843 until 1922, but no official photograph of the building was found, perhaps hinting at the degree of opprobrium in which it was held.

Fig. 7. General view of Bantry around forty years after the famine. Courtesy of the National Library of Ireland, Lawrence Collection.

The present Bantry Hospital, built on its site, has no records of the older structure. However, investigation revealed an undated glass negative in the Lawrence Collection at the National Library showing the workhouse at the edge of a 'General View of Bantry', at the top right of the photo (Fig. 7). This photo in itself is not particularly revealing, but the exceptionally high resolution of the glass negative allowed for considerable detail when enlarged.

In 1841, the site for the Bantry workhouse was 'not settled'.[91] On 22 June 1842, the contract was signed and awarded to Messrs McDaniel and Brown by the architect George Wilkinson.[92] Wilkinson, from Oxfordshire, was the Irish Poor Law Commission's chief architect. The building contract amount was £5,990, but the total amount borrowed for a workhouse with a capacity for 600 on a 6-acre site was £7,750. The date for completion was given as December 1842, but it was not actually finished until 1843.[93] The site purchase price is unclear. It was sold by Lord Bantry for either £5[94] or £500[95] depending on the source, but most likely the figure was £500.[96]

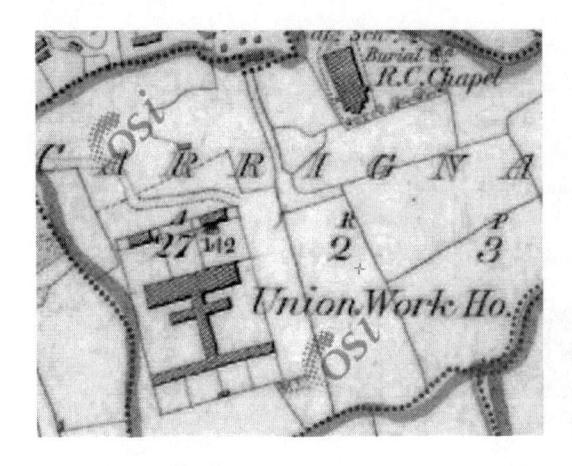

Fig. 8. Bantry workhouse from first OS map, 1845. Fever hospital not yet built.

Construction probably began in 1842. Presumably, local workers were hired for this large project, which must have caused a huge amount of interest and comment in the area but, unfortunately, not in the newspapers. The site adjoined the eastern boundary of Bantry House demesne. Viscount Berehaven could have ridden out on his property to view the foundation excavations.

The floor plans and elevations for the Bantry workhouse have not survived, except for an outline in the first and second OS maps (Fig. 8).

The workhouse resembled one of Wilkinson's standard plans (Fig. 9), except for the reception building at the front; in Wilkinson's plan there was one building, but in Bantry there were two separate structures, with the entrance gate between. No information exists about flooring. Wilkinson had specified bare earth for Irish workhouses, but stone flags had been installed at least in some cases because of dampness. (Measurements of the wards taken by Dr Stephens in 1847 are available in Appendix IV.)

By placing the outline of the Bantry workhouse from the OS map (Fig. 8) over the standard plan (Fig. 9) an approximation of the layout can be made.

EVOLUTION OF A CRISIS

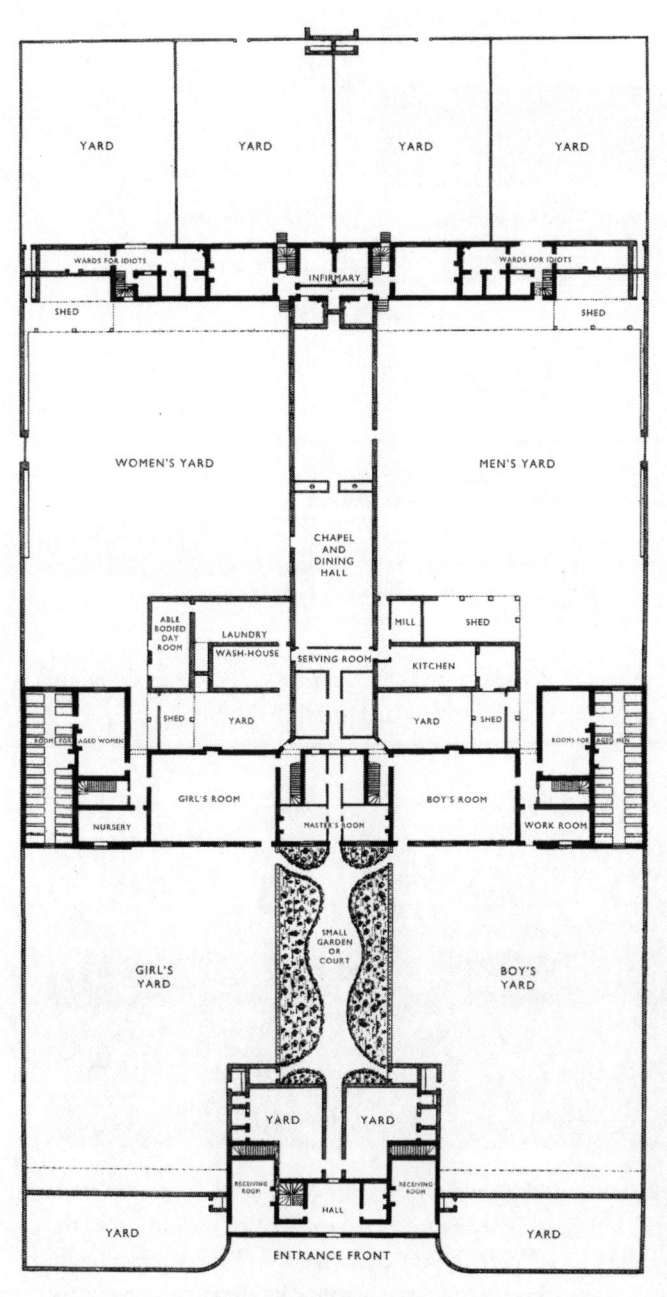

Fig. 9. The standard workhouse floor plan that most closely resembled the Bantry workhouse. Note how the orientation differs from the floor plan in Fig. 10. HC (British Parliamentary Papers), *Fifth annual report of the Poor Law Commissioners: with appendices*, Volume Page: XX.1, Volume: 20, Paper Number: 239 (1839), Plan B. following p. 90. ProQuest: U.K. Parliamentary Papers.

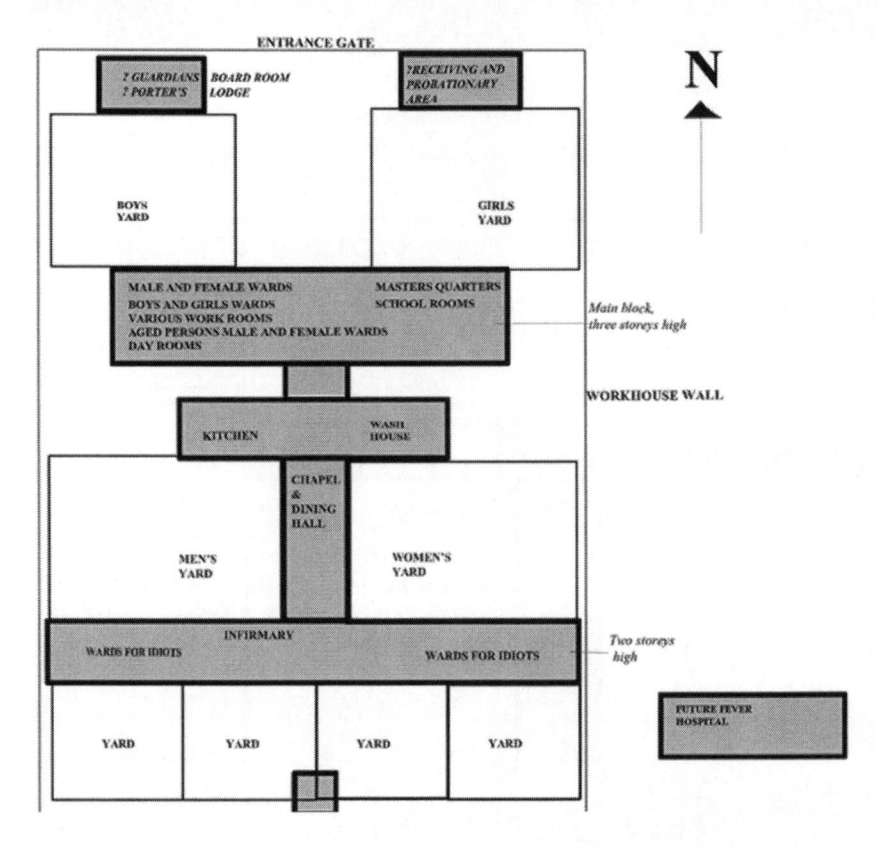

Fig. 10. Probable floor plan of Bantry workhouse in 1842. Author's drawing, derived from historic OS maps and the standard published layout.

Fig. 11. Image of Bantry workhouse and workhouse field from previous photograph (*c*.1890s) enlarged by the author. Two smaller buildings in the foreground probably contained receiving rooms, the porter's lodge and a board room. The main block and entrance gate faced north. Courtesy of the National Library of Ireland, Lawrence Collection.

This layout is further confirmed by an outline floor plan of the later-built Castletown workhouse, which closely resembled the Bantry building.[97] The only visible portion of the entire structure remaining today is part of the foundation of the fever hospital (built in 1846) behind the present-day Bantry Hospital. An underground arched walkway of yellow bricks was discovered during foundation excavation for a new hospital wing in the early 2000s, leading from the fever hospital to the main structure. A photographic record was not made, and the date and purpose of the passage's construction are unknown.[98]

One unwise decision made during the course of the workhouse construction was to ignore the specification that called for a well. It was decided that a nearby stream would provide an adequate supply of water for workhouse needs.[99]

ATTEMPT TO BLOCK BOTH THE POOR RATE AND THE OPENING OF THE WORKHOUSE

In January 1843, the simmering resentment of the more affluent in the union came to a head. Virtually all the resident Bantry Union gentry signed a petition to hold a meeting to protest the implementation of the Poor Law. At this meeting on 18 January, local landowners tried to block payment of all poor rates and to prevent the opening of the already half-built workhouse. The meeting was exceptional in that almost every major landowner in the union was present or represented. Liberals and conservatives, Protestant and Catholic clergy, merchants and townspeople crowded into the courthouse. Several speakers commented that all social classes were in attendance. Only the gentry spoke. The following is a list of those who signed the petition, divided according to the area they came from:

Beara peninsula: John O'Sullivan, JP, Cametrigane, Berehaven; Major Broderick, JP, Castletown, Berehaven; Patrick O'Sullivan, Esq., Berehaven; Phillip Armstrong, Esq., MD, Berehaven; Rev. James Fitzgerald, PP, Berehaven.

Bantry/Glengarriff: Richard White, JP, Inchiclough; John Hamilton White, JP, Drumnbro; Robert Hedges Eyre White, Esq., Glengarriff Castle; The Hon. Robert White, JP, Marino; Augustus Warren Payne, JP, Bantry; Arthur Hutchinson, JP, Cooney; Arthur Hutchins, Esq., Ballylickey; Samuel Hutchins, Esq., Ardnagashal; John Jagoe, Esq. barrister-at-law, Bantry; John O'Connell, Esq., Bantry; Thomas Burke, MD, Bantry; Very Rev. Thomas Barry, PP, VP, Bantry; Rev. John Murphy, Rector, Glebe House, Bantry; Rev. Patrick Begley, CC, Bantry; Messers Shea Lawlor, Downing, McCarthy, Pierson, Donovan, Kingston, Young, Cotter, Tobin and about 200 other names (not specified).

Sheep's Head peninsula: Timothy O'Donovan, JP, Donovan's Cove; Charles Evanson, JP, Cork; Rev. Allen Evanson, JP, Four Mile Water (Durrus).

Other: Edmond William O'Mahony, Esq., Middle Temple; Christopher Gallway, JP, Killarney; Kean Mahony, JP, Killarney.[100]

The list of signatories is a roll call of the pre-famine power brokers in Bantry Union. It contains the names of several guardians. Noticeably absent (but reported to be represented by the Chair) were Lord Bantry and Viscount Berehaven. This was possibly due to the former's age and the latter's travels abroad. John Payne (Lord Bantry's agent) was also absent, and the Catholic landowner

Timothy O'Donovan JP sent his excuses. Since these two individuals were prominent on the Board of Guardians, their non-attendance must have caused comment. Lord Bantry and Viscount Berehaven may have had genuine excuses but equally may have been wary of being seen to defy the PLC in Dublin. The same may have been true of O'Donovan and Payne.

Whatever the reason, it was apparent that all the gentry in attendance were worried about their personal finances. The heavily mortgaged estates in the union could not bear much additional stress.

The newspaper account of this meeting provides a rare insight into the attitudes and beliefs of some of the main players in the politics of Bantry Union before and during the famine. The unspoken message was that no one wanted to spend their personal funds on paupers. The speakers at first focused on the concept of the 'meritorious poor', whom they said, without providing any evidence, would not be relieved by the Poor Law Act. They then turned to anticipation of 'burdensome' taxation, which made the act 'inapplicable to the condition of Ireland', again without offering any substantiation of the claims.

Only two speakers had coherent arguments. The first, the dispensary physician Dr Bourke, said the poor needed to be employed, not sent to workhouses. He believed that the law should be changed to apply only to the infirm, blind and maimed, as nobody would object to poor relief for those individuals.

The second and main speaker was John Shea Lawlor (1798–1876), a Catholic barrister, magistrate and land agent for Lord Kenmare. He expressed the rancour felt by his audience when he referred to the

> Absurd [...] power vested [...] in the [Poor Law] Commissioners [...] they very offensively assert [that] the landowners of this Union [...] would not exercise the functions of charity or kindness unless

> [...] coerced [...] Let it be understood that we are not seeking to restrict the rights of the poor [...] all we desire is that funds raised [...] shall be appropriate to the wants of the poor [It is] nationally insulting to send over to Ireland a set of men thus to lord it over this country, and this on the insolent pretence, that our own gentry were not to be trusted.

He noted with some prescience that 'If the Guardians [...] hesitated to act [...] as the commissioners pleased, they were, like servants, to be turned off, and paid Guardians appointed in their place.'

The meeting unanimously adopted several resolutions, making the points that the Poor Law was 'inapplicable' to Ireland and had been made worse by the Poor Law Commission; that rates from Bantry Union should not be used to pay for the workhouse, which had been foisted on them by 'unrestrained' commissioners; and that the opening of the workhouse should be delayed until the resolutions were passed through parliament.[101] On 28 February 1843, the Earl of Bandon presented petitions 'complaining about the Irish Poor Law' from both the Bandon and Bantry boards of guardians to the House of Lords. Nothing came of them.[102]

It is worth noting that Shea Lawlor, as main speaker at the 18 January 1843 meeting, led the criticism of the Poor Law and the PLC. He later forsook this attitude and became a strong advocate for the poor. He is now mostly forgotten but was a prominent figure during the famine. He was a nationalist with roots in Cork and Kerry and was described as being an improving landlord.[103] He lived at Gurteenroe House near Bantry (now in ruins, just past the Bantry Golf Club). He was described by the contemporary writer Thomas Carlyle as 'a tallow-complexioned, big, erect man with a sharp-croaking Irish voice, small cock-nose, stereotype glitter of smile, and small hard blue eyes, – [who] explodes in talking [...] talks *much*'.[104]

DELAY

It seems that the workhouse building was completed in about August 1843 but stood empty until April 1845 due to further delaying tactics by Bantry Union gentry and landowners. No publicity about this procrastination was found in any of the Cork newspapers, not even in the *Examiner* or the *Southern Reporter*, both of which were more sympathetic to Catholics and the impoverished than the *Constitution*. In this obstructive behaviour, Bantry resembled some of the other recalcitrant unions. For example, the PLC complained in 1845 that Castlerea and Westport unions had not opened their workhouses, and that Clifden and Cahirciveen unions had not yet set a rate. The PLC were suing the Tuam guardians, who had struck a rate in 1842 but still had not collected any money by 1845.

The first sign of real progress in the implementation of the Poor Law came in June 1844 when the PLC prodded the Bantry guardians into action by sending Assistant Poor Law Commissioner Joseph Burke to oversee them.[105] Soon after his arrival, the first poor rate at 10*d* on the pound was struck (on 16 July 1844) for a total rate of £1,738 11*s* 1*d*,[106] and advertisements for rate collectors were published. One month later, in August 1844, the workhouse was declared fit for reception. However, it still took eight more months before it opened, bringing the total time it stood empty to about nineteen months.

An eyewitness account written by Mrs Asenath Nicholson, an American humanitarian, attests to the completed but still-empty workhouse in February 1845. She found in Bantry 'a wild, dirty sea-port, with cabins […] having the most antiquated and forlorn appearance of any town I had seen. A lofty well-finished poorhouse was back of these abodes of misery.' She was shown the slippery uphill path to the gate and found it locked. Her companion told her that although the building had been ready for occupancy for over one year, 'the farmers stood out and would not pay the taxes.'[107] Mrs Nicholson made a tart comment to the effect that instead of wasting money for a keeper to sit in an unused building, the same amount might have helped the starving people avoid the need for such a place.[108]

Mrs Nicholson subsequently witnessed drunkenness at her dilapidated lodgings in Glengarriff. She was told that 'five years before, they were all temperate' but had lapsed since then.[109] So, even before the famine struck, alcohol had again become a problem. In the next few days, in early 1845, Mrs Nicholson visited many cabins around Glengarriff and was appalled by the living conditions. She wondered how she could approach Lord Bantry 'to entreat him to […] visit the cabins and work some change for the better'. But the meeting never occurred due to a series of mishaps, so, as she wrote, 'he escaped what he ought to have heard years before.'[110]

These words of Mrs Nicholson are virtually the only contemporary description of poor people in Bantry Union from less than one year before deaths from starvation began.

THE WORKHOUSE OPENS

The workhouse was finally officially opened by Assistant Poor Law Commissioner Burke at the start of May 1845.[111] Burke continued his visits (once every two months) until December 1846. He was unpopular in Bantry, where he was described as a 'dictator' and publicly accused of nepotism by a *Cork Examiner* letter writer who signed himself 'A Bantry man'.[112]

People were first admitted on 24 April 1845.[113] Bantry workhouse was no different from any others in respect to the harsh regimen well described in the literature, with a master and matron in charge, stringent rules, subsistence diet, severely substandard accommodation and, worst of all, the separation of families on entry.[114] As Alexander Martin Sullivan (A.M. Sullivan, 1829–1884), the writer, lawyer and nationalist politician from Bantry, wrote, 'The warders tore them asunder – the husband from the wife – the mother from the child for "discipline" required that it should be so.'[115]

The guardians appointed Nicholas Roberts as master[116] and Dr Thomas Arthur Tisdall (c.1817–1849), the Bantry dispensary doctor, as medical officer. Tisdall may have had a family connection with the Protestant Murphys of Donemark and Newtown, although his family home seemed to be in Louth. In addition, he seems to have had a chronic heart condition that led to an early death.

At the outset, the guardians' resources were adequate for the workhouse needs. The total number of people who had received relief by the end of September 1845 was only 122, and for the last three months of 1845 the daily workhouse population varied between 68 and 84, with no deaths up to year's end.[117] However, all was not well with the union finances going forward.

THE POOR RATES

Despite Assistant Poor Law Commissioner Burke's visits every two months, the poor rate collection was hopelessly inadequate. By the end of September 1845, only £606 was collected out of the total of £1,738.[118] No information was found as to why that was the case, but it seems likely that the guardians did not make much effort to collect even this fairly low rate, as they had been opposed to it in the first place. In 1844–45, the net annual value of Bantry Union property was £41,725, with a proportion of loan (for the workhouse) to net union valuation in the higher range compared to other unions.[119] The ratepayer tables for Bantry Union published in 1846 reflect the numbers after the 1843 valuation adjustment (Appendix V). On the Beara peninsula fewer families paid rates despite the presence of the copper mines, supporting an impression of greater poverty there. However, the lowest percentage of rate-paying families lived in Kilmacomogue, the area between Bantry and Glengarriff. Many in this electoral division were tenants of Lord Kenmare. It is not clear why in this area only 12 per cent paid rates.

From the table in Appendix V, it can be seen that of the 8,989 families in the union only 2,577 were paying rates. In other words, 29 per cent of families in the union were supporting the remaining 71 per cent. An unexpectedly high percentage of families paid rates in Kilcrohane despite the poverty there (95.1 per cent fourth-class houses).[120] This might be explained by a valuator's discovery in April 1848 that some Kilcrohane ratepayers who owned under £4 property claimed they were on long-term leases, thus being on the rate rolls,[121] possibly in an attempt to maintain enfranchisement.

In contrast, in Skibbereen Union, 45 per cent of ratepayers supported the remaining 55 per cent (7,860 ratepayers and 17,336 families).[122] Thus, Bantry Union carried an unequal burden compared with Skibbereen in this respect.

THE POTATO DISEASE

The momentous event of 1845 was the new fungal disease of potatoes, *phytophthora infestans*. Brought, it was believed, on ships from the New World and capable of spreading rapidly by air-borne spores.[123] It was first reported in Munster in September 1845[124] but not in Bantry until 10 November 1845, when a carefully monitored store of potatoes was found to be blackened and rotten.[125] The neighbouring unions of Killarney and Skibbereen were attacked by disease earlier and held emergency meetings 'in apprehension of blight'.[126] The only records that survive of disquiet in Bantry are letters; one of them, from Lord Bantry, dated 24 November 1845, said, 'the failure of the crop has not been so great in this district [...] the previous season's crops had been so much greater than usual [...] that what is now on hand will be sufficient for the people.'[127] Another letter dated 25 November from Rev. Alleyn Evanson in Durrus was less sanguine, saying, 'the small farmer and labourer, I fear, will be very badly off in the spring.'[128]

Since about two-thirds of the potato crop had survived, shortages did not occur immediately and a sense of urgency was lacking in Bantry Union. In fact, even in January 1846 the focus was on the planning of an extension of the railway line from Bandon,[129] with the prospect that Bantry would become a packet station for America. County Surveyor Edmund Leahy, the Earl of Bandon and numerous Bandon and Bantry gentry met to discuss the subject.[130] Many of the gentry had invested in this project, which was described as having a capital of £500,000 in 20,000 shares at £25 each. Investors from Bantry included Lords Bantry and Berehaven, the Hon. Robert White, John Warren Payne, John O'Connell, Big Pat Sullivan, Richard White of Inchiclough, Jeremiah O'Connell and Samuel Hutchins. This list is valuable, as it shows that these local gentry had discretionary funds in 1845.[131] Another enterprise that was launched at the end of December was the Gurtavallig copper mine on Sheep's Head. It employed sixty to seventy of the local poor people at wages almost double the usual 6*d* to 8*d* per day of agricultural labour.[132]

NATIONAL AND LOCAL MUSTERING OF RELIEF

In October 1845, because of the blight and fear of impending malnutrition, the Mansion House Committee in Dublin was set up by the Lord Mayor, clergy, nobles and gentry. They petitioned unsuccessfully for the establishment of public works, the closure of distilleries, the prohibition of food exports and the setting-up of food depots throughout Ireland. They wrote to Sir Robert Peel, the British Tory Prime Minister, who sent scientists to Dublin to study a possible remedy for blight. Nothing useful came of this. Peel, in anticipation of food shortages, authorised a Temporary Relief Commission in Dublin and purchased Indian meal, secretly importing it to Ireland from America so as not to depress prices and alert his critics. The first of many consignments of Indian corn arrived in Cork on 1 February 1846.[133] Peel decided to repeal the Corn Laws to ease its importation, an action that led to his government's fall in June 1847. The obvious problem was the impossibility of replacing £3,500,000 worth of lost potatoes with the £100,000 worth of corn bought by Peel, but it was 'better than no plan at all'.[134]

Peel's Temporary Relief Commission began to organise itself in early 1846 but issued no guidelines for Poor Law unions until February 1846,[135] and in Co. Cork, not until the end of March.[136] The directives instructed unions to form committees that would distribute relief paid for by local subscriptions. A critical point was that additional grants from Dublin were to be sent in proportion to the subscription amount raised. The Relief Commission in Dublin was chaired by Sir Randolph Routh, head of the commissariat. Aid was co-ordinated by the PLC, the police, the coastguard, the army commissariat and the OPW. In March, Daniel O'Connell, in the House of Commons, spoke about 'the rapid increase in distress in several towns [...] People were now on the brink of destitution.' He questioned what the government was doing to prevent starvation.[137]

In February and March, while other unions in Munster were clamouring that food supplies were running out, Bantry gentry were preoccupied with railway development. The first public alarm in Bantry Union was raised in March 1846 by the Rector of Durrus, Rev. William Moore Crossthwaite, a complex and controversial figure, who appealed in an English newspaper for money 'to keep my poor people from dying of want'.[138] Around the same time a report was sent to the Scarcity Commission in Dublin by Mr Hutchinson, JP of Bantry, stating that 'there will not be a potato by the 20th of May'.[139]

Although elected five years previously, the Board of Guardians had not established themselves as spokespersons or leaders of the union, or taken responsibility for the union as a whole. Due to this lack of leadership, concerned laymen and clergy began to write individually for help to the Relief Commission. A pattern developed of clusters of local petitioners in separate parts of the union.

LOCAL INDIVIDUALS AND THE RELIEF EFFORT

BEARA
Castletown's appeals were almost all from Catholics represented mainly by the O'Sullivan extended family. The Protestant clergy there seldom wrote. The exception, Rev. Nicholas Wright in Adrigole in the Kilcaskan division, was active in written appeals, as to a lesser extent was the parish priest of Kilcaskan, Rev. Jeremiah Sheahan. At the end of March 1846, Rev. Wright implored the Relief Commission for money to build roads, as food would run out in six weeks.[140] In Kilnamanagh, John Reed, superintendent of the Allihies copper mines, wrote for Indian corn for 1,100 men and their families.[141]

BANTRY TOWN
The obvious leader of Bantry was Viscount Berehaven, a man in his early forties with obligations to numerous tenants, but after an initial presence he absented himself for most of the famine. Much of the responsibility was taken up initially by Rev. Thomas Barry, the respected long-time parish priest of Bantry. He wrote letters to the Relief Commission and travelled to Dublin to obtain OPW funds to

employ workers on a chapel. At a Repeal meeting in Dublin, he spoke of 'extreme distress' of parishioners, with no help expected from Lord Kenmare.[142] He was the most committed advocate for the poor in Bantry Union until his transfer out of the parish in 1847.

However, the individual with the greatest power was John Warren Payne, who, as Lord Bantry's agent, represented more than half the property in the union.[143] He was a magistrate, a guardian and a consummate politician. From the pages of the workhouse minutes he comes across as a competent, hard man who attempted to spend the least possible amount relieving the poor of the union. He was assiduous in his duties to Lord Bantry and Viscount Berehaven while at the same time building his own fortune in land and property, becoming a virtual dictator in his later years.[144] He did occasionally make public pleas for famine relief but more often attempted to undercut or delay the efforts of others.

Fig. 12. Richard White (1800–1868) Viscount Berehaven, 2nd Earl of Bantry. Photo courtesy Seana Vida Farrington.

To a continuing extent, the Catholic curates and Rev. Alexander Hallowell, curate to the rector, played a crucial role during the famine years. Rev. Hallowell worked unceasingly, dealing with the bureaucracy in obtaining aid, and he was active in running the soup kitchens. John Shea Lawlor, another natural leader, was a prominent advocate for the unemployed and poor in the union from 1846 until early 1848, when he turned to Repeal politics.

As far as can be gathered from the workhouse minutes, the Bantry guardians, as a group, saw their role as strictly limited to running the workhouse and collecting rates. They did not see themselves as obligated to help the thousands of unemployed who were in danger of starvation.

SHEEP'S HEAD

Rev. Crossthwaite, the Rector of Durrus, was exceedingly active in writing for help and raising funds. The Evansons, a prominent Protestant family in Durrus, and Timothy O'Donovan, the Catholic magistrate, worked together through the famine to procure aid for their area.

Thus, fragmented information trickled out from different electoral divisions instead of a co-ordinated appeal from Bantry Union to Dublin Castle.

FOOD SHORTAGES BEGIN

Bantry Union finally recognised an imminent severe food shortage by the end of March 1846. Government cornmeal was on its way, 10 tons to be stored for future sale, not for immediate use, at the coastguard stations of Bantry and Castletown. More was en route from America.[145] A letter from Viscount Berehaven asked for meal to be sent to Bantry at once.[146] On 15 April 1846, at one of his last public appearances chairing a courthouse meeting, Lord Berehaven said that he and his father, Lord Bantry, intended to increase employment. The inadequacy of this offer was pointed out by both Rev. Barry and corn merchant John O'Connell, who noted that 4,000 people in the district were on the brink of destitution. Rev. Barry said the issue was getting corn to the union and that as the government intended to contribute only in proportion to the amount subscribed by union donors, immediate subscriptions should be taken up. John Payne was reluctant, as were a few others, but they were overruled. (For the subscription list, see Table 1.) A total of £87 was raised, with promised loans totalling £180. No information was found as to whether the loan money was paid out or, if so, ever paid back.

The meeting elected the first Bantry Temporary Relief Committee: Viscount Berehaven, Rev. Barry, Rev. Bennett, O'Connell, Payne, Downing and O'Sullivan. Nothing further was published on this committee until August, but presumably when the government depots opened in May for the sale of Indian corn, they would have bought up amounts for the destitute of Bantry.[147] No confirmation of this is available, and there is no evidence that this relief committee sent a request to Dublin for a grant in proportion to the subscription raised.

In contrast to Bantry town, Rev. William Crossthwaite in Durrus began fundraising quickly and raised £100 in subscriptions. He proposed buying Indian corn 'immediately' and asked that the corresponding government grant be sent out.[148] By June 1846 he had raised over £152.[149]

In Beara, Rev. Alexander Hallowell, at that time secretary of the Beara Relief Committee, sent proof of £267 13s 6d raised in subscriptions (Fig. 13) and said there was no part of the country more destitute. He noted that the subscription was so inadequate that a large grant was needed.[150] On 11 June he wrote to thank the Relief Commission for their 'liberal donation'.[151] In Beara also, Rev. Sheehan and a Eugene O'Sullivan had obtained approval for funds of £25 and £18 to repair roads in their districts.[152]

TABLE 1. BANTRY SUBSCRIPTION LIST, 15 APRIL 1846.

Lord Berehaven £10	Mr John O'Connell £10 and a loan of £50 towards purchasing the necessary food
Mr Payne £5	Mr Jeremiah O'Connell £10 and a loan of £50
Mr Samuel Hutchins £10	Mr Edward O'Sullivan £5 and a loan of £20
Mr Arthur Hutchinson £5	Lieut. Dealy £5 and a loan of £20
Mr Shea Lawlor £5	Mr Jagoe £5 and a loan of £20
Mr R. Downing £5	Mr Godson £5 and a loan of £20
Rev. Bennett £2	Rev. Barry £5

Source: *Cork Examiner* (17 April 1846).

SUMMER 1846: REOCCURRENCE OF BLIGHT, THE LABOUR RATE ACT

In June, the Whig party leader, Lord John Russell, became prime minister. Under the influence of Charles Trevelyan, Assistant Secretary to the Treasury, and other like-minded parliamentarians who believed that self-reliance equated to moral rectitude, a new relief approach was developed. This was organised to promote employment more than it was to ensure a food supply. Furthermore, people expected a good harvest. That hope was dashed when the potato blight recurred in summer 1846 to a much worse extent than the previous year. Even when it was clear that the potato crop had failed completely, grain purchases were not resumed.

In August 1846, parliament hurriedly passed the Labour Rate Act for the employment of the poor in public works, the total cost to be paid out of local rates. The Treasury granted a loan for this purpose

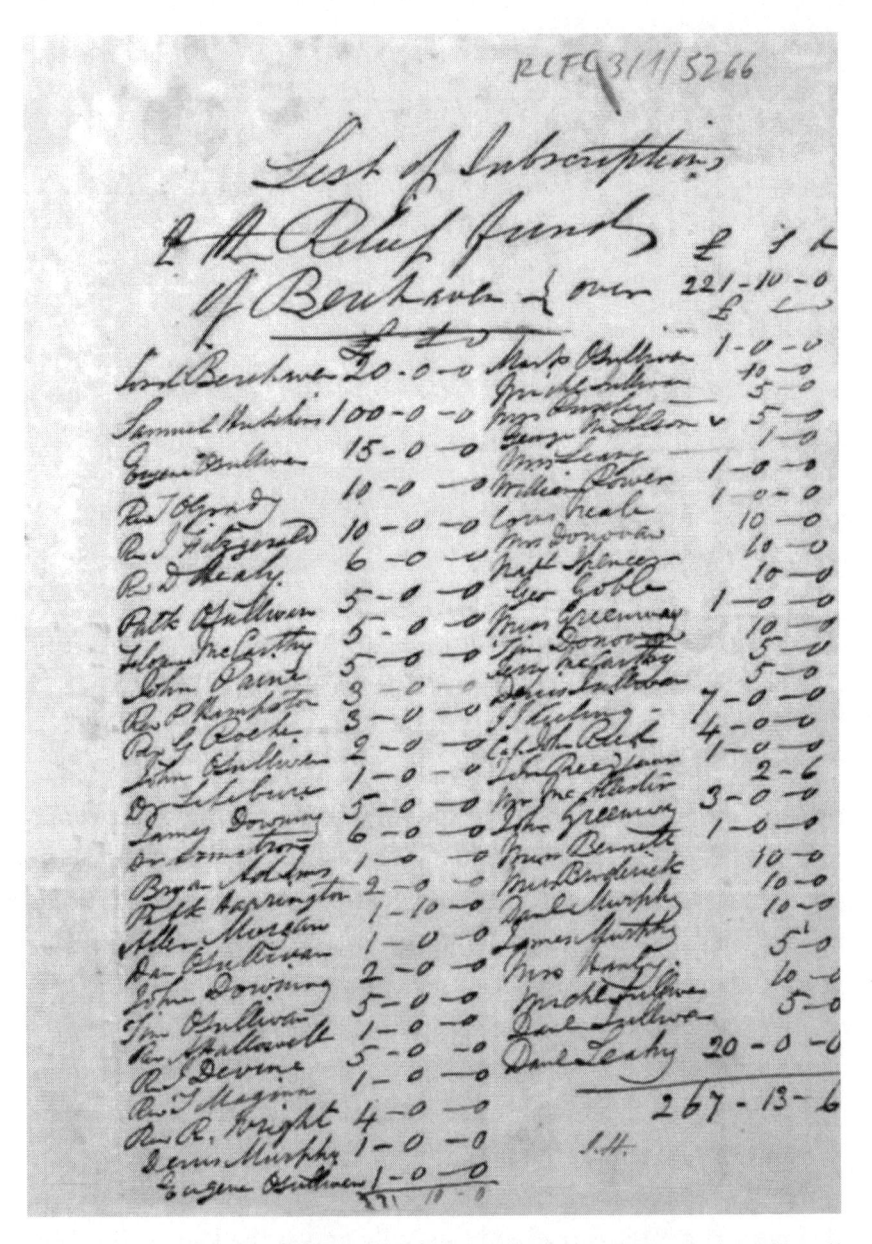

Fig. 13. Subscription list 6 August 1846 from Beara sent by Rev. Hallowell amounting to £267 13s 6d. NAI RLFC 3/1/5266, 8 August 1846 (Famine Relief Commission Papers).

at 3 per cent interest to be repaid in ten years.[153] The central government authorities also took control away from local relief committees on the grounds that tickets for relief and jobs were not being allocated appropriately. Army officers and OPW staff began to check lists of those eligible for public works and veto local recommendations.[154] The Treasury directed the works projects, now the main form of relief. Task work (a system of payment based on individual tasks) was introduced instead of daily wages. In practice, this meant lower pay, and to make matters worse, wages were set too low to keep pace with food prices and to feed a family. This was a critical factor in causing nutritional deprivation in the ensuing months.

In the middle of August 1846, the gentry met in Bantry to recommend works projects to the government worth £9,150. During the discussion, Rev. Barry referred to 6,000 people living in Bantry town. If correct, that would represent an increase of 2,000 since the census of 1841, probably a result of people flocking in to seek employment. It was reported that the meeting 'was densely crowded by the unemployed labourers of the town [...] who evinced the greatest anxiety in the proceedings of the meeting'. John Payne and Rev. Barry in a rare moment of agreement also hoped that a letter to the former government expressing gratitude would help with their 'claim' on the present government.[155] At the end of August, a constabulary report for Bantry Union confirmed the potato crop was almost completely destroyed.[156]

Some comments survive from around that period from a private individual. Jane Besnard Murphy of Newtown, Bantry, Michael Murphy's wife and the rector's sister-in-law, wrote of personal matters and gossip to her daughter Charlotte near Bandon. In an undated letter fragment, she wrote, 'truly awful all the potatoes here are going and gone'.[157]

On 1 September 1846, two weeks after the public works meeting in August, a large assembly of proprietors, clergy and landholders met at the courthouse to discuss the local distress and to ask the government for Indian meal and for employment. The meeting was chaired by Richard White of Inchiclough, a nephew and namesake of Lord Bantry and a respected guardian known as an improving landlord. It became clear that the gentry by then had read about the new Labour Rate Act and the lack of plans to import grain and were worried about the implications. At this meeting, both White and the rector, Rev. Murphy, said that the government must provide food. Rev. Barry said people would starve unless food and employment were obtained. Payne spoke of the financial burden the government had imposed on the union. Rev. Alleyn Evanson agreed, saying that if the public works plan were carried out, Bantry 'would be mortgaged for a debt they could not pay'. Richard O'Donovan (a relative of Guardian Timothy O'Donovan) said the absentee landlords should be made to pay 'instead of having their chariots parade around London'. Shea Lawlor argued convincingly that the wages proposed for the workers were inadequate to sustain them. A resolution proposed by John Payne was passed that said while they gave credit to the government for good intentions, the measures recently introduced were 'totally inadequate for the present emergency'.[158] In the ensuing days, Rev. Barry wrote to the Relief Commission in Dublin for the first time of many, asking for a food provision depot at Bantry.[159] This was an important request. Its effectiveness would have been greater if it had been supported by the mass of gentry and landowners. It is unclear why it was not and why he did not bring up the issue at the 1 September meeting. Rev. Barry also wrote to the Commissary General that the need was urgent because 'there are scarcely any provisions in the town at the present moment [...] We have every reason to fear very serious consequences.'[160]

The Bantry Relief Committee met twice in September 1846, at least one of the meetings being held at the workhouse with Guardian Samuel Hutchins of Ballylickey in the Chair. The meeting there on 10

September was not recorded in the minute book but was reported in the *Constitution*. The committee sent a petition to Lord Russell with concerns about wages, food prices and the difficulty in getting public works started.[161] The committee applied to the government for food, warning of impending starvation, and ordered 20 tons of meal from local subscriptions, to be sent immediately.[162]

On Beara, an acrimonious presentment session for public works was held at Castletown on 18 September. The same Samuel Hutchins (who leased land on Beara) was said to have behaved arrogantly, forcing the meeting into an overcrowded courthouse (he insisted that the larger Catholic church was unsuitable), where the chairman, Lord Bantry, aged 79, was almost overcome with heat. At this meeting Catholic and Protestant clergymen tried with mixed success to steer approvals to help the needy. Lord Bantry spoke up to help the people on Bere Island and also commented that he was almost ashamed to ask the government for so much but had no choice as the people needed the work. (This seems to have been the last time Lord Bantry chaired any meeting in the area.) Applications were granted for the large sum of £38,048. As the meeting broke up, Shea Lawlor entered the courtroom, causing a minor commotion, saying that there was less than £6,000 available for these works.[163] It is not clear what he was talking about, as it seems apparent that the funds approved were expected to be loans from the government. Probably the landowners felt they had no option but to approve enough works to get government funds flowing again to pacify the thousands of unemployed, and perhaps they hoped that the day of reckoning for their finances could be postponed. Shea Lawlor did not buy into this type of reasoning. It is clear from the earlier comments of John Payne that both of them were concerned about the huge debt being incurred by the union.

In October 1846, the Chief Secretary of Ireland, Mr Labouchere, wrote a letter providing for drainage and sub-soiling to be added to public works in the hope that landlords would use the scheme to improve their estates. The cost was a charge on the electoral divisions, not on individuals, and it was seen as being of benefit. Drainage work, though, had a drawback in that it was heavy labour not suited to men enfeebled by hunger. Presentments for drainage were passed, among others, for land farmed by the Earl of Bantry, the Sullivans of Carriganass,[164] Samuel Hutchins, Richard White and John Payne.[165]

FURTHER URGENT APPLICATIONS FOR RELIEF

In the middle of October, John Sullivan of Millcove, the current Secretary of the Relief Committee of Beara, suggested to Sir Randolf Routh that if a steamer was organised to bring meal from Cork, he would undertake to store the meal and keep market prices down to within 10 per cent of Cork wholesale prices. He estimated Beara would need 5,000 tons for the next 300 days and the Bantry district the same (just under 20 tons per day for the entire population of each district). Prices in Bantry and Beara were 30–40 per cent higher than Cork prices, and travel by land was unsafe. The commissariat replied saying, 'the means of assistance was under consideration'.[166] This letter was perhaps vital to eventually getting some help for Beara, the specific estimates of need probably being particularly useful.

Towards the end of October more letters were sent to the Relief Commission pleading for food and money. One from the Beara Relief Committee, stating they only had £200 on hand, asked for a loan or grant to purchase a stock of food 'for the starving population'. They were refused, and the reply lectured them on the necessity of keeping prices up so that private traders did not lose money.[167] The second letter came from a visitor staying near Adrigole in Kilcaskan. He described 'hungry crowds' gathering around him and urged the commission to set up a food depot in the area because no boats existed to get supplies from Cork. It was too far from Castletown and Bantry, and there was no one in the area to help except Rev. Wright.[168] In November, Rev. Wright had sent a subscription list amounting to £123 to Dublin for grants for the Kilcaskan division.[169] A third letter came from Patrick Grant, the head constable in Bantry, who wrote on behalf of the Bantry Relief Committee stating 'the very great scarcity of food'. He hoped a food depot would be established soon, as the meal took over three weeks to arrive from Cork.[170] Nothing was done other than when John O'Connell in Bantry, around the middle of October, 'purchased 2,500 barrels of bread stuffs' and began selling them at cost to the poor. The supply was used up in two months.[171]

Rev. Crossthwaite wrote to the *Times*, reporting that 500 men who walked 4 miles to work did not receive wages for three weeks. He was told by the inspector overseeing them that if he offered to advance money, the OPW would not repay him.[172] He must have been outraged by this response, as he wrote to several newspapers documenting it. Finally, many weeks overdue, at the end of November 1846, a man-of-war steamer was on the way from Cork to Bantry with the 20 tons of Indian corn purchased by the Bantry Relief Committee in September.[173]

APPLICATION FOR ARMED PROTECTION

An event unrelated to food or employment was the decision by Sir H. Pigot, the admiral in command of the Irish squadron, to station a steamer in Bantry Bay for the winter of 1846/47 with an officers' party of royal marines.[174] 'Urgent representations' from unnamed people in Bantry had been made to Mr Redington, the new Undersecretary of State for Ireland, of the necessity for protection of Bantry and

Berehaven. Two days later the answer came that a steam vessel was on the way, despite the fact there had been no breach of peace in the area.[175] One might question the priorities of authorities who supplied armed protection at once while taking months to get a small quantity of meal shipped from Cork to a relief committee. It does, however, point out the apprehension that crowds of hungry people caused. The gentry must have felt justified when, on 23 November 1846, a large crowd of 'under-tenants' gathered near Lord Bantry's lodge at Glengarriff demanding work, food or money. They were arrested in what the *Constitution* called a 'most unpleasant affair'.[176]

SURVIVING WORKHOUSE MINUTES BEGIN

The Bantry guardians faced no major challenges until late 1846. They had set a low rate in 1844 that did not impinge on their personal finances. They had as little contact with workhouse inmates as possible, meeting in the separate building in front. Ragged people may have been visible on Union Hill, waiting to be admitted, but paupers were rarely seen in the boardroom. There is no record of any guardian personally inspecting the infirmary or wards while inmates were present. The earliest surviving minute book begins 4 August 1846. The pages had printed headings dealing with workhouse statistics for the previous week, dates of board meetings and the guardians in attendance, letters from the PLC, reports of the doctor and master, supply lists, wages, rate collections, and the various 'resolutions' of the guardians. These were handwritten by the clerk. In places the ink has faded and the script is illegible, and the pages throughout lack consistent numbering. Often, transactions are spread over many meetings.

Guardian attendance was irregular. Despite a complement of twenty-four, the average attendance from August 1846 to October 1847 was seven. The most dependable was John Warren Payne, followed in order by: Michael Murphy, William Pearson, George Bird, Arthur Hutchins, Arthur Hutchinson, Samuel Hutchins, David Kirby (six-month period) and Richard White (eight-month period). In that time Vice-Chairman Viscount Berehaven did not attend. Timothy O'Donovan, the Deputy Vice-Chairman, was present only a few times, although his brother Richard and a Richard Jr came sporadically. The guardians who attended at least half of the meetings would be presumed to exert the most influence and responsibility for the board's actions or omissions during the months to come, but the minutes give an impression of a passive group led by a few, with a lack of critical discussion in the boardroom. Probably the chairmen exerted the most influence, and their outlook did not vary much. Between August 1846 and October 1847, the chairmen (all Protestant) were as follows: John Payne (who attended fourteen times), Samuel Hutchins (thirteen times), Arthur Hutchinson (eleven times) and Arthur Hutchins (nine times). These men held the fate of thousands of inhabitants in their hands. Of them, John Payne was clearly the dominant guardian.

The minutes from August 1846 began with a squabble about salary. Rev. Murphy refused the Protestant chaplain's job at the workhouse because he considered £20 per annum inadequate.[177] The problem was solved when the salary was raised to £25 and Rev. Alexander Hallowell was brought to Bantry to be Rev. Murphy's curate and workhouse chaplain. The correspondence attached to this exemplifies the disproportionate time spent on trivia at the expense of dealing with issues far more relevant to the welfare of the inmates of the workhouse. The guardians seemed only partially aware of the dwindling union funds and that the rate collection was not replenishing them. In September, under the prodding of the PLC, the guardians demanded that the rate collector for Beara, John O'Sullivan, 'summon and distrain' rate defaulters.[178]

A WANT OF INHABITANTS: THE FAMINE IN BANTRY UNION

By 13 October the number in the workhouse had risen to 395. At the weekly board meeting the clerk said that the union auditor had asked for the union balance for the half-year ending 29 September. He wrote that he had to 'remonstrate strongly with the Guardians on the immediate necessity of examining and certify [sic] the several bills due of the Union up to the 29th of September that the accounts may be closed for audit'. Despite worsening union finances, the board struck a new rate, lowering the percentage in Beara to 7½ d in the pound.

In late October 1846, bowel ailments affecting the workhouse inmates were highlighted by Dr Tisdall, who asked for a 'better description of diet' for the patients. This is the first indication of dysentery. Lack of food then rapidly became the foremost issue. The usual supply of meal had not arrived, and the clerk was instructed to find and buy a ton of meal locally. In early October the PLC wrote that they strongly disapproved of the workhouse serving breakfast to non-inmates. By the end of October there was not enough meal to serve even the inmates their breakfast. Two guardians went to Cork to buy 2 tons of meal, 'wherever it can be found'.[179]

In November, Dr Tisdall requested an assistant, as fever was resurfacing. He was refused on the grounds that when the new fever hospital opened shortly (construction had been ongoing for several months), the medical arrangements would be revisited. (For plans of the fever hospital, see Fig. 14.) In late November the guardians had an unpleasant surprise when Thomas Vickery, the bread contractor, complained that a £95 cheque given to him by the board had been refused by their bank treasurer because the board's funds were exhausted. The board evidently expected that the bank would continue issuing funds even when they had run out of money. Their reaction focused on what they considered atrocious behaviour by the bank manager rather than on how to raise the funds needed by the union.

By the end of November 1846, the union was insolvent. Outside the workhouse the lack of food and employment had reached the point where people were beginning to die of starvation. The period of the next seven months, both never to be forgotten and determinedly 'forgotten' by future generations, was a horror that could not be integrated into the community's collective memory.

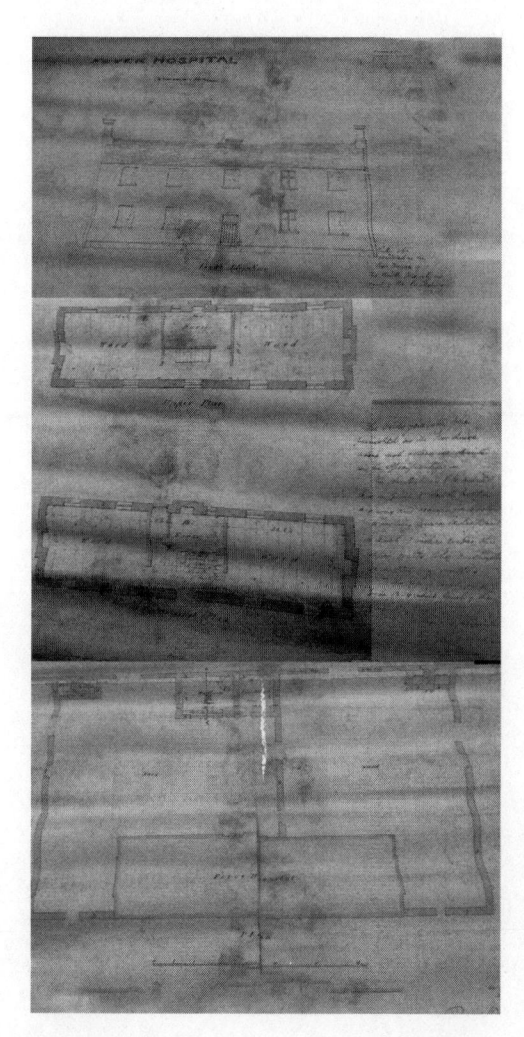

Fig. 14. Water-damaged plans for Bantry fever hospital, completed at the end of 1846. With permission: Workhouse Drawings Collection, Irish Architectural Archive.

3.

DEATH BY MISMANAGEMENT
1846–47

STARVATION: DECEMBER 1846 TO JUNE 1847

Bantry [...] starvation is everywhere. I am at a loss to know what will become of the poor of that locality.

Tablet, 19 December 1846

By December 1846 in Bantry Union, the lack of food and employment had reached critical levels. Thousands of the unemployed had no ability to feed themselves or their families. Deaths from starvation were reported in all parts of the union. Much of the blame for this was laid at the feet of Captain Gordon of the 75th Regiment. As the OPW engineer in charge, he controlled the employment lists. Both Protestant and Catholic clergy complained that he refused employment to needy people.[180] Gordon reported in his journal that 2,000 were employed in Bantry and 1,800 in Beara, and that all farming had ceased, but he said nothing of the thousands of unemployed.[181] On 19 December, the Catholic and Protestant clergy and the constabulary inspector failed to persuade the relief committee inspector[182] to act on the problems with Gordon. The *Cork Examiner* quoted the clergy in a rare instance of sarcasm after an ineffectual reply by the relief inspector:

> Rev. Mr Freeman – And if they starve at all, let them be starved systematically.
> Rev. Mr Barry – There is no doubt at any rate about the mortality whether they are dying systematically or otherwise.

Rev. Jeremiah Sheahan, the parish priest of Kilcaskan, wrote on 14 December to the Relief Commission that in the previous six days twelve people had died in his parish; that 800 of 1,050 families were destitute; that one hundred of these families were living solely on seaweed; and that in the past three months no OPW employment had been available.[183] Reports in the *Cork Examiner* alerted the entire country to the suffering in Bantry Union as 'no less great than in Skibbereen'. They charged that the problem began when the government, through its local OPW official (Captain Gordon), curtailed the efforts of the relief committee. In Bantry town alone, 1,300 men with families were unemployed.

In the week before Christmas the Catholic clergy said they had attended death-beds of forty to fifty people in the previous ten days, 'most caused by cold and exhaustion'. Rev. Freeman told the reporter that he could barely recognise his parishioners, as the facial features were so altered in starvation.[184] The *Examiner* noted that in Durrus more than 1,250 people were unemployed and quoted the incumbent clergyman (probably Father Quinn), 'my poor people – they are in the most frightful state of destitution.'

Similar to the situation in Kilcaskan, the clergyman said that his parishioners were living on a type of seaweed called 'Mivawn' (most likely *Miobhán*, a form of dillisk). Many of the hungry had to walk

DEATH BY MISMANAGEMENT

10–20 miles to buy grain.[185] In addition, the *Examiner* reporter wrote that Nicholas Brien and Timothy Coughlan, road workers on the Sheep's Head, had dropped dead the previous Wednesday on their way home. An editorial in the same edition of the *Examiner* charged the OPW with injustice on account of this. The editorial also said that Rev. Barry had been told by the relief committee inspector that it was uncertain whether a food depot would be established in Bantry, even though without one many would starve.[186]

On 26 December 1846, the *Tablet* excoriated its Catholic readers in England for their indifference towards the starving in Munster.[187] On the same day, even Captain Gordon wrote that there was not enough food in Bantry or Kilcaskan.[188] Three days later the *Constitution*, reporting on Beara, said that 'for every man employed there are five left roving in destitution.' The newspaper noted that the employed did not complain even though they were 'working and walking' in wet clothes for sixteen hours a day, whereas the unemployed were 'crying from hunger'. The report said many Dursey islanders had gathered in Castletown with a plan to kidnap Captain Gordon and hold him until 'he alleviated their distress'. They were barely prevented from doing so by the rector Rev. O'Grady and a Mr O'Sullivan.[189] A report from Castletown complained that death from starvation was aggravated by the 'harsh and unusually severe conduct' of the landlords, and it singled out 'a pair of noble Lords' who impounded cattle daily (presumably Viscount Berehaven and his father). At the end of December, Dr Armstrong, the physician in Castletown, certified two men, Timothy Sullivan and Humphrey Curtin, as dying from starvation.[190] The *Bath Chronicle* reported that 'the inhabitants of Dursey island are dropping hourly for want of food.'[191]

The workhouse guardians met four times in December. Their financial problems continued. The manager of the Skibbereen Provincial Bank, treasurer to the union, wrote requiring guardians' in their individual capacity to guarantee advances made for workhouse expenses. The guardians were affronted. They responded by changing banks and asked Mr Griffin, the manager of the National Bank of Skibbereen, to become the new union treasurer. From him they requested a loan of £600 at 5 per cent, the loan to be repaid from the rate collection. Thus, they pushed the problem further down the road.

One December meeting was attended by Assistant Poor Law Commissioner Burke (his last visit to Bantry). He reported to the PLC that all funds would soon be exhausted because ratepayers were unable to meet the rate and that the result would be that the guardians 'will throw up their offices and make an effort to cast responsibility on the government'.[192] The tone of this letter is both bitter and fatalistic. Burke made no effort to get food to the starving unemployed. He abrogated his responsibility entirely. One can speculate if this was a result of general indifference at the PLC headquarters in Dublin, or whether Burke was personally callous and negligent. Most of the evidence suggests the latter. Poor people had protested vigorously against Captain Gordon; in contrast, it does not seem that anyone importuned Burke for help, even though he was a direct conduit to the Poor Law Commission. Between Gordon and Burke, the people of the union were ill-served.

On 26 December, Randolph Routh wrote to Assistant Commissary General William Bishop asking him to set up soup kitchens in Bantry and Castletown.[193] This was a result of a directive from the government as it realised that failure of Russell's relief measures was resulting in starvation. Named the Temporary Relief Act 1847 (Soup Kitchen Act),[194] it was not passed until February 1847. It was to provide government-sponsored soup kitchens, using boilers and cauldrons provided by the Quakers. It required the unions to form new relief committees to draw up lists of people needing relief. This was to be financed in part from local rates, with loans or grants used only when absolutely necessary. Although this directive was issued in late December, it was not acted on for five months. Nevertheless, Bishop did set up soup kitchens in January 1847 in Bantry and Castletown. These were limited in the numbers they could feed. The large soup kitchens under the Temporary Relief Act did not begin functioning until May 1847.

DISILLUSIONMENT

On New Year's Day 1847, Catholic magistrate Timothy O'Donovan chaired another large meeting of gentry and clergy in Bantry courthouse. It was attended by 'crowds of wretched, miserable and apparently starving people'. O'Donovan stated that the object of meeting was to ask the government for help. Two camps predominated at this meeting: those so angry with the government that they used blame-and-shame strategies, and those, perhaps more cynical, who to varying degrees kept their heads below the parapet.

John Payne, in an unusual anti-government stance, read out the first motion, seconded by Timothy O'Donovan:

> That the condition of this district is most appalling, starvation being universal, deaths from want of food frequent and fearfully on the increase, whilst despair has seized upon the public mind from the apparent indisposition of the government to exert itself for the preservation of the people.

Dr Bourke immediately suggested an amendment, 'that they considered the government had only aggravated the destitution that at present exists.' John O'Connell seconded this motion but Timothy O'Donovan said he 'decidedly' opposed it. Later in the meeting a disagreement arose as to whether Dr Bourke's amendment was too gentle a rebuke to the government or whether a stronger resolution proposed by Arthur Hutchinson and seconded by Richard O'Donovan should replace it. Hutchinson's resolution was to the effect that the government had shown so little sympathy or interest in the 'emergency' that it 'materially weakened [...] the confidence and attachment of the Irish people'. An agitated discussion followed this proposal, both William Sullivan from Carriganass Castle and Richard White opposing it as being too political. Shea Lawlor called for another vote for Dr Bourke's motion, and Bourke's milder amendment was carried. It is interesting to note the cautious position taken by Timothy O'Donovan even though he seconded John Payne's motion.

Resolutions to provide food and employment immediately for the district were proposed both by Protestants and Catholics. The first resolution by Arthur Hutchinson was seconded by Rev. Murphy. Then came two more: the first by Rev. Barry, seconded by Patrick O'Sullivan of Millcove (Big Pat), and the second by Rev. Begley, seconded by Eugene O'Sullivan. Rev. Barry spoke with bitterness about the indifference of the OPW officials. Rev. Begley said that government officials had been 'travelling the length and breadth of the land and they can no longer plead excuses for the neglect of the people'. He knew men who had been working 'two entire days' on the roads 'without ever tasting a morsel of food'. Thirty deaths had occurred in the past week that he knew were from starvation. He denounced the unaffordability of food and 'the obstinate refusal of the government' to establish food depots. He also gave credit to both Arthur Hutchinson and Shea Lawlor for saving many from death by allowing starving people to pick turnips from their fields (the only recorded instance found of Hutchinson showing compassion). Rev. Hallowell spoke to the crisis in unemployment, saying that no steps had been taken by the OPW to start work although all the preliminary steps required for 'reproductive employment' (work that was actually useful) had been completed six weeks previously. He complained that the government forced the relief committee to take men off the work rolls and then did not replace them. He 'implored' the government for relief 'instead of [...] limiting their exertions by useless qualifications and unnecessary delays'. His resolution for employment was seconded by Lieutenant Kirby. The need for a food depot and soup kitchens was emphasised by Rev. Barry and Rev. Murphy.

Shea Lawlor as usual spoke at length. He 'continued with peculiar force and energy to deprecate the present policy of the government'. He praised Robert Peel's actions in preventing starvation. In reference to Lord John Russell, he declared, 'No, Sir, Lord John Russell knew the circumstances of the country, but he preferred to adhere to some mercantile partialities which he had for English speculators [...] running the chance of destroying the people by famine and starvation.'[195]

At the end of the meeting a petition was sent to the Lord Lieutenant saying private charity was drained, people were dying and many more would succumb unless help was sent. Seed corn, seed potatoes and a food depot for the district were needed urgently.[196]

Later in the month a similar petition was sent to Dublin from the relief committee of Durrus and Kilcrohane, signed by both Catholic and Protestant gentry again asking urgently for seed to prevent famine next year.[197]

On 1 January, the *Cork Examiner* wrote again about the starvation occurring in Kilcaskan.[198] The reporter had seen letters Rev. Sheahan had written to Dublin, 'the responses, cold, formal and freezingly polite, assuring the writer of immediate attention and government sympathy and effecting nothing.'[199] Another article on Kilcaskan said that only Rev. Wright and Rev. Sheahan helped the poor, adding that boats were rotting and fishermen were 'too weak to take advantage of the appearance of herring'.[200] A petition from Glengarriff for help was refused by the Treasury.[201] On 19 January, Randolph Routh wrote to Trevelyan saying 5,000 of the starving inhabitants of Castletown who belonged to a copper mining society of Tenby, South Wales would be supplied, presumably with food.[202] The next day Routh wrote to John Payne saying a grant to Bantry was delayed because the subscription list sent in for £118 was not properly certified,[203] another example of bureaucratic indifference. The three-part soup kitchen subscription list (Figs 15a and 15b) was eventually accepted.[204]

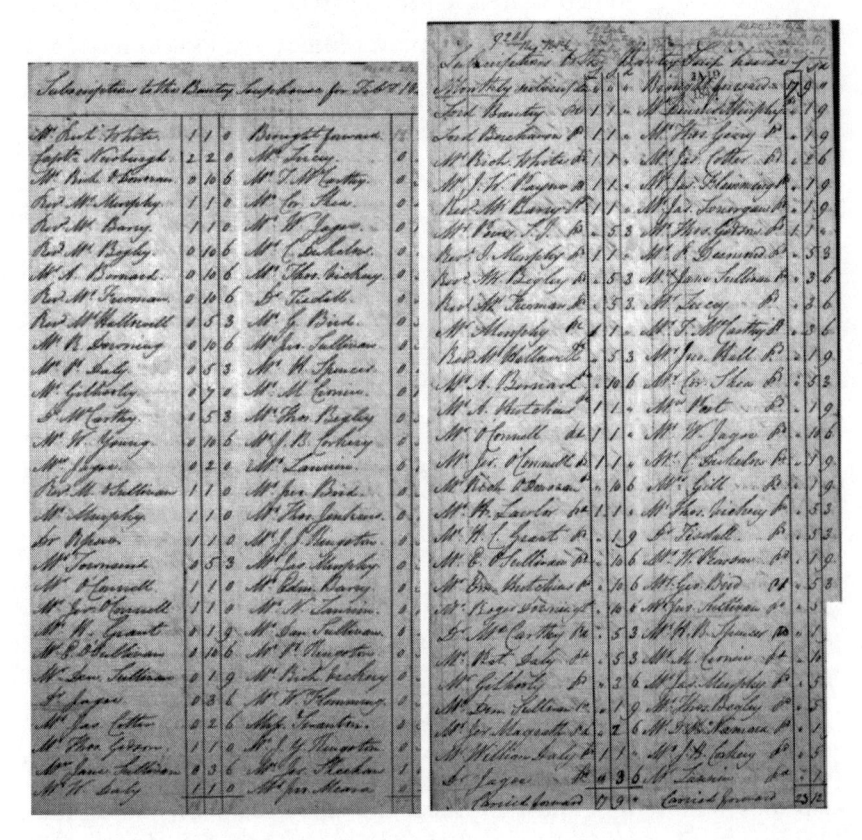

Fig. 15a. First and second page of the Bantry soup kitchen subscription list, February 1847.

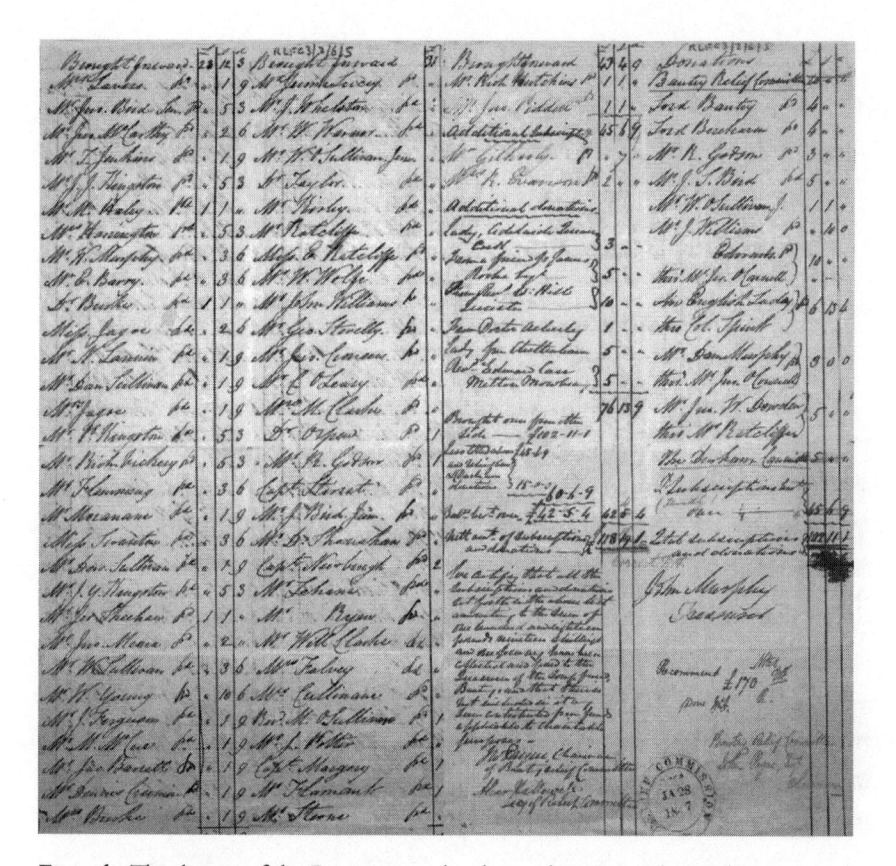

Fig. 15b. Third page of the Bantry soup kitchen subscription list, February 1847. NAI RLFC 3/2/6/5, February 1847.

JANUARY 1847: DEATHS INCREASE WITH SCANT RELIEF

The first Bantry inquest on deaths caused by starvation – of which, in this case, there were six – was held on 5 January 1847.[205] The jury, which included Guardians Richard White and Samuel Hutchins, stated that if the government refused to lower food prices, 'the result will be a sacrifice of human life from starvation to a frightful extent and endangerment of property and public peace.'[206] Another inquest took place at the end of January when ten deaths from starvation were recorded by local doctors. One of the victims, a John Whoolehan from Durrus, had been refused admission to the workhouse earlier the same day and was found dying at Custom Gap (a small street in the centre of Bantry town). Local people refused to take him in for fear of infection, so he was carried to the workhouse, where he died an hour later.[207]

The *Southern Reporter* wrote that 'the inhabitants are falling in hundreds in the huts all around the bay. The deaths on distant hills [...] and on roads none can calculate.' The *Times* said the scenes of 'extreme misery appear to have been transferred from Skibbereen to Bantry'.[208] A report to the Society of Friends from their unnamed correspondent in Bantry said that 10,000 people were absolutely destitute. The workhouse was full and temporarily closed to admissions and, terribly, 'the ties of natural affection, previously so strong a feature of the Irish, seem to be completely torn asunder.' Daily deaths occurred from starvation, and more than one hundred people were at the writer's door that morning seeking relief.[209] Two days prior in Bantry at a presentment session (where local JPs considered requests for money for local projects) it was noted that only 2,100 heads of families were employed, while 4,600 heads of families were unemployed.[210] This suggests that the 10,000 reckoning of 'totally destitute' was an underestimate.

The soup kitchen set up by Assistant Commissary General William Bishop was open in Bantry by 16 January 1847, producing 120 gallons of a brew of unknown quality per day.[211] By May 1847, three were set up: one near the rectory for people coming from Sheep's Head; one 1.3km north-east of Bantry town near Michael Murphy's Newtown residence at 'soup house field', where a LIDL supermarket now stands; and the third at the 'Black Bridge', for people coming from the east.[212] The last location is unclear, complicated by a similar name later attached to a railway bridge. None of the soup kitchen locations is marked with a memorial plaque. Lord Kenmare was reported to have contributed £150 to the soup depot, while most of the shopkeepers and people of the town of Bantry were in the main 'doing their utmost [...] with two marked exceptions, the noble lords who have both given only £4 to the Relief committee', referring to Viscount Berehaven and Lord Bantry.[213]

Bishop visited Castletown and described great distress and suffering, a dysfunctional relief committee and a soup kitchen in chaos because of sectarian infighting. At Adrigole, Rev. Wright operated a small soup kitchen with a private fund.[214] Rev. Crossthwaite in Durrus received funds from Lord Bandon that allowed him to provide breakfast to school children.[215] Also in the Durrus area, a Mrs Beamish, one of the Evanson family, ran a soup kitchen from her farm in Ardogeena. As Susanna Pyburn wrote in the 1930s schools' collection, 'There was a regular staff [...] who distributed the soup throughout the day [...] Food was stored [...] in a storehouse the ruins of which are still in [...] Friendly Cove. None except the wealthy was able to purchase it.'[216]

BANTRY UNION'S MISERY BECOMES PUBLIC KNOWLEDGE

In early February 1847, after another fifteen certified starvation deaths, the Bantry magistrates stopped holding inquests, claiming they were too time-consuming.[217] The *Southern Reporter* said, 'Famine and pestilence are sweeping away hundreds [...] as to holding more inquests, it is mere nonsense. The number of deaths is beyond counting.'[218] The *Freeman's Journal* reported that the Bantry jury foreman wanted to bring in a verdict of wilful murder against Lord John Russell. Rev. Barry intervened, recommending 'starvation' as the verdict and appending a note considering 'how far it was attributable to the neglect of Lord John Russell in yielding to the interests of a class of greedy monopolists'.[219]

In parliament on 8 February 1847, Daniel O'Connell spoke for the last time, three months before his death. Appearing weak and unwell, he made an appeal for help, saying that 'the House was not sufficiently aware of the extent of the distress in Ireland.' He was reported as saying that '25% of the people were perishing through destitution and that the people were starving [...] in hundreds, thousands, nay, even millions.' He asked the government to release funds 'so there might be some prospect of staying the progress of the famine'. He ended without submitting any specific proposal, perhaps because of his feeble health, although this was not made clear.[220]

On 13 February in the House of Commons, William Smith O'Brien, MP for Limerick, asked whether Mr Labouchere (Chief Secretary of Ireland) knew of the starvation deaths in Bantry. Labouchere replied that the 'destitution in that part of Ireland was most severe and that he had no doubt the attention of the Irish Government has been called to Bantry.'[221]

Several relief organisations, governmental and private, received reports during February showing the extent of the crisis in the union. A crucial help for Bantry Union was the British Relief Association (BRA).[222] One of its agents, a Captain Harston, wrote that deaths were rising. He had given food and money to Rev. Crossthwaite and a grant to Bantry widows and orphans.[223] He described 'the intense misery, raging fever and perfect absence of food that they are truly suffering from down on the sea coast'.[224]

A report to the Society of Friends from Castletown begged for warm clothing, particularly shoes for barefoot men on the roads who became 'struck with the cold', leading to early death.[225] A W.H. Mackintosh wrote to the OPW, initially describing the people in Beara as 'perfectly peaceful [and] completely servile, with all the accompanying vices, low cunning, a disposition to cheat and a want of common honesty'.[226] Later in the month, he changed his tone, saying that the people did not have strength to work and he needed to pay them more to avoid the 'dreadful scenes of other places'.[227] On 16

February Rev. Barry wrote to send his heartfelt gratitude to the men employed on the London Gasworks who sent a £20 contribution to the poor of his parish.[228] A report in the distress papers said that the labourers in Bantry were too weak to work hard; that they were quiet, non-violent and in despair. Agriculture was neglected. The farmers had not been able to procure seed for sowing.[229]

Drainage works under the ratepayer-funded Labouchere scheme finally began in Bantry in February 1847 under Samuel Hussey (1824–1913). In later years Hussey became well known as a harsh land agent who wrote a book about his experiences. He was critical about a lack of care and detail in the way the works were specified in the union.[230] However, the main square in Bantry was filled in, a road from the docks was built and 'glebe walls' of Bantry house were rebuilt.[231] It is probable that the well-known 100 steps at Bantry House were constructed at this time, financed by the Labouchere scheme and not by Viscount Berehaven individually as is sometimes implied.

Much later in 1904, Hussey wrote, 'The state of things round Bantry of which I had accurate knowledge was appalling. I knew of twenty-three deaths in the poorhouse in twenty-four hours. On a relief road, two hours after I passed, on my ride home I saw three of the poor fellows, stretched corpses on the stones they had been breaking.'[232]

At the end of February, Rev. Wright reported to Dublin that he was unable to feed the poor any longer. His meal supply would run out that week. His wife, servant and niece had all fallen sick. He asked the government to step in.[233] Meanwhile, in London, Viscount Berehaven wrote to his younger brother William (later the third Earl of Bantry), dealing with personal and legal affairs until he broke off to say, 'dreadful accounts from Bantry. Mr J. Payne writes 40 deaths daily of Rev. Barry's parishioners.' Many of these were his own tenants. Perhaps he was trying to avoid culpability by calling them Rev. Barry's parishioners.[234]

THE WORKHOUSE AND DR STEPHENS' REPORT

The workhouse guardians held three poorly attended meetings in January 1847.[235] Dr Tisdall pressured them to limit admissions and to open the fever hospital. They agreed to both. They also agreed to hire an assistant for him but then did not carry through with this. This was the second time they had failed to provide the help that Dr Tisdall said was needed. Several months before, the PLC had suggested building more accommodation, but apart from the housing of fever victims, the guardians would not consider expansion, despite large numbers of starving people. By the end of January, a rise in fever cases had caused overflow in the fever hospital (which had a capacity of forty). Guardian Michael Murphy showed concern about the crisis. On New Year's Eve his wife Jane wrote from Newtown House, Bantry to her daughter Charlotte saying, 'your dear papa is I trust safe in England by this time [...] He hopes to make some good purchases that we may be enabled to supply the neighbouring people better food. Alas, the state of things here is fearful [...] woes of the *crowds* that are at this door every hour of the day.'[236]

The Bantry guardians wrote to the *Constitution* in early February to warn that because of lack of funds, they might be forced to close the workhouse and 'turn everyone out'. On 2 February, the inmates received only one meal because of this situation.[237] This letter was perhaps a means of pressing the PLC to act, or maybe a pre-emptive defence against charges of neglect, since deaths were occurring amongst people being refused admission. The minutes record Rev. Hallowell saying that patients were five and six to a bed in the fever hospital, and Dr Tisdall confirmed a similar state in the infirmary.[238]

On 9 February, Dr Tisdall wrote that he was seriously ill and had arranged for a Dr McCarthy to take his place at the workhouse. The board granted him two months' leave. On 13 February, whilst at home,

Dr Tisdall sent a letter to the *Constitution* saying that the workhouse had become a 'perfect pest house', with people dying within hours of admission, thirty-six in the past week. He hoped readers would help. Though ill, he continued to send letters to the guardians, worrying about the increasing deaths (over fifty per week) and recommending measures to alleviate problems. Then, for reasons unexplained in the minutes, the board decided to replace the substitute chosen by Dr Tisdall with a Dr Jagoe. This decision was made only four days before an unanticipated inspection of the workhouse and fever hospital on 19 February 1847 by Dr Richard Stephens from the Central Board of Health. Dr Stephens reported that no doctor had been in attendance since Dr Tisdall had left, although he stated later that a 'medical man from the town' (perhaps Dr McCarthy) had visited two days before. Dr Jagoe had not yet started in his new position. This resulted in the absence of any doctor in the workhouse from 9–19 February with the exception of the brief visit from the 'medical man' on 17 February. Whatever the explanation for this lack of medical coverage, it showed atrociously poor management by the guardians.

When Dr Stephens arrived, he found patients *in extremis* in the fever hospital and was forced to give emergency aid to a dying woman whose new-born infant was 'nearly suffocated'. In his report he detailed the major problems as lack of medical attention, absence of water (because it had to be carried from the stream) and filth. He described the main workhouse as being in fair order but the fever hospital being in a 'heart-sickening' state with the dead lying next to the dying and, 'above all [...] incessant cries for water'. No doctor or nurse was present, only a hired inmate 'unfit for duty'. He called together the master, the matron and the only three guardians that could be found and he laid out their immediate medical and ethical responsibilities (see Appendix VI for full details on Dr Stephens' report).[239] Rev. Hallowell wrote that he accompanied Dr Stephens 'bed to bed through the hospitals'. He described emaciated children and a 'dying child nestling close to a filthy corpse'. He quoted Stephens as saying that in the course of twenty years' medical experience, he had never witnessed anything so frightful.[240]

At the beginning of March, the workhouse weekly death rate peaked at seventy, forty of whom were children (Fig. 16). The PLC sent a copy of Dr Stephens' report to the guardians. In a defensive response, they replied that they 'deplored' the state of the fever hospital but denied any responsibility. As they said, 'We cannot be expected to visit it', and if food and water were lacking, it was the 'fault of the attendant'. Nor did they admit responsibility for the gap in coverage after they had fired Dr McCarthy. They allowed the PLC to blame Dr Tisdall. However, the board, in a sudden flurry of changes to past policies suggesting consciousness of guilt, agreed to substitute rice for Indian meal to stem dysentery and to hire a temporary apothecary; they also told Dr Jagoe to hire 'two efficient nurse tenders', whatever the expense. It must have been a bitter pill for Dr Tisdall to learn that the items requested by him in November (a better diet for inmates and an assistant), plus extra nurses and an additional doctor, had been given to Dr Jagoe with no effort on his part.

WORKHOUSE LIMITS ADMISSIONS

The guardians may not have admitted culpability in writing to the PLC, but their actions showed otherwise. Later in March 1847, both Dr Stephens and Dr Phelan, an assistant Poor Law commissioner, travelled to Bantry to attend a board meeting with the apparent purpose of sorting out the workhouse problems. They did hire a Dr Nagle on a temporary basis to work alongside Dr Jagoe, but neither Stephens nor Phelan advocated expanding either the workhouse or the numbers permitted in the workhouse. Instead they tacitly acquiesced in the closure of the workhouse to further admissions until the guardians considered the numbers low enough to reopen. This, despite the fact that the workhouse was less crowded than in the two previous months and dying people were at the gates begging for admittance.[241] While it is not clear why Stephens and Phelan went along with this plan, it seems to have been an entirely self-serving move on the guardians' part, maybe out of fear of catching the fever themselves or as a way to improve the workhouse death statistics. Richard White was the sole guardian to oppose this plan.

This was the worst possible time for the workhouse to close its doors to further admissions. A 'gentleman' who said he had been travelling through Skibbereen and Bantry 'administering part of the relief funds collected by our deputation in England' wrote a private letter subsequently obtained by a newspaper and published in early April. It quoted him as saying that 'hundreds and thousands seem to have laid themselves down to die.'[242] (This may refer to the extreme apathy and cognitive indifference that is a recognised symptom of starvation.) In the *Constitution*, Rev. Hallowell wrote that there was scarcely a house in Bantry unaffected by fever or dysentery. He gave many examples of the families he visited:

> A poor man named Carthy [...] died this night [...] his wife [...] in a dying state [...] his daughter, fifteen years of age [...] her body swollen and covered with blisters [...] the little baby whose throat was mortifying [...] Now the father and two children are numbered with the dead.[243]

Rev. Hallowell also pointed out that the sick in their cabins could not get food or water because their neighbours were too afraid to venture inside.

SOUP KITCHEN ACT: FUNDING DELAY IN BANTRY UNION

On 20 March 1847, six hundred Bantry labourers for the OPW were abruptly dismissed with no relief available to them except the small soup kitchen in Bantry and some private soup kitchens, none of which had yet received government funding. Although the Soup Kitchen Act, first mooted in December, had finally passed on 26 February, almost nothing was in place for these suddenly unemployed workers. Funds were only going to be available from Dublin once newly established relief committees had submitted financial estimates and lists of the needy. The new Bantry Relief Committee had not even formed at that point,[244] but they did get organised toward the end of March. Chaired by John Payne, its members consisted of John Shea Lawlor, Rev. Begley, Rev. Freeman, Rev. Murphy, Timothy O'Donovan, Dr Orpen, Richard O'Donovan, Arthur Hutchinson, Samuel Hutchins, Emmanuel Hutchins and William Vickery. By 13 April the committee still had not done the necessary work to obtain government funding.[245] Shea Lawlor and Captain Morgan, the new Poor Law inspector in Bantry, both wrote in complaint, the former to the newspaper and the latter to the PLC.[246] In addition, Shea Lawlor wrote to the Relief Act commissioner[247] saying nothing had been done by the committee despite the fact that hundreds were dependent for their lives on its speedy action.[248]

In April, deaths from starvation and fever continued unabated in the union. One correspondent described 'heart-rending' scenes in Bantry town, dying people lying outside houses and, in one house, thirty-five people dead and dying.[249] In a response to the Archdeacon of Cork, who said no one should be 'permitted to die of starvation on the streets of Cork', Rev. Barry said he wished the guardians of Bantry Union felt the same. He accused them of closing the workhouse and letting six people who failed to gain admittance die the same day.[250]

Bantry Workhouse August 1846–July 1847

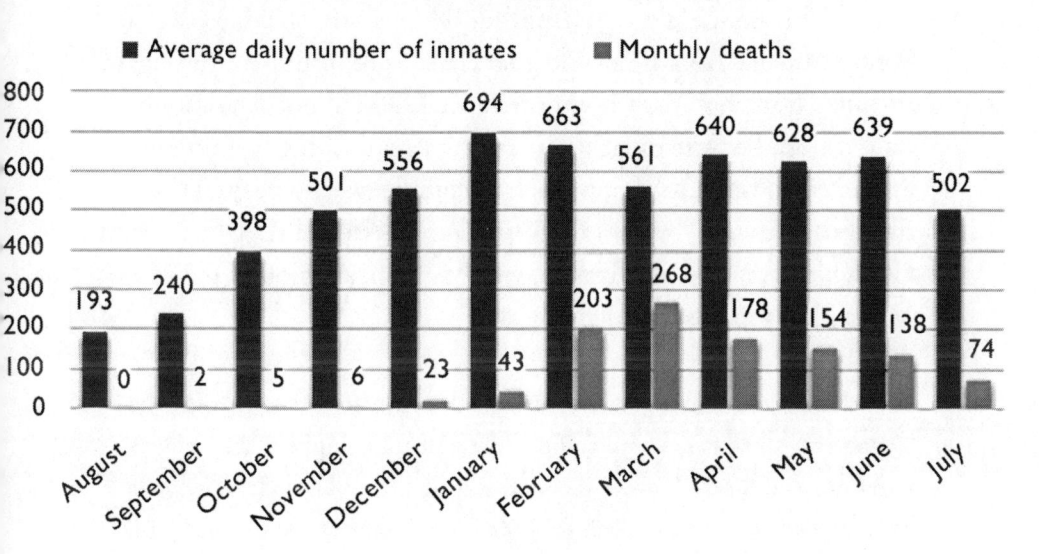

[Bar chart showing average daily number of inmates and monthly deaths:
- August: 193 inmates, 0 deaths
- September: 240 inmates, 2 deaths
- October: 398 inmates, 5 deaths
- November: 501 inmates, 6 deaths
- December: 556 inmates, 23 deaths
- January: 694 inmates, 43 deaths
- February: 663 inmates, 203 deaths
- March: 561 inmates, 268 deaths
- April: 640 inmates, 178 deaths
- May: 628 inmates, 154 deaths
- June: 639 inmates, 138 deaths
- July: 502 inmates, 74 deaths]

Fig. 16. Bantry workhouse inmates and number of deaths, August 1846–July 1847. Chart drawn by author from the statistics in the workhouse minutes. CCCA BG/43/AA1, A2.

Unfortunately for the union, at this juncture Rev. Barry was moved to Cork, but once there, he continued to advocate for Bantry parishioners. On 18 April 1947, a large meeting was held in the Catholic church in Bantry by Rev. Begley; it was attended by Shea Lawlor (who spoke at length) and 4,000 others who pleaded with the OPW and relief commissioners to continue employment to preserve life. Rev. Begley hoped the meeting would rouse the energies of the new relief committee in Bantry because, he said, 'even in a remote district a legal duty cannot be neglected with impunity.'[251]

Despite the need, the workhouse was still open to admissions only intermittently in April. The clerk said that on 6 April, because of fear of catching fever, the guardians remained only a short time at the workhouse before deciding to hold future meetings at the courthouse. This concern was not unfounded, as one of them, Richard White, was ill. Because of the guardians' lack of funds, they again threatened to close the workhouse if the PLC did not send money.[252] In addition, because of lack of money for coffins, the board resolved that 'shell coffins' (also known as trap coffins) were to be used to carry the dead to the pit, but not for burial. A well-known clergyman from Cloughjordan, Rev. F.F. Trench, who visited the union at the end of March, left this description:

> At Bantry I saw lying at the corner of the street two coffins for the poor; they call them 'trap coffins;' the bottom is supported by hinges on one side, and a hook and eye at the other. In these coffins the poor are carried [...] to a large pit [...] at a little distance from the road, and the bodies are dropped into it.

He went on to say that most in the district were not carried in these coffins but were buried in their rags and sometimes these were stripped off to cover someone still alive.[253]

Toward the end of April, Dr Nagle, who had been hired temporarily, left the workhouse assuming that Dr Tisdall was returning to replace him. However, the Central Board of Health, thinking that Dr Tisdall was responsible for the deplorable state of the fever hospital, refused to rehire him despite pleas from the guardians, who knew perfectly well that Dr Tisdall had not been remiss in his duties. The guardians simply were not prepared to admit their own negligence to the authorities. As for Dr Tisdall, he died two years later, at 32 years of age, of heart disease at his father's home in Louth, leaving a wife, child and posthumous son.[254]

Before his departure, Dr Nagle presented the guardians with a list of problems: the master and matron systematically opposed his orders, told other staff he had no authority and were generally verbally violent and abusive; new inmates, many in a dying condition, were forced to wait shivering in wet clothes prior to admission; patients were dying from severe dysentery, and the bread and meat were 'unfit for human consumption'; no whey was available for thirsty fever patients; and smallpox was spreading. The board declined to address these problems. At least, nothing was written in the minute books to suggest that they did, but they did complain about Rev. Barry's previous public accusation that they had refused admissions to the workhouse, agreeing again that it was better to close it than have overcrowding. A letter in the *Southern Reporter* from a 'rate payer' complained that the Board of Guardians had a 'complete disregard for the truth' and an indifference to the poor. The writer said 'they try to avoid culpability by blaming their doctor.'[255]

Better news came at the end of April when the New England Relief Committee met in Cork to allocate food from America that had arrived on the *Jamestown*. Rev. Barry was present and said no place needed relief more than Bantry Union, 'Nearly 4,000 had died in Bantry alone.' He requested 100 tons of meal, but in the end Bantry was allocated only 32 tons.[256] This is one of the few contemporary estimates of the number of deaths. Also, at the end of April, Captain Harston of the BRA said that because of the inactivity of the new Bantry Relief Committee, he had given monetary grants to private soup kitchens in Bantry.[257] Here, he said, 'the full amount of distress [...] has only begun to show in the last few weeks [...] deaths averaging from fifty to sixty per day [...] mainly from dropsy, dysentery and effects of want of food.' He told the BRA that a supply of provisions once per week to Bantry would be needed.[258]

It is not clear if the BRA responded then, but in early May, Shea Lawlor wrote to the *Cork Examiner* that the original relief committee (from 1846) had met and succeeded in procuring a three-week meal supply from Society of Friends representatives who arrived fortuitously on 6 May. Four thousand rations were given out on 10 May, and the supply was sufficient to continue until 24 May.[259] Shea Lawlor was less successful in an application to Undersecretary Thomas Redington asking for a sessions hearing to complete roads left in a dangerous state. A scribbled reply informed him there was no intention of doing that.[260]

'WILFUL MURDER'

On 5 May the *Cork Examiner* devoted four-and-a-half columns to report on the continued inaction of the Bantry Relief Committee. The April meeting was exceptionally rancorous and bitter. It was discovered that no tally of the needy or financial statements had been sent to Dublin. Chairman John Payne chose to ignore Captain Morgan, the Poor Law inspector, when he stated that no lists had been put forward. Instead, Payne focused on censuring Shea Lawlor for publicly criticising the committee. Shea Lawlor spoke passionately and at length. He said that since 20 March he had been trying to get the committee 'to move' so people would not starve. He accused Payne of being

> the weighmaster of starvation and wretchedness – the calculator of life and death – the thermometer of misery. Yet underneath your very window hourly pass the remains of the uncoffined dead. God of mercy! How can you endure such a sight? So young and yet so heartless.

At the meeting's end, Captain Morgan told Payne, 'Circular after circular has been sent [by the PLC], and yet nothing has been done by you [...] All you want is to pay a little devotion to the task.'[261] The *Cork Examiner* castigated the committee for its 'criminal slowness', saying 'thousands of starving wretches' depended on it.[262]

The publicity increased when on 18 May in the House of Commons, the MP for Stroud, George Julius Poulett Scrope (a passionate speaker in the House of Commons with ideas for bettering the life of the Irish poor) said the delay of the Bantry Relief Committee, if deliberate, could be described as wilful murder. He also accused Viscount Berehaven and his agent Payne of stopping their subscriptions to the soup kitchen and of not employing anyone.[263] His attack was later countered in the House by Labouchere, who read a letter from Viscount Berehaven in which he claimed he employed as many as possible, and although he and his agent had withdrawn their subscriptions, they were giving other relief. Scrope was unimpressed by this, saying he had many confirmations of the viscount's neglect from resident gentry and clergy in Bantry.[264] All this negative publicity may have stirred the new relief committee to action. Government soup kitchen relief finally began in Bantry on 23 May.[265]

FAMINE FEVER CONTINUES

During May, illness and death in the workhouse continued at high levels, with over seventy patients in the fever hospital built to accommodate forty. The guardians had been obliged by the PLC to replace the master and matron because of their behaviour toward Dr Nagle. They also hired a Dr Abraham Tuckee, who became chief medical officer. Dr Jagoe remained as fever hospital doctor. Rates were still not being paid, and the guardians continued to have problems with bad cheques they had issued. On 18 May, Dr Jagoe told the guardians that the master had allowed putrefying dead bodies to be piled up without any covering in the dead house and outside it. The smell was so disgusting he could only stand it for a few minutes. This was widely reported, the *Cork Examiner* saying the dead were left unburied, 'in exposed places, where they are torn by rats [...] we hope the Poor Law Commissioners will instantly interfere to put a stop to such infamous proceedings [...] Duties amongst the Bantry guardians are honoured in the breech not the observance.'[266]

On 10 May, Guardian Richard White, the landlord of Inchiclough, died of fever, leaving a wife and eleven children.[267] He had been universally highly regarded, and his death shocked the community. He had tried to keep the workhouse open and was active in public meetings to seek relief. He might have become an enlightened union leader if not for his premature death. In 1877, A.M. Sullivan, the Bantry-born author and politician, said that the people of Bantry still mourned him.[268]

On 12 May 1847, 23-year-old Augustus Gallway (son of Christopher Gallway of Killarney) wrote to the *Tablet* saying he had been sent by the Relief Commission to 'manage' the 'dissensions' (presumably sectarian) in the Castletown area. More to the point, he found that people all around him were starving and dying, with no one there making any noticeable effort to help. He asked for monetary contributions.[269]

Fig. 17. A famine soup pot at Newtown House, 2018. Photograph by author. The pot was suspended over a larger container containing coals, according to a local source (personal communication, Alex Hamilton).

In late May, an English visitor, Rev. John East, travelling past Bantry workhouse, observed 'pestilential bed-rags [...] just rinsed in the running stream' and a 'solitary woman crouched at its bolted door'. He spoke with Rev. Hallowell, barely recovered from illness, who told him that during the nearly six weeks he had been ill, whole families had died and been replaced twice in the same hovel. East commented on the paucity of young children, saying the current mortality was seventy times higher than that of London. He met the 'overworked' Rev. Wright in Adrigole, who told him that Rev. Sheahan (the parish priest) was 'half-starved'. In Castletown, he was shown a hut next to the doctor's house where fourteen people 'lay in famine fever'.[270]

DR KIDD'S VISIT TO BANTRY

In the midst of all these happenings, Dr Joseph Kidd, a young Quaker originally from Limerick, made a mildly bizarre but helpful visit of mercy to Bantry. A member of the British Homeopathic Society, he travelled from London to Bantry impelled by accounts of terrible suffering and mortality. He spent sixty-seven days in the town from April to June 1847 treating the sick on daily rounds. He kept mortality statistics on his almost 200 patients with fever and dysentery[271] (Appendix VII), which, along with detailed notes and his patients' names, were recorded in a short book.[272] Kidd described the cruelty of the 'barely convalescent' standing outdoors at a Bantry soup kitchen, semi-naked, for up to twelve hours to receive 'six to eight ounces' of food.[273] In a journal article he reported that Bantry suffered even more than Skibbereen because of lack of active help from the resident gentry, 'both as to personal exertions and pecuniary assistance'.[274] Kidd did not make any mention of Protestant ladies' aid societies in

Bantry Union, nor were any records found. This is surprising because, as mentioned in Chapter 1, ladies belonging to Protestant societies in Bantry and Durrus in the 1820s collected clothes and blankets for the destitute.[275] The rector's family is not mentioned anywhere as being involved in famine relief efforts. It seems likely that they would have helped Dr Kidd; it is also likely that they would have helped Rev. Hallowell run the soup kitchens, but no information on this is available. Dr Kidd was helped by Rev. Murphy, Rev. Hallowell and Archbishop Whately and was sent rice and money by the BRA. In her memoir, Kidd's daughter recalled her father as saying that the decision to go to Bantry was the turning point of his life.[276]

Dr Kidd's time in Bantry coincided with the peak of daily deaths from starvation. He wrote that he was sure he had contributed to the survival of many of his patients, and his notes bear him out. However, this was most likely due to the extra rations he brought them and not to his homeopathic approach. He seems to have kept apart from the frictions raging in the relief committee and to have socialised only with the clergy. Apparently, he kept a low profile and was discrete and diplomatic except for his comments quoted above, which were published after he went back to London. In his book, he published several notes of appreciation that he received after he left Bantry from Revs Murphy, Hallowell and Begley.[277] When he returned to London, he ceased practising as a homeopath and devoted his long life to a large medical practice. Much later he became physician to Benjamin Disraeli.

MORE CRITICISM OF BANTRY RELIEF COMMITTEE

A *Cork Examiner* editorial in early June said that the 'inhuman and wicked policy' of the Bantry Relief Committee for the 'past four months' had been to remove the destitute, not by killing them, because that might have 'inconvenient consequences', but by 'withholding relief until the people who are half dead are wholly so'.[278] The *Southern Reporter* was even more critical of the relief committee. When reporting on a trial proceedings for manslaughter at the petty sessions in June, where Shea Lawlor testified that the deceased died of starvation, the newspaper pointed out 'that hundreds have died in the district from the same cause and hundreds are daily perishing [and] that this horrid condition of the people has been brought about by the criminal delay into bringing into operation the Relief granted by law under the Temporary Relief Act and [...] I am of opinion that this delay has been given to that relief by design.'[279] Lawlor brought with him Rev. Hallowell and the two Catholic curates to support his contention, but they were not allowed to testify. The chairman of the sessions was none other than John Payne, the man Shea Lawlor was accusing of malfeasance. In what appears to have been a cowardly move, the Protestant rector John Murphy said he felt too ill to testify.

In June, at a meeting of the new Bantry Relief Committee, Shea Lawlor faced off with John Payne, who wanted to remove people from the relief lists because they had been 'added irregularly'. Lawlor fought this plan fiercely, publicising Payne's intentions in the *Southern Reporter*; he pointed out that people had been added without Payne's signature (as head of the finance committee) because they would have died otherwise, and that the reason they had not been added in regular fashion was Payne's refusal in March and April to make up lists of the needy. Payne actually backed down under this pressure and no one was struck off at that time.[280]

Shea Lawlor, in his customary convoluted style, mused aloud to the petty sessions court in Bantry on 9 June 1847, complaining without actually naming him, that the chairman John Payne had a finger in too many pies, 'This is a daily result, in this district, of three multiplied functions in one person.'

One wonders what could have been achieved in Bantry Union if Lawlor and Payne had worked together. It was probably an impossibility: Lawlor a Catholic with a fiery energetic temperament, and Payne a Protestant – hardworking, lacking in compassion – who on one hand was 'monarch of all he surveyed',[281] and on the other hand was required to be endlessly attentive and subservient to Viscount Berehaven and the Earl of Bantry.

INACTION OF VISCOUNT BEREHAVEN

By this time, Viscount Berehaven had completely abdicated his role as the natural leader of the union. He had inherited a debt-ridden estate that had been through two resettlements,[282] but unlike his father Lord Bantry, who had helped in providing food for his tenants when famine threatened in 1784,[283] he showed little interest in the welfare of those who worked his lands and evinced no desire to improve their lives or their methods of farming. He had a second residence at Belgrave Square, London and an income of £1,500 per year from a settlement in 1825. In 1836 his marriage brought a dowry of about £30,000. This seems to have funded his frequent travels in Europe, where he bought art and expensive furnishings for Bantry House.[284] It appears that his income was also to be augmented at his marriage with 'a considerable estate' in Beara. However, no specific amount was quoted, and it is unclear how much it was eventually worth.[285] (On his death, however, his personal estate was reported as being 'under £90,000'.)[286]

When his £4 monthly contribution to the soup kitchen was made public, he withdrew all help, apparently in a fit of pique, and isolated himself in Bantry House whenever he was in Ireland.[287] In addition, his and his father's investment in the railway scheme diverted funds they might possibly have used to help their tenants. Later on, both also used only a small portion of their Land Improvement Act funds (in a scheme where the government lent money to landlords so they would employ labourers to work the land) to give local employment before returning most of the loan. In addition, both Lord Berehaven and Lord Bantry tried to avoid paying rates. In 1849 a reference to rates unpaid by Lord Bantry was made in the workhouse minutes,[288] and in 1849 John Payne made an unsuccessful attempt to get the valuation of Bere Island reduced for Lord Berehavan.[289] In December 1850, Lord Berehaven refused to pay a rate amount owed of £259 16*s* 7*d*. The PLC threatened to take proceedings against him in one of the superior courts in Dublin, but it was unclear what, if anything, was done.[290]

The lifestyle chosen by Viscount Berehaven was expensive and left little room for famine relief. Considering his priorities, it is not surprising he did not act responsibly, did not choose to represent his community to the government and failed to unite the union as he might have done to mitigate the disaster. If he had shown compassion for his starving tenants and, instead of spending money on the Continent, had bought a few hundred tons of Indian meal for his district, that action might have encouraged John Payne to lead the guardians in a more enlightened direction, potentially saving many more lives by expanding the workhouse and allowing more of the destitute to enter.

However, that did not happen and, regrettably, the combination of soup kitchens opening and healthy-looking new potatoes growing in June 1847 discouraged help when it was still desperately needed. It gave not only Westminster but also some of the union gentry a sense of respite from the horror of the previous months. Unfortunately, the feeling of relief was as false as it was brief.

4.
BATTLING FOR SURVIVAL
1847–48

FALSE HOPE AND ARBITRARY NEW RULES

June 1847 was a time of transition. In the early part of the month many died from a combination of dysentery, fever and starvation, but as the soup kitchens fed increasingly more people, the death toll lessened, leaving thousands who were barely surviving. Unlike many other unions, Bantry Union received only loans, no grants, under the Temporary Relief Act, perhaps because John Payne's new relief committee had been so slow in returning financial estimates of need.[291] Castletown had a food depot, but despite continuing pleas to Dublin, Bantry town did not.[292] The situation in the union was still desperate.

A.M. Sullivan was an 18-year-old eyewitness to events in the town. He recalled how, in June 1847, Rev. Hallowell hailed him from the door of a hovel in Custom Gap and asked him to buy wine for the dying man inside, a naked hunchback named Richard O'Brien. When Sullivan returned, he found that Hallowell had dressed the man in his own flannel underclothes and his shirt. Sullivan wrote that Hallowell dared death daily in his efforts to save 'the perishing creatures' around him.[293]

Sullivan also wrote of terrible scenes at the soup kitchens in Bantry, 'Around these boilers on the roadside there daily moaned and shrieked and fought and scuffled crowds of gaunt cadaverous creatures that once had been men and women made in the image of God.'[294] One of the common sights in Bantry Union at that time was the 'body man', who drove a horse and cart picking up corpses along the roadsides.[295]

By July, due to the continuing work of the soup kitchens, conditions continued to improve slightly in the union. Canon John O'Rourke, in his history of the famine published in 1875, reported that the kitchens made 'good meat soup', distributing 17,000 pints daily in the 'twenty-six soup kitchens from Skibbereen to Castletown'.[296]

Perhaps because of this modest easing of the situation, Shea Lawlor's newspaper letter writing campaign changed from a theme of attacking John Payne and the new relief committee to a focus on electioneering for Repeal candidates in the approaching general election in August 1847. He may have felt that he had succeeded locally in alleviating starvation and now needed to campaign further afield for candidates who would advance the cause of tenant rights, an important concern of his.[297] However, neither he nor other poli-

Fig. 18. Soup pot sunk in the ground for use as a pond at Donemark (in a property near 'Soup-house Field'), approximately 112cm (44in) in diameter, 61cm (24in) in depth. Photograph by author.

ticians used the famine as an electioneering theme. This seems odd to modern analysts, who found a similar lack of urgency about the famine nationwide among all candidates in that important election.[298]

In fact, Shea Lawlor allowed himself to become involved in a ridiculous verbal dispute with William Sullivan Jr of Carriganass for unclear reasons. A few weeks later, in the *Cork Examiner*, Sullivan libelled Lawlor as follows:

> Notice, John Shea Lalor [*sic*] of Gurteenroe, having wantonly and unprovokedly insulted me, and having dexterously evaded giving the usual and required satisfaction, I hereby proclaim him to be a shuffling swaggering coward, and only worthy henceforth of the notice that gentleman extend to blackguards – Carrignas Castle, Bantry.[299]

Towards the end of July, both were arrested in Killarney with pistols at the ready.[300] Lawlor continued to have legal difficulties, but after a couple of months he extricated himself from them.

In July, the early potatoes were reported as generally healthy and bread prices had gone down.[301] In that month, over 20,000 'gratuitous rations' were given daily in Bantry Union soup kitchens.[302] The highest number of rations supplied in one day was 35,126, probably at the end of July.[303] However, in the same month Jeremiah O'Callaghan wrote in the *Cork Examiner* that in Durrus village (described by him as 'a collection of catacombs'), he found a 'human form' trying to mix his rations from the Carrigbuí Relief Committee, 'the beans [...] almost consumed by worms [...] and totally unfit for even brute consumption.'[304]

Despite these problems, the soup kitchens were keeping thousands alive. July 1847 was an all-too-short interlude between the starvation of the spring and the hardships to come.

A WANT OF INHABITANTS: THE FAMINE IN BANTRY UNION

WITHDRAWAL OF DIRECT SUPPORT FROM WESTMINSTER

During July, when the soup kitchens were operating at their peak, Westminster was becoming less disposed to help Ireland, particularly under the influence of the Whig Charles Wood, Chancellor of the Exchequer since July 1846. He believed the Irish were exaggerating the famine and, like Trevelyan, 'opposed interventionist policies in Ireland'.[305] He made the following meretricious statement to parliament, as reported by Hansard (the official report of Parliamentary debates), in July 1847:

> When the pressure of the calamity was most severely felt, the gentry and landlords of Ireland said, 'Tax us as much you will, but for God's sake save the people from starvation.' And the Government had […] saved the people. The Government had been successful, as irresistible evidence demonstrated, in checking the progress of famine and mortality; and he firmly believed that the measures adopted by the Legislature […] had, under the blessing of Heaven, preserved thousands of the peasants of Ireland from famine and death.[306]

At the time of this statement, deaths in the Bantry workhouse were still greater than seventy per month and at least 30,000 people in the union were receiving free food each day. Yet, Prime Minister Russell's government began to claim success, implying that the worst was over and that outside help for Ireland was no longer warranted.

It is true that in the summer of 1847 the potato blight for the most part did not return in Bantry Union. Some newspapers reported that the famine was over.[307] Charles Trevelyan clearly agreed, as his book *The Irish crisis: being a narrative of the measures for the relief of the distress caused by the great Irish famine of 1846–7*, published in January 1848, put it firmly in the past.[308] Unfortunately, as there was no employment and the potato crop was small due to lack of seed being planted the previous spring, thousands of people were still without food, the soup kitchens providing their only sustenance.

At this juncture, changes made in Westminster were to drastically curtail even this relief. In a major reversal, the British government legislated that all support for the poor in Ireland must come from within Ireland, from the poor rate. All relief was transferred from the Treasury to individual Irish unions – in other words, to Irish ratepayers.[309] The new Irish Poor Law Amendment Act allowed outdoor relief (funds or Indian meal outside the workhouse) only for certain classes of paupers:

1. The aged
2. The sick and the disabled
3. Widows with at least two dependent children

Aggravating the situation was the Gregory clause, which denied any relief to occupants of more than one quarter-acre of land, forcing these tenants, when they began to starve, to give up their small plots to enter the workhouse and giving landlords a way to clear estates.[310] These tenants had to make out 'notices of surrender' six months prior to giving up occupation. According to the *Cork Examiner*, the notices were being 'bought up' eagerly by small tenants who now saw land as less important than getting relief.[311] If correct, that report indicates what dire straits they were in. Tenants who occupied poor, rocky land, similar to that found in Kilcaskan, were worst affected, as 2 acres there would produce much less food than a small area of fertile soil.

In respect to Kilcaskan and Glengarriff, a Rev. Garret Roche P.P., newly appointed to the area around Glengarriff, reported on 7 August that the blight had reappeared there. He also complained that the Protestant rector had a lot of money and was distributing charity to such an extent to Catholics that he feared 'perversion', meaning they would be persuaded to convert to Protestantism. This, he said, made him far more uneasy than 'the physical wants of the people'.[312] Fortunately, the blight seemed to remain contained in that area.

THE SOUP KITCHENS CLOSE

Because Westminster had determined to stop sending funds to Ireland, including the money to run soup kitchens, the Relief Commission in Dublin warned all the unions in July 1847 that the kitchens would soon close and instructed districts to reduce the relief lists and organise local employment.[313] Ironically, on 2 July the OPW placed a newspaper notice saying that all roadworks had to stop immediately, as no funding was available for them.[314] The PLC sent warnings to all workhouse guardians that after the soup kitchen closure, they would be responsible for all the outdoor relief listed above. Relief would only be given to the able-bodied if the workhouse was full, and then only under special orders from the Poor Law Commission.

That is why, only two months after government money began to fund Bantry Union soup kitchens, and despite the fact that thousands depended on them for survival, the news came that they would close on 12 September. In fact, food was stopped for many in August.

As for the Bantry guardians, they had been told in June by the PLC that they must raise the rate to more than three shillings in the pound to repay government loans for the soup kitchens. No rates had been collected in Kilcatherine, Kilnamanagh, Kilcaskan or Kilcrohane in the last rate collection. Samuel Hutchins, a guardian, had also refused to pay his rate and actually left the area for two months.[315] The new rate varied from 3*s* 2½*d* in Beara to 5*s* in the Kilcrohane division (presumably to make up for arrears), but the guardians told the PLC that it was impossible to find rate collectors who were willing to do this unpopular work.

RELIEF DISTRICTS ARE FORMED

In preparation for the major development of outdoor relief, a large number of guardians attended the board meeting held on 3 August 1847 at the workhouse. Their task was to divide the union into nine relieving districts and to elect relieving officers to distribute the relief. The first relieving officers elected were: Edward Power, for Kilmacamogue and Bantry; Nathaniel Evanson, for East and West Durrus and Kilcrohane; William Murphy, for Kilcaskan; and Mortimer O'Sullivan, for the remaining Beara electoral divisions.

Beara had four relief sites: Glengarriff, Adrigole, Eyeries and Castletown. Other sites were located in Kilmacomogue and Bantry. On Sheep's Head there was one in Kilcrohane and one in Durrus. The 'alms-house' in Kilcrohane still stands.[316] Although some preparation for outdoor relief was begun, no attempt was made in August to initiate outdoor distribution of meal or money.

Fig. 19. View of a portion of the steep road up to the Kilcrohane alms-house (now privately owned), showing the hill that had to be climbed by the semi-starving to obtain food. Photograph by author.

PROTEST AND UNREST

In late August the PLC told the guardians no more money would be sent to Bantry Union until they began collecting the rate. Amazingly, the board appeared unconcerned and the last meeting in August was cancelled for lack of a quorum. The minutes give the impression that the board was just not interested.

Others, however, were perturbed. Hundreds of 'squalid applicants' gathered outside a Bantry Relief Committee meeting at the beginning of August at the courthouse, agitating against being removed from soup kitchen relief. One particularly 'unpopular' but unnamed landlord barely escaped violence.[317] It would be interesting to know the name of this landlord. It was not John Payne because he would have been described as an agent. Nonetheless, at some point either just before or around this time, it is clear that Payne had ceased his activities on the relief committee, perhaps because of the bad publicity and hostility it had engendered a couple of months earlier.

In the middle of the month, the reporter Jeremiah O'Callaghan wrote of seeing a crowd of 'skeletal, and bloodstained' hand-cuffed prisoners being led by the police into Bantry at 5.00 a.m. He was told they were from Letterlickey, tenants of Arthur Hutchinson, a Bantry magistrate and guardian. When Hutchinson had arrived to seize their cattle, they tried to prevent him with all 'available war instruments' and he had been beaten back. At that point Hutchinson had 'proceeded to a magistrate and had the parties indicted and dragged from their beds'.[318] It is unclear what ensued in that particular instance, but in a separate, similar case, Hutchinson was indicted for assault and battery against a tenant.[319]

At a second relief committee meeting on 25 August 1847, Shea Lawlor accused the committee of striking people off relief lists under pressure from the commissary inspector. He proposed that they should instead request an extension of relief. The rector Rev. Murphy, who chaired the meeting, asked whether the destitute could not enter the workhouse and was told emphatically that people were terrified of the high mortality rate there and, more importantly, of having to leave their tools and cabins unprotected. A case in point was twenty weavers who had received no food for three weeks but feared going to the workhouse because their cabins would be tumbled and their looms destroyed.[320] Shea Lawlor said the relief committee should be ashamed to be 'thus led by the nose [...] and made the instruments of injustice'. He demanded that everyone be restored to the relief lists, and for the committee to resign *en masse* if the commissioners objected. With the exception of Arthur Hutchins of Ballylickey, Rev. Murphy and all the committee signed the agreement.[321]

This is a telling example of how disengaged Rev. Murphy was at that time from the reality on the ground but how he was persuaded to act to protect the needy by the others on the committee. Their action was noted by the *Southern Reporter*, who criticised the PLC for forcing destitute Bantry artisans into the workhouse and praised Shea Lawlor for 'trying to save a few'.[322] At the same time, the *Cork Examiner* warned landlords that if the poor rates were enforced, 'change of ownership was inevitable'.[323] It also criticised the PLC for having 'shifted' the intention of the legislation to 'an interpretation of their own making', that relief was 'solely' to be for one season.[324] However, in late summer, the destitute state of Bantry Union was officially recognised when the Poor Law Commission and the BRA, in correspondence between two of their principals[325] and Treasury Secretary Trevelyan, designated it as one of twenty-two distressed unions.[326]

After several relief committee meetings, Shea Lawlor wrote to Undersecretary Redington saying he feared people would not remain peaceful (Fig. 20).[327]

A WANT OF INHABITANTS: THE FAMINE IN BANTRY UNION

At a later assembly in September 1847, called to promote fishery development and employment by union landlords, Shea Lawlor presented a petition signed by 750 working men with suggestions for useful works for the union, including a detailed statement from masons showing the works needed and the costings. However, 'no proprietor came forward with an offer of employment.' Information about Bantry's fishing potential was sent to an interested company in London, but otherwise the meeting achieved nothing.[328]

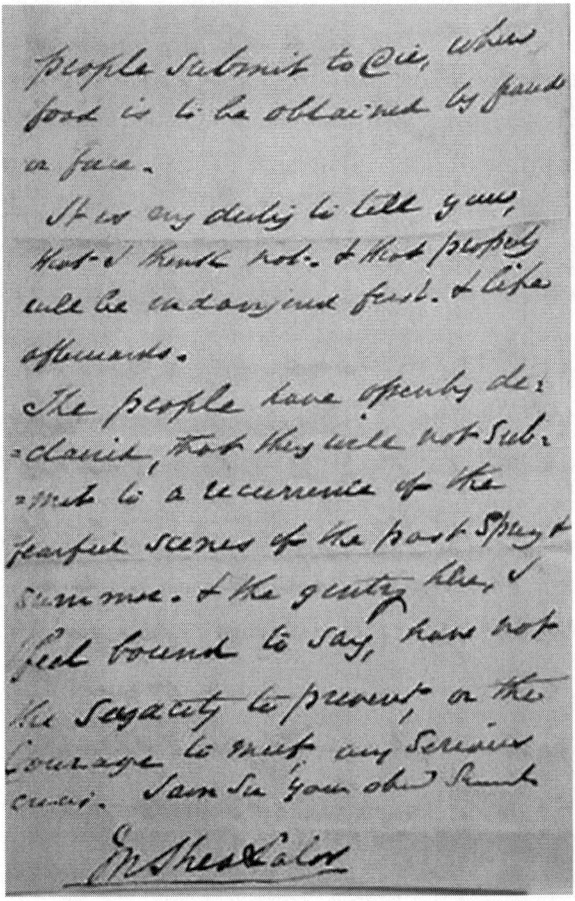

Fig. 20. Part of the letter from Shea Lawlor to Undersecretary Redington, 3 September 1847.

RENEWED HUNGER, FEAR OF STARVATION, DISSOLUTION OF BOARD OF GUARDIANS

By the end of summer 1847, it was clear that employment was not going to materialise from either the government or local landlords. Distress was inevitable when the limited harvest was exhausted. Due to lack of seed, lack of work on the land, illness and movement to towns, less acreage than usual had been sown with potatoes the previous spring. Also, some districts did suffer blight. Rev. Wright said that in Kilcaskan no potatoes survived. However, people still had hope that works approved in the past would continue. The fishermen in Dursey sent a petition to the OPW asking for work to begin on a pier.[329] The OPW refused, saying no money was available, as the funds sanctioned for roads had been spent on food.[330] The gentry in Durrus also hoped that employment could be coaxed from the authorities. They sent a petition to Dublin asking for funds from English fishery sources to build piers in Durrus. Written by Rev. Alleyn Evanson and signed by the Catholic and Protestant gentry and clergy, it showed their ability to co-operate.[331] Nothing came of these petitions.

On 6 September 1847, a hunger riot occurred outside the Bantry workhouse. The new master, Henry O'Brien, made the unlikely claim that out of 800 people gathered at the workhouse gate, not one of them 'accepted admission'. He had to 'call the military' to stop them 'digging up potatoes' growing in the workhouse field. Three were arrested.[332] A strikingly different account was published in the *Cork Examiner*. The reporter said the crowd consisted of 'famished' people who had walked from neighbouring parishes but were refused admission to the workhouse. Large numbers of police under the control of Arthur Hutchinson forced them to disperse, and as they did, some grabbed and ate turnips on the way out.[333] Toward the end of September, the *Cork Examiner* reported that distress had reached the trader and the shopkeeper.[334] A letter in the same paper enclosed £42 for Rev. Freeman, saying that recent Bantry emigrants to Massachusetts had contributed half the amount. The report ended with a gruesome account of the Abbey cemetery, where 'a thousand corpses were stacked nine-deep in the ground'. The report said the 'two noble lords who [...] owned most of the district had not helped to relieve the suffering.'[335]

On 14 September the union guardians, in the presence of Assistant Poor Law Inspector Crawford, asserted that the 3s rate was impossible to collect and asked 'respectfully' to keep the lower rate. In reply, the PLC warned that they might disband the board. This threat energised the board enough for them to develop a plan to make workhouses self-sufficient by reclaiming and working wasteland.[336] This plan was mentioned in the newspapers as 'The Bantry Circular' and was ridiculed by *The Globe*. It came too late. If they had bestirred themselves earlier, maybe their legacy would have been different.

By late September the people of Beara were so short of food that Rev. Enright, the parish priest of Castletown, and a Morty Sullivan, of the same town, petitioned the new Chief Secretary, Sir William Summerville, in person in Dublin, saying that of 21,000 people, three-fifths were in danger of starving. No employment was available from landlords, most of whom were absentee. Those nearby were themselves in arrears and could not help even if they had been willing. Summerville said he would ask the PLC about building a workhouse in Berehaven (the first time this possibility was raised).[337] Rev. Enright was quoted as saying that Viscount Berehaven had branded every cow on Bere Island with the initial 'B' as a new method of distraint.[338] That the situation in Castletown was desperate was confirmed in a horrible account a few days later of two hookers arriving at Bantry 'with 240 human spectres from Berehaven'. The reporter Jeremiah O'Callaghan watched them crawl and totter towards the workhouse, with 'famished infants' screaming and adults moaning. They clung to the iron railings until Rev. Begley and one guardian let them inside, where the reporter was told provisions were due to run out in twelve hours.[339] However, the *Southern Reporter* said that of the paupers who arrived from Berehaven on 2 October, only a hundred were admitted, the rest left to wander in the town. The workhouse was unable to provide even one meal for them.[340] Following this, a *Cork Examiner* editorial excoriated the management of the Bantry Board of Guardians and the Bantry Relief Committee, harkening back to the delay in soup kitchen relief, 'What [...] can be expected from those men who by a vicious management, contrived to defraud of relief a perishing community [...] from seven [months] to four.'[341] In these last words, the paper is referring to the fact that the soup kitchens only operated fully from June to the end of August instead of from the beginning of April, as should have been possible if the relief committee had not delayed.

The Bantry guardians met twice more in October; all, with the exception of Richard O'Donovan, refused to raise the rate. O'Donovan said the 3*s* rate was for the subsistence of the poor and should be paid. He was supported by Shea Lawlor and Rev. Begley, who both attended as spectators. The board still refused to raise the rate.[342] On 9 October, the PLC issued 'an order for dissolution of the Bantry Board of Guardians', on the grounds that 'through the default of the Guardians, the duties of the Board have not been duly and effectually discharged.'[343] The board met for the last time three days later and said that if the PLC insisted on the higher rate, the union would be plunged into anarchy and bankruptcy. Being now relieved of an 'onerous and disagreeable duty' that they felt they had discharged well, they did not think the commissioners' censure 'justifiable'. (Bantry was the fourth board to be dissolved, the first being that of Ballinrobe Union on 23 June 1847.)

A REFLECTION ON THE FIRST BOARD OF GUARDIANS

There is no doubt that the bungling and uncaring management of the Bantry workhouse by the elected Board of Guardians from August 1846 to October 1847 caused unnecessary misery and suffering among the poor and starving who sought help there. The guardians' degree of ineptitude and indifference is difficult to overstate. When elected, they delayed striking the first rate for about one year, losing the opportunity to build up reserve funds, and they also delayed the opening of the workhouse for almost two years. They made little attempt to collect the rate and were outraged when the bank refused credit. Because they refused to expand the workhouse, starving people were turned away to die. Only Richard White of Inchiclough disagreed with that policy. Just one or two guardians organised private soup kitchens. Dr Tisdall's pleas for help went unheeded. Inmate meals under the original board were not described in any available workhouse minutes, but several entries suggested an inadequate diet, particularly in October 1846 when Dr Tisdall requested better food to deal with chronic bowel complaints. Dysentery, aggravated by coarse Indian meal, could have been managed with the addition of rice to the diet, but rice was more expensive. Rice was not supplied to the inmates until after the scandal involving Dr Stephens' visit. It is not surprising the guardians were heavily criticised in the press, in the House of Commons and by Dr Kidd. The decision to dissolve the board seems justified by the derelict performance.

It is clear also that the PLC did not adequately supervise the first Board of Guardians. Assistant Commissioner Burke visited the first elected board only every two months. Subsequent to the dissolution of the board, the PLC sent a resident Poor Law inspector, whose reports seemed to have more credibility with the commissioners than reports from guardians. The presence of this inspector played a critical role in obtaining essential funding. If the first board had had a resident inspector, some deaths might have been prevented.

It is a pity that the innovative work scheme that the guardians devised on the brink of dissolution was not thought of earlier. It showed that under pressure they were capable of creative and constructive thought. But it was too late.

OUTDOOR RELIEF BEGINS UNDER THE NEW VICE-GUARDIANS AND CAPTAIN GORDON

One week later, on 19 October 1847, the PLC appointed paid vice-guardians: Denis Clarke (a Catholic from Co. Galway)[344] and Augustus Gallway (previously posted to Beara).[345] They also appointed a Captain H.W. Gordon of the 59th Regiment as Poor Law inspector of the union (a different person from the previous Captain Gordon of the OPW).[346] Fifteen weeks of workhouse minutes are then missing that cover the beginning of outdoor relief and a tumultuous period in which Gallway was dismissed on false charges of embezzlement, brought by Rev. Crossthwaite (who appeared to have been suffering from paranoia at the time or, at the very least, mistaken beliefs).[347] Voluminous documentation of this bizarre episode can be found in contemporary newspapers. The PLC viewed Gallway as guilty and appointed a replacement vice-guardian long before the charges were dismissed.

Outdoor relief, the only barrier between life and death for thousands, began in the middle of November when Captain H.W. Gordon started it in Beara with BRA funds.[348] The exact number of people on outdoor relief is unavailable until the end of January 1848, when the workhouse minutes begin again, showing over six thousand people in receipt. In addition, the BRA provided money to feed bread to schoolchildren. A rate of 3s in the pound was struck on 12 November by the new vice-guardians.[349] In his frequent letters to the PLC, Gordon wrote that he found the rate collectors negligent, especially in Kilcrohane, where in addition to very poor collection of rates, some tenants under £4 valuation had been entered as ratepayers. However, he said this had been corrected.[350] Presumably the rate-paying obligation was changed to the immediate owners or lessors of the properties (principally the Earl of Bandon and Timothy O'Donovan).

Gordon reported that the able-bodied were 'certainly in a starving state' due to the previous guardians' refusal to strike the rate. He complained it was impossible to find anyone in Castletown trustworthy enough to distribute relief. He wished the landlords would exert themselves to apply for loans under the Land Improvement Act.[351] Gordon reported in early December that the new rate was starting to come in; that the priests supported the rate collection; and that employment under Lord Bantry was about to begin (in Kilcaskan) under the Land Improvement Act.[352] It is not clear if Viscount Berehaven's name was also on his father's application. It may have been, but no documentary evidence was found.

Remarkably, in about a six-week period, Vice-Guardian Clarke and Poor Law Inspector Gordon had taken stock of the situation facing them and had begun to tackle the union's problems. There was also no doubt that their remit extended to the entire union and not just the workhouse.

Dr Thomas Willis arrived as the replacement for the dismissed Gallway before Christmas 1847.[353] He was a Catholic and an apothecary, as well as a doctor, a writer on social conditions and a co-founder of the St Vincent de Paul Society in Ireland. He worked with Denis Clarke to manage the union for just over one year. The minutes reveal that both were conscientious and hard-working. They saved many who would otherwise have died. They were well paid, but it is difficult to estimate the value that Clarke's salary of £250 per annum would represent today. Using only the retail price index, it would be about £25,000, but using the relative wage or income worth, it would come to £194,000.

WORKHOUSE MINUTES RESUME

The vice-guardian minutes resumed on 25 January 1848, with new printed forms allowing columns for auxiliary workhouse accommodation and for outdoor relief statistics. A glance shows that although numbers of inmates exceeded those of the year before, death rates were much lower (Fig. 21). Outside the workhouse, deaths from starvation were reported less frequently in the newspapers but no specific figures are available. Those that became known to the PLC were investigated individually by Captain Gordon, who found that several fatalities occurred because of refusal to give up land to enter the workhouse. Unlike the previous board, Gordon and the vice-guardians had face-to-face contact with workhouse inmates. Gordon reported that the vice-guardians worked late every night.

Gordon wrote to the PLC detailing his efforts to prod landowners into granting employment. He worried about labourers with no shelter whose cabins had been tumbled when they had entered the workhouse, and he reported to the PLC that two of the relieving officers (Powers and Eccles) were not doing their jobs properly. He expressed frustration that Lord Kenmare and Robert White (related to Lord Bantry) had done nothing to help their tenants under the Land Improvement Act but later wrote that applications under this act had been sent in from Timothy O'Donovan, Richard O'Donovan and Rev. Alleyn Evanson (for Kilcrohane), and from Richard Evanson (for West Durrus).

A WANT OF INHABITANTS: THE FAMINE IN BANTRY UNION

Bantry Workhouse August 1847–July 1848

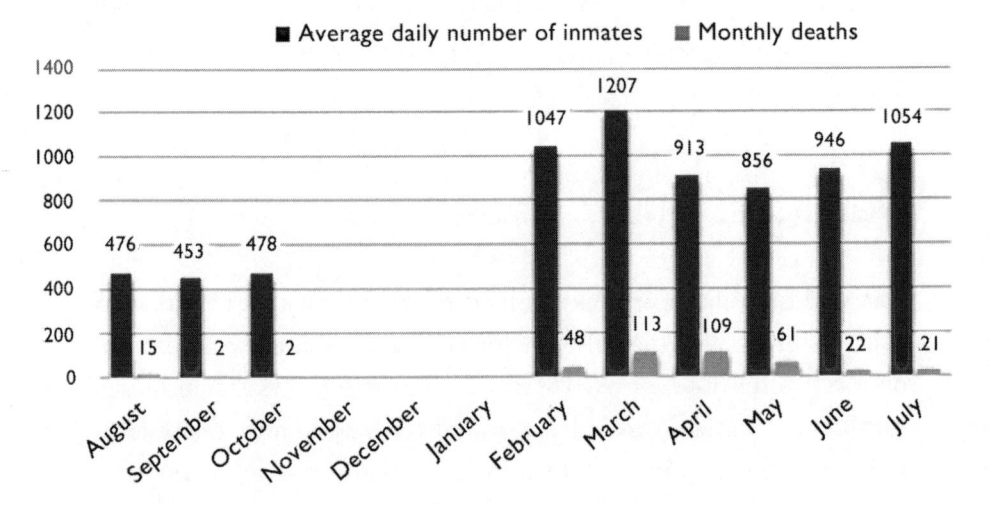

■ Average daily number of inmates   ■ Monthly deaths

Month	Avg daily inmates	Monthly deaths
August	476	15
September	453	2
October	478	2
February	1047	48
March	1207	113
April	913	109
May	856	61
June	946	22
July	1054	21

Fig. 21. Inmate numbers and workhouse deaths, August 1847–July 1848. A gap occurs where workhouse minutes are missing. Drawn from weekly statistics in workhouse minute books. CCCA BG/43/AA1, A2, A3.

In early January 1848, Gordon wrote that a mob of 500 persons had surrounded the workhouse, presumably looking for relief, but this incident was not reported in the newspapers. In the same month, in disquieting counterpoint, Viscount Berehaven complained (in a letter from Bantry House to his brother William) that he could not buy an egg for breakfast and did not venture out at all 'for fear of trifling demands'.[354] There is no evidence that Berehaven, the previous vice-chairman of the Board of Guardians, attempted in any way to alleviate suffering in the district or support the efforts of the vice-guardians and the Poor Law inspector at this time.

Gordon also explained to the PLC that rates were difficult to collect in Beara because land ownership and occupancy were in such an extraordinary tangle that it was impossible to tell who was liable.

By 16 January, Gordon reported that large numbers of paupers from Beara had swelled the total workhouse number to 1,164, which Gordon felt was a deliberate attempt (by persons unnamed) to force outdoor relief for the able-bodied. To 'counteract it', he and Dr Willis raised the workhouse threshold to 1,600.[355] Gordon and the vice-guardians worked together to discharge inmates who were eligible for outdoor relief in order to have room to admit the unemployed 'able-bodied' who were starving. (To twenty-first century ears it seems strange to describe a starving person as 'able-bodied'. What was implied was that if these individuals were not starving, they would be able to work.) The vice-guardians employed these tactics to the benefit of the starving unemployed over the next few months.

The rate collection of £2,013 in January 1848 was twice that of the previous year under the old Board of Guardians. However, despite the increase to a three-shilling rate in November 1847, the amount collected was not enough to wipe out the £6,884 in arrears from the late board, leaving the union still insolvent.[356]

Throughout January and the first half of February, Gordon was frustrated by what he termed 'the idleness of those discharged [from the workhouse] for work, many of whom try to return, sooner than take task-work'. He was particularly unsympathetic towards the men working on Lord Bantry's drainage works in Kilcaskan.[357] This was uncharacteristic of the usually compassionate Gordon. The *Cork Examiner* said the wages were inadequate and laid the blame with the engineer, a Mr Gilman, for setting too low a rate of pay, 'that would destroy men as rapidly as disease and starvation'.[358] Some of Gordon's attitude at this time might possibly be attributed to sickness. He became dangerously ill and his letters stopped abruptly. His duties were taken over by the Poor Law inspector for Skibbereen, Mr Marshall.

During February 1848, there were reports of 'hordes of paupers inundating Cork City', some from Bantry.[359] In Bantry Union itself, 'emaciated figures in rags staggered through the streets, all their efforts directed at obtaining food.'[360] At the Bantry Sessions, a Timothy and Mary Leary, 'both obviously very poor', were indicted for stealing twenty turnips and fifty parsnips and sentenced to seven years' transportation.[361]

VICE-GUARDIANS RECEIVE HELP FROM THE BRITISH RELIEF ASSOCIATION

In February the PLC insisted, against the vice-guardians' advice, that the vice-guardians go to court to force John Puxley, owner of the Berehaven mines at Allihies,[362] to pay a higher rate. The result was a victory for Puxley, as his rate was lowered by the court from £1,200 to £450.[363]

In March, fever increased and the deaths in the workhouse rose to about thirty per week for the ensuing two months. The vice-guardians borrowed £3,500 with interest paid by the BRA for six months. They ordered fifty-three coffins, an indication that they had ceased to use the hinged coffins.

Rate collectors were listed as follows in the March workhouse minutes, three of them (Hutchinson, O'Donovan and Payne) being former guardians: Cornelius O'Donovan, for Kilmacomogue and Bantry; Arthur Hutchinson, for Durrus East and West; Richard O'Donovan, for Kilcrohane; John Payne, for Kilcaskan; and John O'Sullivan, for Beara. O'Sullivan deserves special note. His brinkmanship had exasperated both the old and new guardians. No doubt his job was unpleasant, but his ability to obfuscate, procrastinate and deflect criticism year after year was prodigious.[364]

During the month of April, union funds were again augmented by a £1,000 loan from the BRA. When the milk allowance for children was increased by the vice-guardians, fewer of them died and the overall mortality in the workhouse was lowered (Fig. 21). New relieving officers were added as pressure for outdoor relief accelerated.[365]

CAPTAIN GORDON SURVIVES

Captain Gordon came close to death but did recover, and while convalescing in early April, he resumed his close co-operation with the vice-guardians. He sent expense estimates through September 1848 to the PLC and said the rate collection was going well. He was concerned that the BRA would be ending school relief in September. This was a serious prospect, as that organisation had given £4,999 3s 6d for feeding 10,386 children in the union from October 1847 to April 1848.[366] He described the debts of the previous board as 'a serious evil' and hoped that the PLC would sanction further loans to the vice-guardians 'to support the farming preparations' going on.[367] Gordon returned to work in May and reported that many landowners and tenants were growing potatoes again with renewed energy because of the small but healthy potato crop of 1847 and that he and the vice-guardians had agreed to rent 4–5 acres from John Payne to plant potatoes without delay.[368]

Because of slightly lower workhouse numbers, the vice-guardians decided to stop renting the two storehouses in Bantry town where children had been lodged due to workhouse overcrowding since early 1848. They received another £1,000 loan for day-to-day expenses from the BRA and, on 23 May, struck a new rate (between 2s 11d and 4s 7d) for all divisions in the union.[369] By May 1848, on very limited funds, the vice-guardians were managing a workhouse population of around 950 and supplying outdoor relief to about 31,000 people per month. If one assumes the union population had sunk to 45,000 by then (a conservative estimate), the vice-guardians were keeping at least 70 per cent of the union alive in the month of May 1848, or at any rate, preventing outright starvation.

EMIGRATION AND LACK OF FACILITATED EMIGRATION

Many people had been emigrating voluntarily, paying their own way. During the spring of 1848, the vice-guardians must have seen one of the main emigrant ships from Bantry Union, the *Dealy*, at anchor from their vantage point on Union Hill.[370]

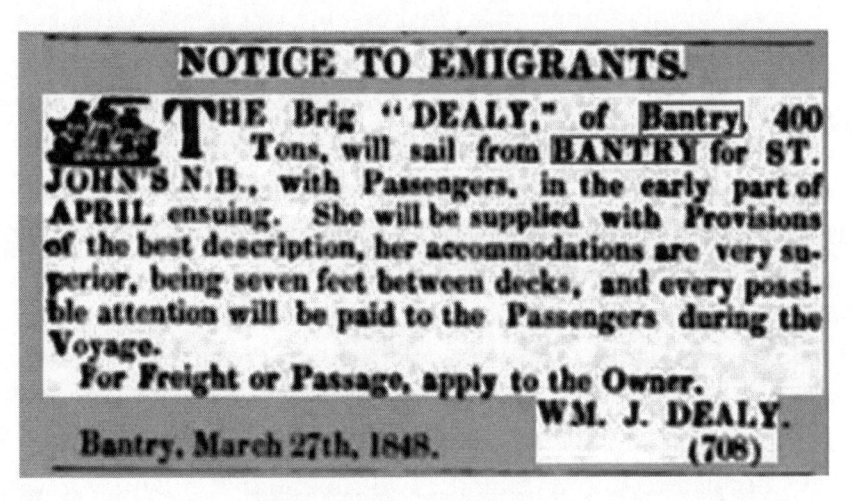

> **NOTICE TO EMIGRANTS.**
> THE Brig "DEALY," of Bantry, 400 Tons, will sail from BANTRY for ST. JOHN'S N.B., with Passengers, in the early part of APRIL ensuing. She will be supplied with Provisions of the best description, her accommodations are very superior, being seven feet between decks, and every possible attention will be paid to the Passengers during the Voyage.
> For Freight or Passage, apply to the Owner.
> WM. J. DEALY.
> Bantry, March 27th, 1848. (708)

Fig. 22. A typical newspaper notice of sailing. *Shipping and Merchantile Gazette* (13 November 1848). Some names of passengers who died on arrival in St John can be found in *Saint John New Brunswick Courier* (7 August 1847) and in Daniel F. Johnson, *Irish Emigration* to *New England Through the Port* of *Saint John, New Brunswick, Canada, 1841 to 1849* (Clearfield Company, 1997).

Fig. 23. Brig *Tantivy* by Miles Walters, 1830s. Oil on canvas. With permission: New Brunswick Museum-Musée du Nouveau-Brunswick, www.nbm-mnb.ca. Accession number 1957.10.

The *Dealy* was a brig said to closely resemble a sister ship, the *Tantivy* (Fig. 23). It was built in 1839 at St John, New Brunswick and owned by William J. Dealy RN of Bantry. The *Dealy* made numerous crossings with emigrants from Bantry to Quebec and St John between 1841 and 1848 before it was wrecked in 1848 off the coast of St Ives, Cornwall. Dealy was an ex-Arctic explorer and owner of a Bantry timber yard. Since the 1820s some of his family members had emigrated to St John, New Brunswick, as had members of the Kingston, Bird, Clarke, Pattison and Dukelow families.

Paddy O'Keefe, a local historian in Bantry, researched the *Dealy* in great depth in the 1960s. In various letters found in the Cork City and County Archives, the ship is described as a two-masted square-rigged craft with a hold space of 70 x 20ft on two decks with headroom of only 5½ft. Into this space were crammed up to 200 people and their provisions.[371] On the return voyage the ship carried timber. The *Dealy* made voyages from Bantry to Quebec and St John in 1841, 1842, 1843, 1844 (two crossings), 1845, 1846 and 1847.[372] O'Keefe did unearth crew lists for the *Dealy*, but despite years of searching, he was unable to locate any passenger lists. Recently, some information has become available about emigrants from Bantry who died in Canada after the voyage (Appendix VIII).

An 1882 illustration of an unidentified ship entering through the mile-long 'Narrows' entrance to St John harbour was found in a Victorian publication for girls (Fig. 24). This must have been the first glimpse seen by surviving emigrants of their point of disembarcation in the New World.[373]

Fig. 24. Entrance to St John, New Brunswick.

Other immigrant ships were *Brothers*, from Bantry to St John, May 1846, and *Themis*, from Bantry to St John, June 1846. In addition, ships with unknown destinations were: *Triumph* from Bantry, *Pons Aelii* from Berehaven and *Renewal* from Berehaven.

For those immigrants arriving in Canada with no money, conditions were not promising. An official communication in June 1848 from St John, from Emigration Officer M.H. Perley to Provincial Secretary John Saunders, testifies to that:

> I HAVE to report the arrival of the barque 'Springhill' from Donegal, with 103 passengers, and brig 'Dealy' from Berehaven, with 128 passengers, for which vessels ship returns are enclosed.
>
> The passengers by these vessels are in general very destitute. Those who have sufficient means go at once to the United States. For those who are compelled to remain there is no work, and the amount of employment appears to decrease every week, owing to the depression in the timber trade. As the season advances it is quite probable that hundreds who are now engaged will be thrown out of work altogether.[374]

Despite the discouragement by Canadian officials, those who emigrated faced a brighter economic future than those who stayed. This was attested to by the sums of money sent back to Ireland in the years after the famine.

The possibility of emigration of Bantry workhouse inmates to Australia was first brought up by the PLC in May 1848. Lists were made of youngsters in Bantry workhouse eager to go to Australia, but eventually it all fell through, despite the vice-guardians' initial interest. When the opportunity arose to act in 1849, the vice-guardians could not afford the £5 charge per person. Thus, during the 1840s no pauper in Bantry workhouse received assistance to emigrate. No record of facilitated emigration could be found in respect to Bantry

Union, and no one from Bantry appears to have emigrated under the Earl Grey scheme.[375] This scheme, which took young Irish girls from overcrowded workhouses to work in Australia, was managed from 1848–50 by the British Secretary of State for the Colonies, Earl Grey.

MAY 1848: STIRRINGS OF HOPE AND REPEAL

As summer approached, small signals appeared that life might be getting back to normal. Jane Murphy wrote a fairly cheerful letter from Bantry on 7 May to her daughter Charlotte, living near Bandon (Fig. 25). Referring to the rector (her brother-in-law) and his family, she remarked, 'They are all gay at the Glebe house. Margaret keeps appearing wearing new things.' She also remarks on Rev. Hallowell's recent marriage,[376] which had occurred two days before.[377] This letter had a more hopeful tone than the year before and matches the faint notes of optimism in the newspapers and in the workhouse minutes. Another encouraging report was that of Captain Thomas of the Gortavallig mine in Kilcrohane. He reported shipping out 88 tons of copper ore, evidence of some employment on Sheep's Head.[378]

During May 1848 accounts of destitution were also competing with other news. The Young Irelanders, the Irish Confederation and William Smith O'Brien filled the papers. About 1,000 people marched through the streets in Bantry, cheering loudly when they heard that Messrs Smith O'Brien and T.F. Meagher had been acquitted of sedition charges.[379] Repeal of the Act of Union was the political theme of the day. (In 1800, Ireland was force-marched into a parliamentary union with Great Britain. The Repeal Association, against this union and fostered by Daniel O'Connell, was non-violent. However, The Young Irelanders, of whom William Smith

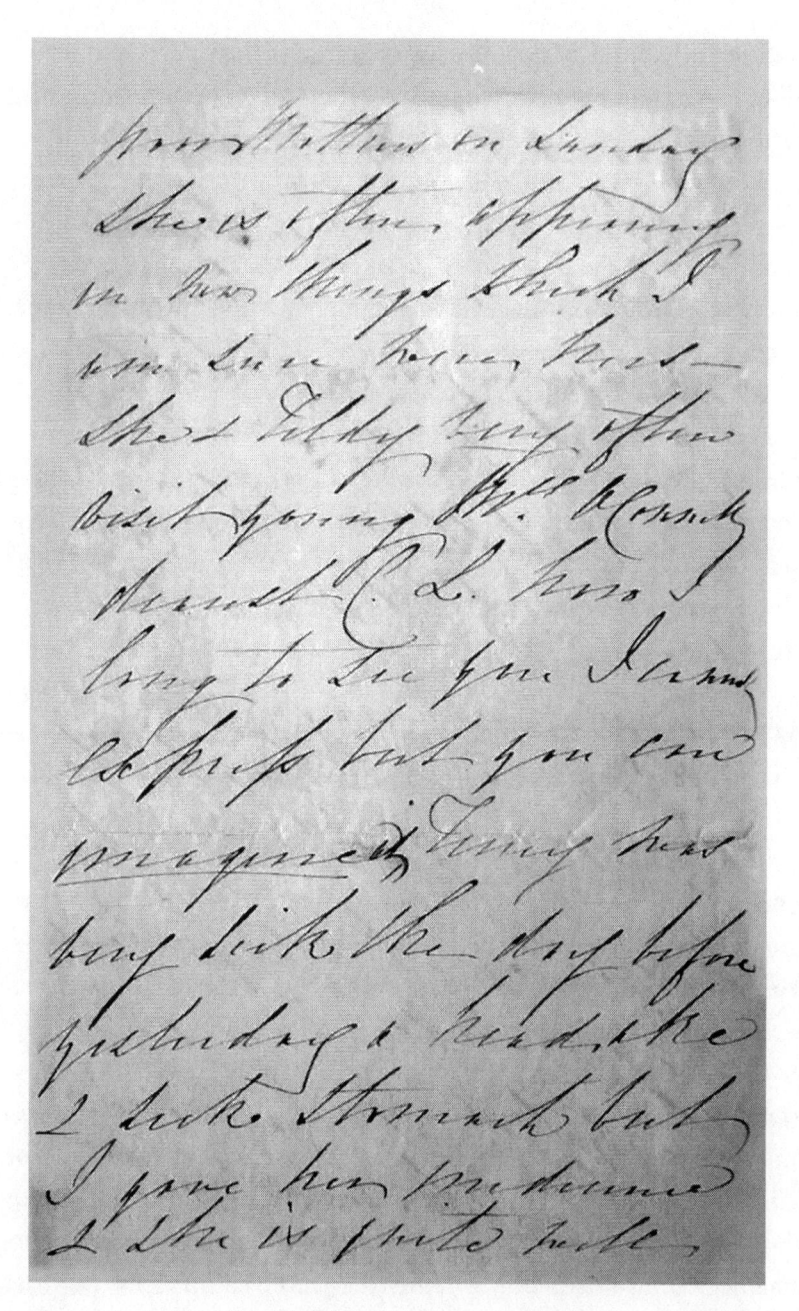

Fig. 25. Part of Jane Murphy's letter, with gossip and innuendo, May 1848.

O'Brien and John Mitchell were prominent members, had broken off to form their own confederation. Their views became radicalised by the famine, and this eventually led to armed rebellion.)[380]

Bantry's Repeal Club was founded around then by Shea Lawlor, a self-professed 'non-violent' Repealer.[381] He had not been engaged in advocacy for the destitute since the vice-guardians had taken over in the workhouse but instead was actively involved with the Repeal Club. In later years he was an instigator of, and committed to, the tenants' rights movement.[382]

Later reports said, 'almost every parish in County Cork is organised into Repeal Clubs.'[383] The *Cork Examiner* reported that Viscount Berehaven had ordered that no Repealer enter his estate,[384] and a regiment was stationed in Bantry due to widespread concern that a revolt of some sort might be imminent.[385]

JUNE–JULY 1848: APPROACH OF THE HARVEST AND OTHER PROBLEMS

In June 1848, the vice-guardians were approached by Thomas Vickery, who said he was under legal pressure as a result of bad cheques from the previous Board of Guardians. This was followed by an appeal from John O'Connell, the meal supplier, who complained that the vice-guardians owed him £640. Taken with what was owed to him by the previous guardians, the outstanding amount totalled £1,400. The vice-guardians asked the PLC for another £1,000 loan, as it was impossible to collect more rates until the harvest. They pointed out that they had collected almost all the rate struck in November 1847, allowing for the devaluation of the Allihies mines, with only £900 uncollected. It was unclear whether they received this loan, but there was no indication that it was refused.

The vice-guardians also had to deal with the discontented Henry Spencer, clerk of the union, who had previously resigned twice over pay issues, changing his mind and being rehired each time. He now resigned again. When he tried to return, he was not allowed back, and a new clerk, Maurice Healy, only 20 years old, was elected. Spencer, incensed by what he considered an injustice, later became a thorn in the vice-guardians' sides. He formed an alliance with John Payne and built up a practice advising landowners of ways to avoid paying rates, calling himself a Poor Law Union accountant.[386]

In July 1848 the vice-guardians were occupied with prosecutions against the heads of families who had deserted their children. No explanation for the desertions was found, but maybe the men had left the area to seek work elsewhere. The vice-guardians said the relieving officers must 'seek out the wretches who would abandon those they are bound to support'. Showing concern for labourers discharged from the workhouse, they urged relieving officers to make sure the men received cash payments daily for the first week and thereafter weekly. The vice-guardians also became concerned about the poor quality of meal available for outdoor relief for close to 6,000 recipients. In an effort to ensure better quality, they changed the relief to money: ninepence per week for each adult and four pence and a halfpenny for each child under 10 years old. At the vice-guardians' last meeting in July, Denis Clarke raised the possibility of the blight returning, while the *Constitution* actively played down similar rumours.[387]

On 8 July, a major distraction occurred when William Smith O'Brien, the nationalist Protestant MP for Limerick and leader of the Young Ireland movement, visited Bantry.[388] The Cork Grand Jury, fearing imminent violence, asked for a ship to be sent to Bantry Bay 'for the purpose of protecting the peaceable inhabitants of that part'. Her Majesty's sloop *Pilot* was immediately dispatched and a visit of a ship of the line, *Blenheim*, was planned to 'give confidence to the loyal portion of Her Majesty's subjects'.[389]

On 31 July in Tipperary, the abortive Repeal 'rebellion' occurred. A week later, O'Brien was arrested. Following the failed revolt, Bantry and Castletown, among other districts, were placed under the operation of the Crime and Outrage Act, a bill passed by the British government the previous December because of growing nationalist agitation.[390] Proclamations decreed that all arms had to be delivered to the authorities in Bantry by 7 August.[391]

O'Brien was sent for trial and convicted of high treason. His sentence to be hanged, drawn and quartered was eventually commuted to transportation to Australia.

BLIGHT STRIKES AGAIN

Reports of blight appeared in early August 1848.[392] Captain Gordon told the PLC that in Kilmacomogue and Bantry, half the crop was gone. Durrus and Kilcrohane were worse off. On Beara, three-quarters was gone. Kilcaskan was not quite as bad as the others.[393] Bantry Union poor who had starved in 1847 and barely made it through the spring of 1848 now faced the awful prospect of another devastating loss of the large potato crop sown in anticipation of a healthy harvest. The vice-guardians, who daily passed by the rotting tubers in the workhouse field, must have felt dread. The first noticeable change in the workhouse minutes was the dropping of any pretence of politeness towards the Bantry gentry. Saying that destitution had always existed in 'this wretched district' because of an 'almost entire disregard of that protective power that should be extended towards the poorer classes', the vice-guardians wrote that unless 'coercive measures are adopted [...] they cannot hope to raise enough money [...] to prevent calamity.'

Resistance to the rate collection continued, including passive resistance by magistrates who did not appear for cases taken against those who had rescued seized cattle. However, the Catholic clergymen in and around Bantry still encouraged rate collection and the vice-guardians hoped to persuade the Castletown clergymen to do the same.[394]

At the end of August, school relief to the 9,411 children in the Bantry Union concluded,[395] despite an unfulfilled promise by Prime Minister Russell that the Treasury would continue to provide food and clothes for them.[396] A farewell letter from Captain Gordon, who had finished his tour of duty, expressed his appreciation to the vice-guardians for preventing absolute starvation in 1848 but anticipated severe want in the winter and spring of 1849, a prediction that unfortunately came true.

5.

FROM BAD TO WORSE
1848–49

THE BLIGHT RETURNS

During early August 1848, newspapers throughout Ireland and England were filled with conflicting reports on the potato harvest. In addition, the Liverpool Corn Exchange reported that farmers, fearing the disease would appear in their tubers, were forcing 'their potatoes on the markets in great abundance, and at extremely low prices'.[397] In Ireland, by 19 August, all except the most determined optimists had given up hope. According to the *Bristol Times and Mirror*:

> The intelligence from all parts of the country [is] really appalling. The potato fields in all quarters are rapidly decaying. The passenger along the roads will be convinced by the offensive effluvia that potato-fields are becoming a mass of rottenness.
> The Poor Law Commissioners […] describe […] the blight as rapid and most destructive in its progress […] at this moment some of the poor law unions are absolutely insolvent and […] now [the commissioners] disburse as much as £10,000 weekly amongst the unions so circumstanced.[398]

The *Weekly Chronicle* described the rot in Ireland as being so virulent that potatoes laid aside in the evening for use the next day were decayed by the following morning. The report continued, 'How is it to be expected that the crop [...] will last through the next winter and spring and provide food [...] until [...] summer of 1849?'[399]

During the months of September and October 1848, almost 17,000 people in Bantry Union were kept alive through the system of outdoor relief, whereby they received either meal or money on a weekly basis from the relief officers appointed by the vice-guardians. These numbers increased as the weather grew colder but no deaths from outright starvation were reported.

TABLE 2. NUMBERS GIVEN OUTDOOR RELIEF IN BANTRY UNION IN OCTOBER 1848

Electoral division	Number given outdoor relief
Kilmacomogue	1,507
Bantry	5,688
Durrus	1,195
Kilcrohane	567
Kilcaskan	1,507
Kilcatherine	1,562
Killaconenagh	2,036
Kilnamanagh	1,763

Source: CCCA (Cork City and County Archives) BG/43/A3 (Bantry Board of Guardians minute books), October 1848.

SEPTEMBER 1848: BANTRY UNION

The workhouse minute books are almost the only source of information for events in the union at this period. The notes recorded that a significant improvement in the workhouse water problem had been achieved with the digging of two wells by inmates over the summer, finally giving everyone there 'an ample supply'. However, the vice-guardians wrote that rate payments were coming in too slowly. John Payne, responsible for collection of rates from Kilcaskan, had not deposited any funds but still found time to write an unpleasant letter criticising the vice-guardians' expenditure of £6 for an altar for inmates in the workhouse chapel. The vice-guardians also reported on the dangers facing the rate collector in Kilcrohane, where hostile and intimidating crowds gathered on the collector's arrival.

One of the much-needed educational talks given by agricultural experts occurred in early September 1848 in Bantry. A Mr John Hinds was sent by the Royal Agricultural Improvement Society of Ireland to help local farmers learn how to diversify their crops and increase yields. Some farmers were eager to attend, but the only members of the gentry who came to be educated were both vice-guardians, John Payne, John O'Connell and Michael Murphy from Newtown House.[400] This indifference by those who should have been eager to lead the community in better farming practices was seen throughout the 1840s; it was repeated in the response to another agricultural instructor (a Mr Fawcett) who came to Bantry a few months later to lecture on turnips, carrots and parsnips. He was reported as saying that he found the farmers 'despondent and fearful they would lose their holdings'.[401] Again, few of the gentry attended. John O'Connell, the corn merchant who attended the talk, said he 'deeply regretted that those who ought to be the people's guides [...] absented themselves'.[402]

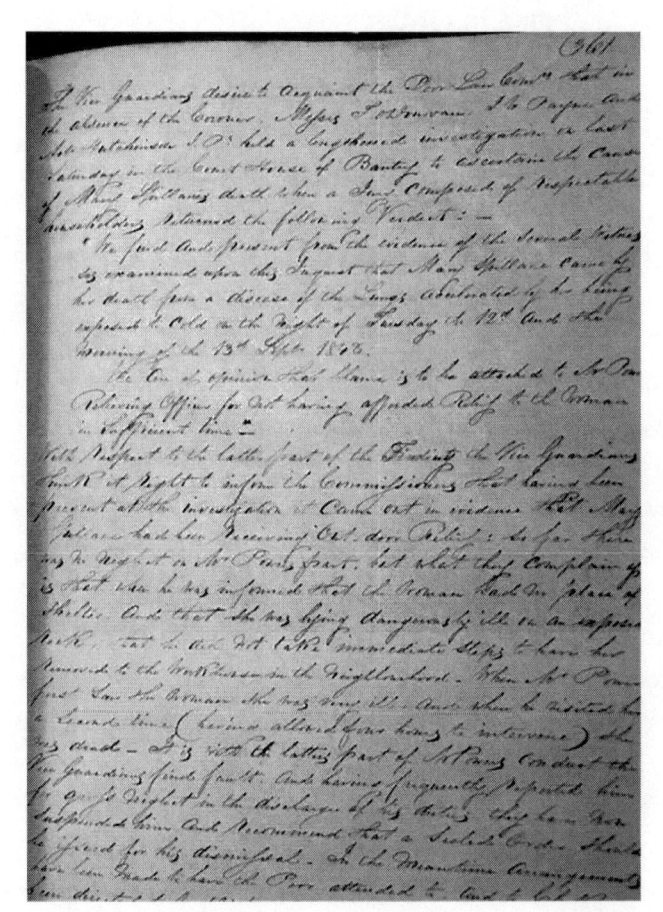

Fig. 26. Workhouse minute book account of Mary Spelling's death, 19 September 1848. CCCA BG/43/A3 (September 1848).

The minute books record the dismissal of the relieving officer for Kilmacomogue, a Mr Power, by the vice-guardians for callous negligence. He was called in September to help a Bantry woman, a Mary Spelling, whom he found lying 'dangerously ill' on a rock. He left her where she was, without offering any aid. He returned four hours later to find her dead. This was not his first offence, but it was the final straw for the vice-guardians, who were outraged by his behaviour.[403]

NOVEMBER 1848: PROBLEMS INCREASE

By November 1848, the reduced and demoralised population of Bantry Union was facing another nine-month period of destitution. Pressure on the vice-guardians increased as outdoor relief numbers grew, and although the workhouse inmates were optimistically reported as being in 'excellent health', their numbers were also growing. Because of overcrowding, two store buildings in Bantry were leased again to accommodate the boys and girls. At the workhouse, a visiting committee was upset by the 'extreme filth' of 800–900 inmates wearing rags, with no bedding but straw. Because of this, the vice-guardians felt forced to buy ready-made clothes despite the constant work of the 'workhouse tailor [...] six pauper boys [...] and sixty sewing women'.[404] They were reprimanded by the PLC and had to apologise for the 'extravagance'. In addition, the bank threatened not to honour cheques for material for inmate clothing and demanded repayment of debt.

In November, a Kilcrohane committee reported tenants running away, rents going unpaid and land remaining untilled; they also pointed to an increase of want and how the collection of the poor rate was 'crushing' those who tried to stay. The vice-guardians wrote to the PLC saying that Kilcrohane was exceptional in its poverty and was the worst in 'this miserable Union':

> It has contributed more inmates to the workhouse than any other division since its opening. The current proportion is above one-fifth of the total number. The most extreme misery exists [...] in Kilcrohane as throughout the Union and the condition of the [...] people is *immeasurably below what the most heartless would consider the <u>lowest</u> depths of wretchedness.*[405] [Reproduced as in the original]

They enclosed a list of twelve people paying the highest rates in the Kilcrohane division, showing even their limited ability to pay (Appendix IX),[406] and begged the PLC for help. They were sent £500 from a BRA fund that had been donated to the Poor Law Commission.[407] To add to their difficulties in the same month, three legal cases for debts against the union were pending, one of those a writ from Thomas Vickery, who had never been paid for bread he supplied to the workhouse during the tenure of the previous Board of Guardians.

In November the PLC published the rate and collection history of different unions. The total amount of rate struck in Bantry from January 1844 to May 1848 was £10,277 15s 4d. The amount collected was only £4,378 3s 4½d (42 per cent). In Skibbereen the total rate amount from July 1842 to May 1848 was £35,364 5s 8d, of which £19,609 7s 1d had been collected (55 per cent).[408] This difference might have been less if the Bantry guardians had not delayed in striking a rate and had collected the rate more energetically.

CAPTAIN LANG ARRIVES

The PLC appointed a Captain J. Lang to Bantry Union as its new Poor Law inspector. He was transferred from the Granard Union after a reprimand by the PLC when a private letter he had written to them had been published inadvertently by the commissioners. He had implied that the priests in Granard were fostering rebellion among lazy parishioners. He wrote an apology, which the clergy refused to accept. Prior to that, he had been acknowledged as performing well as a temporary Poor Law inspector.[409]

Captain Lang arrived in Bantry on 12 December 1848. The overcrowded workhouse and fever hospital, with twenty-one deaths in the previous week, horrified him. He wrote to the PLC the same day, detailing a crisis situation with a one-day supply of bread and no meat or rice for the next day, as well as threats from debtors. He described how he had persuaded the meal contractor John O'Connell to continue supplying the workhouse until Christmas Eve. No staff in the workhouse had been paid for nearly six months. The PLC, on receiving this, wrote to Sir George Grey, the Home Secretary. They urged him to release money from the BRA fund for Bantry Union, saying, 'if funds are not found [...] people will starve as in winter 1846–47.'[410] In return, Grey sent £10,000 in aid for all distressed unions. However, the financial pressure continued. By the end of December, several traders in Bantry town refused to supply goods to the workhouse without a guarantee of weekly payments, an impossibility for the vice-guardians. Lang wrote to the PLC to say that relieving officers reported daily increase of destitution and no employment in the union.[411] In a subsequent letter he said that 'the people present the most revolting picture of squalid filth and rags ever beheld in a Christian land.' Many people had to remain in the workhouse 'from the absolute want of clothes'.[412]

Again, in December 1848, the vice-guardians wrote about the plight in which local inhabitants found themselves, excerpts of this communication being quoted later in the House of Commons. They explained that during the previous spring, the people had made huge efforts to put land under tillage and had used up all their resources so that when the blight had reappeared in August, they had no reserves whatsoever:

> sufferings of a large proportion of the people in this wretched union: without food, without clothing, without employment, with no hope whatever, save from the relieving officer, or from the chilly protection of the workhouse [...] we are compelled to express our fears, that their wants and sufferings will very considerably increase.[413]

In early January 1849, dysentery, deaths and numbers on outdoor relief all increased.[414] The Indian meal for this relief was stored in seven depots across the union, meaning that people in a weakened state of health were forced to walk long distances to obtain any nourishment.[415] A native of Kilcrohane told this author that his grandfather talked of his father tramping miles to and from the depot to get a tin ('about the size of a coffee tin') filled with meal for his family.[416]

Captain Lang wrote to the PLC in January describing the 'terrible appearance' of people being admitted to the workhouse, saying bad weather and lack of clothing were more of a problem than lack of food. This comment is confirmed by a report saying the diet in Bantry workhouse was better than that in Skibbereen. At breakfast, able-bodied men received stirabout made of seven ounces of Indian meal, one ounce of rice and a half-pint of milk. For dinner they were given one pound of 'very excellent bread, and one quart of porridge'. The diet of women and children was 'equally good'. Those who were on outdoor relief received money to pay for seven pounds of meal per person per week.[417]

But Captain Lang wrote that the rate collected was insufficient for future months and there was no seed or capital, or the will, to prepare for spring crops. He criticised the local proprietors for their lack of planning and lack of land improvements, and the lack of instruction of their 'half-barbarous' tenantry. He disagreed with the landlords who blamed the Poor Law for all their distress, saying the 'canker lies deeper' because those proprietors had previously mortgaged their estates far beyond their marketable value.[418] The vice-guardians wrote that the outdoor relief population would suffer more than the workhouse inmates in the near future. The union needed £8,700 up to the middle of August 1849, much more than the best-case rate collection of £5,500. Many who had paid the last rate were now inmates of the workhouse.[419]

NEWSPAPERS COMMENT ON THE CRISIS IN BANTRY UNION

The *Cork Examiner* analysed the financial situation, showing that although Bantry Union's tax base was less than one-third that of Skibbereen Union, it contained three-quarters of the numbers of paupers. To erase its debts and to feed the people on outdoor relief, the union would need to raise £35,000 from the rates, an 'utter impossibility'. Farmers were leaving 'with realisable property and rents' while they still could. It was inevitable that the land of those unable to meet the rates would be sold. The town traders had been severely affected by debts owing from the 'late Board [of Guardians]'.[420] The *Times*, responding to this article, said that the 'uncivilised' people of Bantry had procreated with 'animal nature instead of moral prudence [...] If the landlords have to sell up [...] that is the price of their mismanagement but we cannot prevent it and certainly are not answerable for it.'[421] At the end of January 1849, the *Shipping and Merchantile Gazette* reported, 'In the rural districts there is no want so observable as the want of *Inhabitants* [...] the lands lie waste and desolate.'[422]

At that point, the PLC posted Dr Willis to the Cavan Union.[423] No reason for, or discussion of, this move was found. Willis was described by Canon O'Rourke as a 'kind and generous man';[424] this remark is supported by occasional comments in the workhouse minutes to the effect that he had admitted emergency cases out of usual hours. Willis took away from Bantry three crosses he had made from the wood of one of the hinged coffins. A surviving cross is now in Maynooth and has an inscription by Willis, which reads in part:

> During the frightful Famine Plague which devastated [...] Ireland in the years 1846–47, that monstrous and 'Unchristian Machine', a sliding coffin, was, from necessity used in the Bantry Union for the

conveyance of the Victims to one common grave. The material of this Cross […] is a portion of one of these Machines, which enclosed the remains of several hundreds of our countrymen, during the passage from the wretched huts or waysides, where they died, to the pit, into which their remains were thrown.[425]

FEBRUARY 1849: THE LIMITS OF ENDURANCE

The *Southern Reporter* wrote on 10 February 1849 that Bantry Union was bankrupt, warning that everything was 'confusion' and that the vice-guardians would have to stop outdoor relief and close the workhouse unless they received government aid.[426] Two days later, the *Cork Examiner* reported that the cess collector for the union had resigned because he could collect no money in the district.[427] On 16 February the *Examiner* reported the workhouse as still open.[428] Three days after that, the same reporter stated that there were 2,130 people in the workhouse and 8,690 on outdoor relief.[429] The four union rate collectors were under duress trying to collect arrears from the previous August and had to travel with large forces of policemen as protection.[430] On 24 February, the *Southern Reporter* said there had been no outdoor relief for two or three weeks. The only reason the workhouse had not closed was because Captain Lang had guaranteed payment for the food for two weeks out of his own funds.[431] However, it appears from the minute book that only one week of outdoor relief was missed.

About this time, Captain Lang fell ill with the fever that would kill him. The onset of his illness was not mentioned in the workhouse minutes, which were disorganised and illegible during February 1849. This was partly due to the clerk falling 'dangerously ill' and probably partly due to Vice-Guardian Denis Clarke being left unaided in such a crisis. On 28 February, in the midst of this chaos, Captain

Lang died.[432] No obituary notice or further information was discovered relating to him, despite a thorough search – a surprising finding considering his major contribution to the union's welfare, but perhaps understandable in the circumstances. The Poor Law inspector for Skibbereen had also died earlier in the month.[433] The PLC sent a temporary vice-guardian, a Mr Peard from Fermoy, to help Vice-Guardian Clarke in Bantry.

In early March, two ships left Cobh with supplies of Indian meal and biscuits for Bantry.[434] Despite this aid, Clarke and Peard said they feared starvation if the rates were the only fund to help the union.[435] A litany of misfortunes then occurred: the master of the workhouse became ill, went on leave and died a few months later; the matron became ill; Peard left, leaving Clarke alone again until a Richard Lodge came to fill in for a few weeks; and Anthony Nicholson, the relieving officer of Kilcatherine, was dismissed because he had twice embezzled relief funds. (In April a second relieving officer, James Sullivan of Kilnamanagh, had to be dismissed for defrauding paupers of their relief money.) By the end of March, the outdoor relief rolls had risen to 10,002 people.

One wonders about the thoughts and feelings of Vice-Guardian Denis Clarke by the end of March 1849 as the union teetered on the brink of collapse due to the depletion of funds and the illness and death of workhouse officers. Somehow, he and the late Captain Lang had managed to keep the workhouse open and to continue outdoor relief, except for one week. This effort is not adequately documented because of the confusion at the time, but it is certain that many more people would have died if not for the perseverance of Clarke and Lang. This is clear from the workhouse statistics below. The main support from the community for Clarke's efforts seems to have been the meal supplier John O'Connell, the clergy of both persuasions, and perhaps ex-Guardian Michael Murphy, who lent them money at some point.[436]

Bantry Workhouse August 1848–July 1849

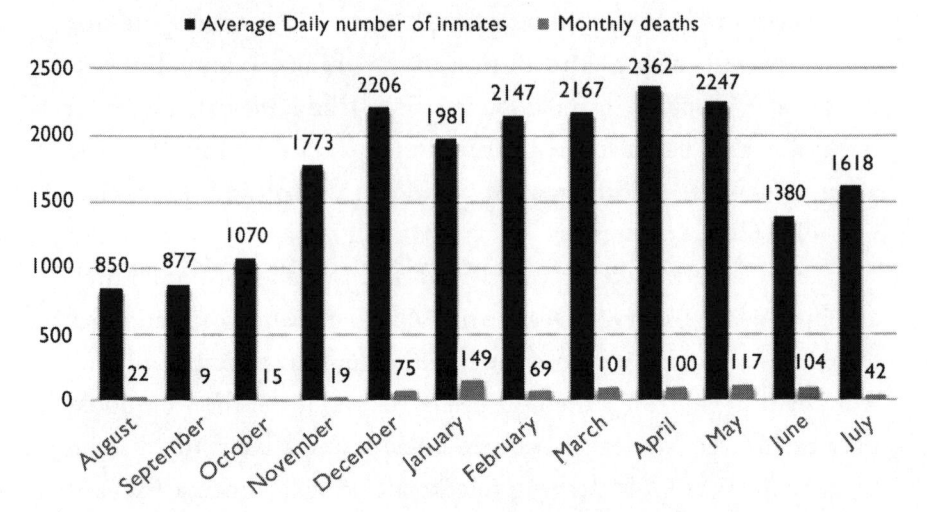

■ Average Daily number of inmates ■ Monthly deaths

Month	Inmates	Deaths
August	850	22
September	877	9
October	1070	15
November	1773	19
December	2206	75
January	1981	149
February	2147	69
March	2167	101
April	2362	100
May	2247	117
June	1380	104
July	1618	42

Fig. 27. Inmate numbers and workhouse deaths, August 1848–July 1849. Drawn from weekly statistics in the workhouse minutes. CCCA BG/43/ A3, A4, AA2.

MARCH–APRIL 1849: DERELICT LANDLORDS AND OTHER MATTERS

Toward the end of March, letters from the late Captain Lang discussing the Bantry Union landowners' lack of responsibility towards tenants were read out in the House of Commons by George P. Scrope MP.[437] Supporting Scrope's and Lang's criticism, the *Cork Examiner* said that Dunmanway Union tenants were less destitute than those in Bantry because Dunmanway landlords made more effort to give employment.[438] Also revealing Bantry landlords' indifference to tenant welfare was information disclosed in April by Rev. Somers Payne, the father of John Payne.[439] He stated that Lord Bantry and Viscount Berehaven had returned £9,700 of their £12,000 loan under the Land Improvement Act, because they found that giving employment did not help in lowering their rates.⁴⁴⁰ It seems that their primary motive when applying for the loan was an attempt to lessen their own financial burden and not to help their tenants. Captain Lang had worked hard to persuade landlords to obtain those loans. Some of his work seems to have been wasted.

The other topic that was discussed nationwide in March was the proposed Rate-in-Aid scheme, where better-off unions were going to be forced to support poorer unions, a scheme from which Bantry would derive a modest benefit (by 1851, the union was to receive £7,808 10s).⁴⁴¹ On 30 April, when the Rate-in-Aid bill passed in the House of Commons, the *London Standard* described it as 'a foolish and criminal expedient', saying that even if the whole of the Rate-in-Aid was collected, it would fall seven-eighths short of what was necessary for Ireland.⁴⁴²

Closer to home, in April, the civic authorities in Cork city decided that the influx of paupers from Skull, Skibbereen and Bantry could no longer be tolerated. The Cork Health Committee allotted £100 'for clearing the streets and carting paupers to some distance from the city boundaries [...] as these paupers had become exceedingly obnoxious by taking possession of shops and enforcing their demands'. Later the Cork corporation gave £150 for the same purpose. These moves were denounced by a Cork city poor law inspector.⁴⁴³

APRIL–JUNE 1849: A HOST OF TRIALS FOR BANTRY UNION

FOOD SUPPLIES AND DEFICIENT FUNDS FROM THE TREASURY

Bantry workhouse remained crowded in April with about 2,300 inmates, of whom over twenty were dying per week. Close to 10,000 people were on outdoor relief but no death statistics exist for them. Extra relieving officers had to be hired for the Kilmacomogue and Kilcrohane divisions. In a major change in agricultural practice, oats and vegetables were sown in the workhouse fields instead of potatoes.

At this point, on 12 April 1849, a large public meeting was convened in Bandon by the lord lieutenant of the county, Viscount Bernard. Lord Bernard said the purpose was to bring before Her Majesty's government and parliament the extreme distress in two unions, Skibbereen and Bantry, of which Bantry was in the worst state of the two; indeed, it was worse off than at any time previously. The meeting resolved that these unions were unable to pay the rate and were entitled to receive aid from the Treasury.[444]

Despite this resolution, a serious problem arose at the end of April when the Treasury stopped sending the PLC the full amount of funding needed to sustain Bantry Union (Table 3). In the House of Commons, a Mr Horsman said that the relief commissioners had been given less funds than were necessary and that the new (unnamed) temporary Poor Law inspector in Bantry had stated deaths from want and exposure were daily increasing. The present relief was barely enough to support existence, but if the reductions continued, 'the natural consequence would be starvation and death'.[445]

Between 25 April and 23 May, the PLC, who often seemed unsympathetic to struggles in the union, engaged in a major tussle with the Treasury in an effort to prevent starvation. The PLC succeeded in getting the minimum monthly relief amount – £350 – fully reinstated and reimbursed by 11 June.

In May, the *Southern Reporter* published a petition to Lord Russell from an unidentified group of people in Bantry Union requesting that the amount per day of Indian meal for outdoor relief should be increased from an 'inadequate' nine ounces to fourteen ounces. They also wrote, 'Our gentry are crushed and unable to help themselves or others. The burden has become too oppressive.'[446] It is disappointing that the authors of this petition could not be identified. It would be interesting to know who in Bantry Union was still active on behalf of the destitute. The *Southern Reporter* continued, 'The work of the

Vice-Guardians is blameless. They have had to contend with insuperable difficulties.'[447]

TABLE 3. DEFICIENT FUNDS SENT BY THE TREASURY TO BANTRY UNION IN SPRING 1849

Date	Amount requested by the PLC (£)	Amount sent by Treasury (£)
25 April	315	268
2 May	350	229
10 May	345	60 (plus 130 a few days later)
18 May	410	315
23 May	not noted	200
2 June	410	410
11 June	465	465 (plus 105 to make up deficiencies)

Source: HC (British Parliamentary Papers), *Papers relating to the aid afforded to the distressed unions in the west of Ireland*, Volume Page: XLVIII.7, 77, 87, 121, 171, Volume: 48;77;87;121;171, Paper Number: 1010 1019 1023 1060 1077 (1849). *ProQuest: U.K. Parliamentary Papers.*

A Captain Haymes, who replaced the late Captain Lang as Poor Law inspector,[448] wrote to the PLC saying that half the people in the union had no means of existence until harvest time. Outdoor relief deaths had decreased in the past week, which he attributed to a recent decision to give relief in Indian meal instead of money,[449] but people had become so weak and emaciated that few were able-bodied. He had instructed the relieving officers to give extra meal to those who were capable of a full day's work, to keep up their strength. He also reported that 74 per cent of the rate had been collected. The outstanding balance was due on lands long since abandoned.[450] However, despite clear evidence of near starvation, the PLC remained concerned that people were faking distress and frequently urged the vice-guardians to be alert for deceit in applicants for relief.

POPULATION, VALUATION AND LEGAL MATTERS

On 25 May 1849, the *Cork Examiner* estimated a drop of 11,000 in the population of Bantry Union since 1841 due to 'extermination, emigration, famine and plague'. Immediate government support was called for.[451] In the next few days many newspapers took up the cry that the famine was spreading and deaths from starvation were once again occurring in the Bantry area.[452] An appeal to the Irish General Relief Association, which had just reconvened, was reported from a Mr McCarthy, the only resident magistrate in Beara, who said the situation there was appalling.[453]

Also, in May the solicitor T. McCarthy Dowling reported to a select committee on the Poor Law for both Skibbereen and Bantry that the valuation of Bantry Union was no longer £37,000 but about £25,000, and that the tradespeople who had supplied Bantry workhouse were in great distress. This was one of the few times that the plight of Bantry shopkeepers was mentioned in contemporary sources. He stated that the Skibbereen guardians thought it unfair that Bantry Union was entirely supported by the PLC, but he acknowledged that the rate collected in Bantry Union was much less than in Skibbereen.

On 17 May 1849, as a result of the lawsuit brought by Thomas Vickery, the contents of the workhouse were sold for £38.[454] Despite the sale, the goods were not physically removed. Accounts of what happened are obscure, but it seems there was a court order to pay Thomas Vickery £38 19s at once and then yearly amounts of £100 until the remainder of the previous Board of Guardians' debt to Vickery was satisfied.[455]

PRISONER WELFARE

The plight of prisoners dying at the Bantry Sessions had been addressed the previous February by the *Cork Examiner*.[456] It was again taken up in early June by Walter Berwick, a well-known Cork judge who complained to the Cork County Grand Jury of many deaths of prisoners who were conveyed in open carts between Bantry and Cork for the session hearings. They were often drenched with rain on the journey and then left for days in cold, damp cells in their wet clothes in the Bantry bridewell, where a high number expired.[457]

BIGOTRY

As if matters were not bad enough, religious bigots on both sides again raised needless acrimony. Rev. Jeremiah Cummins, in Kilcrohane, urged money donations for a Catholic school to prevent children from losing their faith 'in frequenting the Protestant schools'.[458] Not to be outdone, Rev. Crossthwaite of Durrus gave a talk in Essex to the Irish Society. He said priests prayed from the altar that children who went to Protestant schools would get cholera.[459]

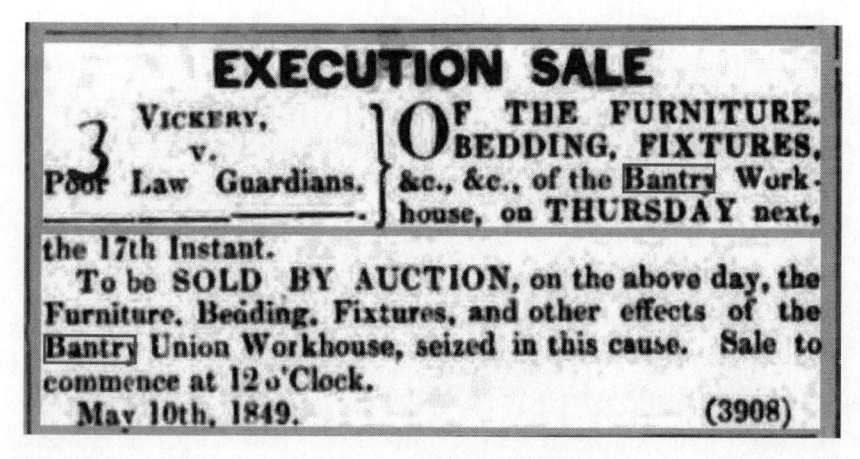

Fig. 28. Notice of sale of workhouse effects. *Southern Reporter* (15 May 1849).

THE CHOLERA OUTBREAK, MAY–AUGUST 1849

The first cholera case in Bantry Union occurred at the end of May 1849. The vice-guardians, warned in advance, had already planned to use a detached shed in the grounds of the workhouse for cholera patients and to rent a building for the same purpose in Castletown. The workhouse numbers rapidly diminished as people feared they would become victims of the disease.[460]

In early June, the most pressing workhouse problem was lack of burial space for the increased number of deaths from the epidemic. Three acres 'adjacent to the workhouse' were contracted by John Payne for this purpose. Part of this land is still preserved as a mown field with the name 'Killeenagh Burial Ground' across a small road from present-day Bantry Hospital. The plaque mentions that the field was used for unbaptised babies, and before that, for famine deaths. It does not mention that cholera deaths were the impetus for its existence.

At the same time, in early June, Denis Clarke fell ill and John Peard returned as a vice-guardian to assist for a while. Clarke recovered after a few weeks. He, Peard and Haymes managed the union through the cholera epidemic. By 12 June, fifty-five cases of cholera were reported. The doctors reported that people collapsed and died suddenly, one being Denis Sullivan, the relieving officer for Kilmacomogue. Another illustration of how sudden the onset could be came from Jane Murphy of Newtown in an undated letter on 'the cholera' to her daughter, 'A daughter [...] of an old friend of your papas [...] died of it [...] has left an infant 7 months old and five children [...] she was in your uncle's kitchen talking to your aunt who had given her a warm drink when half an hour later she was seized with it.'

Cholera deaths were reported separately, so were not included in the workhouse statistics. On 19 June, the total number of cholera cases was 102, with 44 dead, 27 cured and 31 under treatment. That week may have been the peak of misery for 1849, with a reoccurrence of starvation deaths, the onset of cholera and large numbers of barely surviving people on outdoor relief (nearly 17,000 in June, an increase of almost 10,000 since March).

By 3 July, the doctors said cholera was abating, but twenty-five patients remained under treatment. In Castletown, fourteen cases had occurred, of whom eight died and five remained under treatment.[461] The cases continued to diminish. By 21 July, the workhouse cholera shed was closed. However, eleven new cases of cholera were treated at the workhouse in early August (probably in the fever hospital) with two deaths. The last new case was reported on 23 August. By the end of the epidemic, the total number of cases in the union was 185, of whom 82 died, a mortality of 44.3 per cent.[462]

OUTDOOR RELIEF AND OTHER PROBLEMS DURING THE CHOLERA EPIDEMIC

OUTDOOR RELIEF

The greatest challenge was the ever-increasing numbers on outdoor relief. In early July 1849, the *Dublin Evening Post* published an eye-witness account of this programme, exposing how critical the relief was in saving the lives of those barely clinging to existence. The writer described the distribution of meal in an unidentified location in Bantry Union as 'harrowing':

> Several hundreds of men and women appeared, young aged and infirm [...] presenting the appearance of walking skeletons to claim their weekly allowance. Many were pointed out to me that but two years ago were powerful men who now retained nothing but height of their former appearance, youth with hollow cheeks and staring eyes

> [...] with hardly anything left of humanity, mentally or physically. Children [...] staring at the window whence the relief tickets were issued with such anxiety for their turn to be called. Through the whole proceeding I was struck by the kind and feeling manner [...] of the Guardians and other officials.

The unnamed writer said he had not been prepared for the extreme wretchedness he saw, and also not for the gentleness he observed. Earlier in his report he noted that West Cork 'has been sinking in a frightful manner' and described one-fourth of the shops as being abandoned, as well as a quarter of the houses 'unroofed and deserted'. In Bantry he reported that the weather was good and early potatoes were growing well. Fish were abundant but boats were few.[463]

If it had not been for the vice-guardians (Clarke and Peard) and the Poor Law inspector (Haymes) stoutly defending the outdoor relief lists, there is no doubt that Bantry Union deaths in early summer 1849 would have been as bad as or worse than in 1847. In response to the PLC's weekly letters questioning the need for such large amounts of relief, the vice-guardians told them it should come as no surprise that the numbers on outdoor relief had risen so greatly, as the only place that gave employment was the Berehaven mines. On 7 July 1849, 19,562 people were reported on outdoor relief, the highest number reached.[464] The vice-guardians also reassured the PLC that the relief lists were frequently reviewed and 'doubtful cases' were offered tickets of admission to the workhouse. By 19 July they wrote that the outdoor relief numbers had been reduced to about 15,000 and further weekly reductions would take place. They reported that the number of vacancies in the workhouse was due to dread of cholera. People would rather almost starve than enter it. One reason for the reduction in people needing relief may have been that some summer crops were becoming available at that time. There is no source confirmation of this, but it seems likely.

A less serious annoyance suffered by the vice-guardians were pay demands from the workhouse doctors. Initially they refused them but later compromised by recommending a smaller increase than requested.

RATES COLLECTION ISSUES

Continued resistance to payment of rates continued on all sides. The vice-guardians were forced to press claims at the Bantry and Carrigboy (Durrus) petty sessions to recover rates. In July, eighty-four summonses were issued at Bantry and fifteen at Carrigboy, and the defaulters were directed to pay.[465] Around the same time, the vice-guardians' attempts to retrieve rate payments suffered a setback when their solicitor, McCarty Dowling, in what appears to have been unprofessional conduct, decided to defend Lord Bantry's non-payment of rates. Since Dowling was the union's appointed solicitor, the vice-guardians felt he should have recused himself.[466]

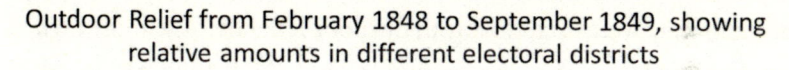

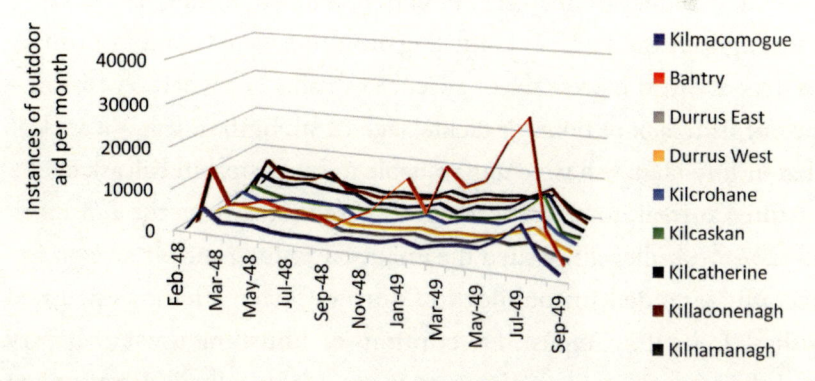

Fig. 29. Chart showing outdoor relief in the nine electoral divisions of Bantry Union, February 1848–September 1849. The numbers represent persons who were 'relieved' (given money or meal). Drawn from the outdoor relief numbers written weekly in the workhouse minutes.

A WANT OF INHABITANTS: THE FAMINE IN BANTRY UNION

John Payne again caused a problem when he wrote complaining that the rate for Bere Island (belonging to Viscount Berehaven) was too high. The vice-guardians disagreed, saying they could prove the property was actually worth more than the valuation; they also pointed out that after the union valuation was revised in 1843, the total was lowered by 20 per cent, against the wishes of the PLC – the reason for the reduction, the depreciation in the price of agricultural produce. The vice-guardians referred to minutes from April, May and June 1843, a reference to a minute book now unavailable, that contained information on the opposition of the gentry to setting rates before the start of the famine. This episode gives an insight into the vice-guardians' tougher stance by July 1849 and their refusal to concede to Lord Bantry's son or his agent.

SOME PEOPLE WERE STILL STARVING

On 23 July 1849, the electoral division of Kilcaskan was still destitute, as a petition for help made clear. People were 'starving', with no employment, and they were excluded from outdoor relief because most owned more than a quarter of an acre of barren land. All fishing had failed.[467] (Throughout the famine, confusing accounts were found in primary sources about the presence or absence of fish.) For whatever reason – lack of fish, lack of boats or tackle, lack of strength to fish – it is clear that in July 1849, fish were not available to the people in Kilcaskan.

On a surreal note, a reporter and sketch artist from the *Illustrated London News* allegedly visited the union on 30 June and wrote a bizarre account intended for publication during Queen Victoria's planned visit to Ireland in August. Descriptions of a bustling town of Bantry with herring boats at the quay and, most ironically, illustrations of well-nourished peasants on a mountain near Kilcaskan make it difficult to believe anyone actually had visited, or if they did, makes one wonder at the motivation in supplying such misleading information.[468]

THE TIDE TURNS

The end of July 1849 marked the turn of the tide in the famine in Bantry Union. On 27 July, healthy potato crops were reported,[469] and more importantly, these reports remained consistent during August and September. But, for the depleted and weakened inhabitants, there was no rejoicing. The damage had been overwhelming. Real recovery and reinstatement of the union to its position in the early 1840s would not be possible for many years. Any long-term improvement that did occur was slow and uncertain. However, as the summer of 1849 progressed there was at least a short-term change for the better. By early September, H.J. Fawcett, the agricultural instructor, said 'the green crops were thriving and firmly established' in Bantry Union. Before then, they were virtually unknown. 'The farmers were vying amongst each other' in their cultivation and eager for advice. The harvest was expected to be the most abundant in many years.[470]

AT THE WORKHOUSE

The vice-guardians finally had time to partly remedy the lack of an educational program for children who were inmates. On 20 July they wrote to the PLC, in an explanation for the neglect of education, that

> the master of the Bantry workhouse having died sometime since, the male teacher of the school was appointed to act as master until another should be elected. The attendance books had not been kept for three months because of the master's illness. The female teacher was dismissed for incompetency [...] and the female appointment is now in abeyance. The free stock of books has been lost or worn out, and there have been no regular accounts kept for some time.

However, they said the situation had improved since a new master, John Woulfe, was appointed on 7 July. The male teacher had resumed teaching then. They had been unable to get a female teacher. The Education Office wrote back to say a stock of free books for the school would be sent as soon as possible.[471]

On the issue of outdoor relief, the vice-guardians reported the numbers down to 7,195 by 21 August. One week later there were only 2,656. Presumably people were employed in the harvest and getting enough to eat to replace the relief Indian meal. The vice-guardians said that only the blind, bedridden and those who could not be moved remained on outdoor relief. This 'happy change in the condition of the poor classes is chiefly owing to the plentiful harvest'. By September's end, only 281 people continued on outdoor relief in Bantry Union.[472]

The PLC were still pushing to get the rate collected. The vice-guardians replied more assertively than previously that they were doing everything they could and, 'considering the opposition which their collectors faced', thought their lodgements 'very satisfactory'. Despite that reply, they began to put still-greater pressure on the rate collectors, forcing even magistrate Arthur Hutchinson to co-operate.

By the middle of September 1849, finances had improved so much that they were able to order a great many supplies of all sorts for the workhouse, including cloth, dishes, tools, brushes and glazing material.[473] Dunmanway Union, angry about their Rate-in-Aid payments, made a formal protest to the PLC about 'mismanagement' and 'extravagance' in Bantry Union.[474] How much attention the vice-guardians paid to complaints from the Dunmanway Union is questionable.

QUEEN VICTORIA AND OTHER VISITORS

Almost the only news published in August was that of Queen Victoria's eleven-day visit to Cork, Dublin and Belfast on 2–12 August 1849.[475] Her presence in Ireland caused great excitement in West Cork, even though she did not visit the area. Most of the local newspaper accounts discuss the disappointment caused by changes in her published schedule and the severe congestion of carriages around Bandon, which prevented many of the curious from actually getting to Cork city in time to see her. The Queen was reported as graciously expressing appreciation to her hosts, autographing the Book of Kells and being warm in her farewells on her departure. She was welcomed with a degree of enthusiasm that today seems surprising. She said nothing publicly about the famine.

Overall, there was a greater local impact from ordinary English tourists visiting the union[476] and from the resumed service of a three-horse car that ran daily from Bantry to Killarney.[477] The *Constitution* reported that since the spring of 1849 the hotels around Killarney and Bantry Bay had been filled, mostly with tourists from London, by virtue of an arrangement between the Irish and English railways.[478] In September, Windele, the antiquarian, went on an archaeological excursion to Beara.[479] Letters in the archives from his friends, including a James Dowling in Castletown, detail the journey by train, horse and gig and finally boat from Bantry to Berehaven. He was assured that a 'sure-footed' pony would be available for him to explore the countryside.

In the same month Lord Lieutenant Clarendon and his party travelled to Killarney, where a stag hunt was put on for their benefit.[480] On their return journey they visited Lord Bantry and were shown around his grounds in Glengarriff. This visit was reported by the *London Illustrated News* as an 'Autumn Idyll'.[481]

PRELIMINARY STOCKTAKING OF FAMINE DAMAGE

Toward the end of August 1849, a report on the Irish agricultural returns for the whole country was published for the years 1847–48 and was commented on by many. The report said no one had been prepared for 'the wholesale annihilation' of small farms, which the returns demonstrated. This was certainly the case in Bantry Union,[482] where tenancy of farms under 5 acres had decreased by more than half.[483] The authors of the report saw 1849 as an auspicious year nationwide, with more land than ever before under tillage (obviously in larger farms) with more diverse crops.[484]

BANTRY UNION BECOMES SMALLER

In 1848 the Poor Law Boundary Commission was formed with a main purpose of reducing the size of some overly large unions to make their administration more efficient. The commission originally proposed fifty new unions so that no property was more than 8 miles from the workhouse. Only thirty-three were created.

On 29 September 1849, the boundary commission formally divided Bantry Union into two separate unions, the Bantry and Castletown unions, each of which would revert to electing local guardians to replace the vice-guardians.[485] New and smaller electoral districts were created for each of the new unions:

> **Bantry Union electoral districts**: Bantry, Ahil, Douce, Durrus East, Durrus West, Glanlough, Whiddy, Glengarriff, Kealkill, Kilcaskan, Meelagh, Scart, Seefin, Sheep's Head (with a total of fifteen guardians).

> **Castletown Union electoral districts**: Adrigole, Bere, Coulagh, Curryglass, Kilcatherine, Killaconenagh, Kilnamanagh (with a total of ten guardians).

The old Bantry Union had 137,256 acres; the new union, 82,441 acres. The valuation of the new Bantry Union was reduced to £21,510.

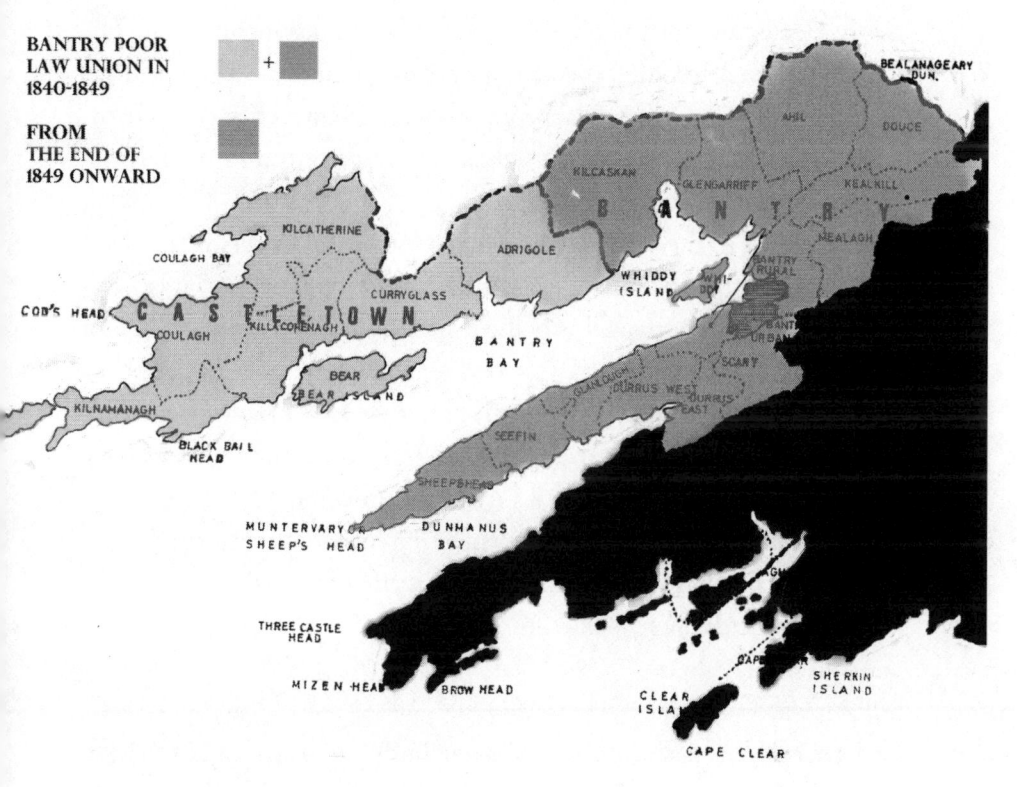

Fig. 30. Map of Bantry Union before and after September 1849. Map courtesy of Cork City and County Archives.

HANDING OVER THE UNIONS

In early October an announcement was published for the re-election of boards of guardians for both Bantry and the new Castletown Union.[486] The Bantry vice-guardians continued to meet in October while guardian elections took place and relieving officers were reassigned.[487] On 16 October, William Geraghty of Ballina, Co. Mayo replaced Captain Haymes as Poor Law inspector. He and Denis Clarke were together for the last three board meetings before the newly-elected boards took over. The workhouse was inspected by Dr Phelan before he handed the union over to the newly-elected Bantry Union guardians. Only trivial problems were discovered and recorded in the minute book, typical of which was a boy found in the female area and a teacher temporarily absent.

The tenure of the paid vice-guardians ends with no personal reflections, and no expressions of gratitude or regret. Denis Clarke was reported in the newspapers as being posted as an assistant guardian to the Carlow Union, but there is no evidence that he took up the position.[488] He and his wife had a small daughter and a two-month-old baby. It is unclear where they went.[489] From that time, his whereabouts could not be traced until his death notice on 7 October 1887, where he is described as a widower living at Morehampton Road, Dublin, with only £5 in effects.[490] (For a listing of the paid vice-guardians see Appendix X.)

UNPAID VERSUS PAID GUARDIANS

In Bantry Union the paid vice-guardians far outperformed the unpaid elected board. The motivations involved were probably very different. The first elected board may have sought prestige, influence over merchant contracts and power over thousands of people. The vice-guardians probably saw their job in more pragmatic terms and less in terms of image or local standing. With just two of them, they did not have to deal with shifting and unreliable board attendance or antagonisms among multiple members. If the paid vice-guardians had been in place during spring 1847, maybe deaths would have been fewer, even if, like the original board, they had been surprised by the suddenness and severity of destitution and the torturous bureaucracy of government aid. This conclusion is supported by the dramatic differences between the tenure of the original guardians and the paid vice-guardians (Fig. 31).

FROM BAD TO WORSE

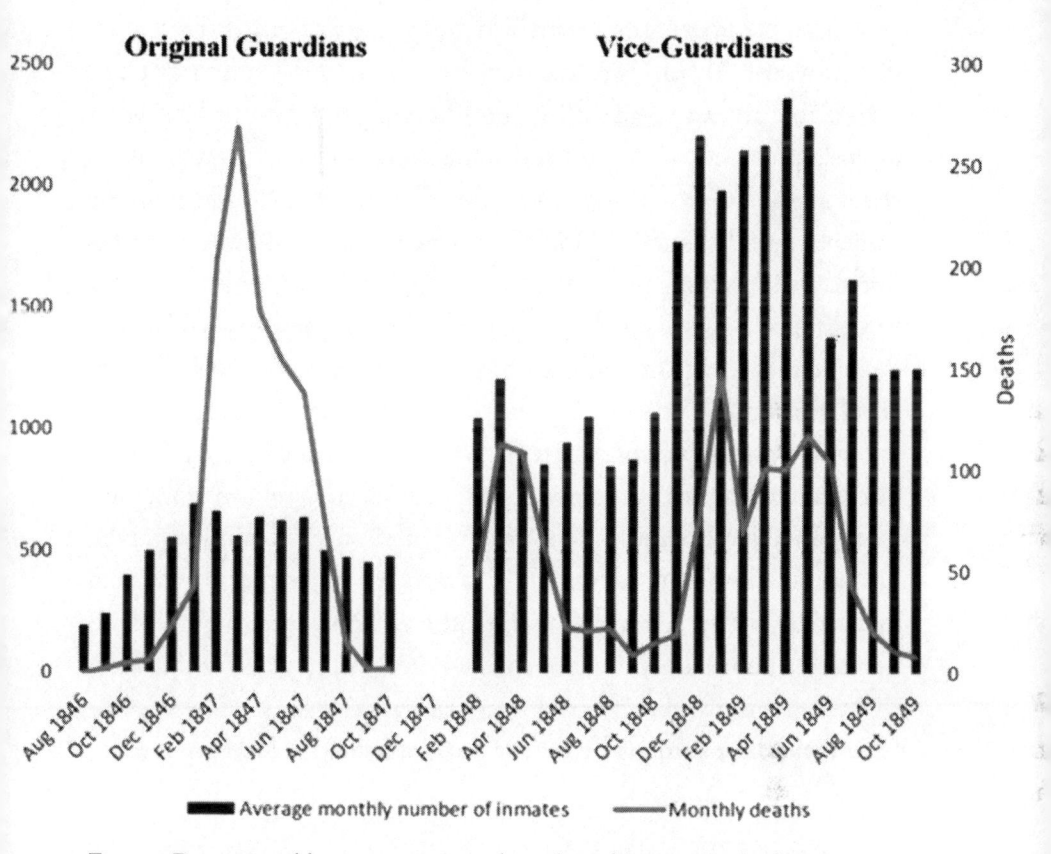

Fig. 31. Bantry workhouse inmate totals and workhouse deaths from August 1846 to October 1849 drawn by the author from weekly statistics in the Bantry workhouse minute books. The gap represents the three months of missing minutes.

A WANT OF INHABITANTS: THE FAMINE IN BANTRY UNION

Although inmate numbers trebled during the vice-guardians' tenure, the number of deaths was less than half those in the spring of 1847, remarkable given the weakened condition of people in the later years of the famine. The workhouse diet under the vice-guardians was almost certainly superior to the diet under the original board. In addition, the paid vice-guardians and the local Poor Law inspectors showed a dedication to their task that was absent in the original board. In letters to the PLC, the vice-guardians showed empathy for the destitute when they described the 'chilly protection' of the workhouse. They fought to give adequate outdoor relief to thousands of people despite the Treasury's attempts to withhold funds. The vice-guardians made heroic efforts to discharge their duty, as did the Poor Law inspectors sent to work with them, notably Captain H.W. Gordon in 1848 and Captain Lang, who died in 1849 as a result of his work. As reported in the newspapers, and made clear in their letters to the PLC, the vice-guardians showed kindness to the poor, something not apparent in the original board. Overall, the evidence shows that the paid vice-guardians worked hard, were competent and did a better job than the board made up of local grandees.

LOSSES

By the end of the 1840s, Bantry Union had been dispossessed of thousands of families and small farms. The loss of population in the union between 1841 and 1851 (using the census figures) was not evenly distributed among the electoral divisions (Fig. 32). How accurate the census figures are is in doubt, but they are the only ones available. Beara lost 21.9 per cent of inhabitants, the Kilmacomogue area lost 24.7 per cent and Sheep's Head lost 46.8 per cent. (More detailed figures showing the losses in each electoral division can be seen in Appendix XI.) Overall, the entire union lost 27.4 per cent of inhabitants through famine or flight. This is less than Skibbereen Union, whose population was depleted by about 35 per cent.

In September 1849 the boundary commission estimated the new Bantry Union population at 25,200, while it put the number for both unions at an erroneous 56,000. Both figures were inaccurate on two counts: they do not take into account famine losses, and they continue a long-standing error for the population of Kilcatherine.[491] From the 1851 census it is difficult to calculate the total population in the new Bantry Union because the boundary between the two unions cut through Kilcaskan. The highest it could have been, including the whole of Kilcaskan, was just under 22,000. The 1851 population of Kilcaskan was 3,992, so a reasonable estimate of the new, smaller Bantry Union's population in 1851 would be just over 20,000; a reasonable estimate of the new Castletown Union would be about 17,000, giving a total for both unions of about 37,000.[492]

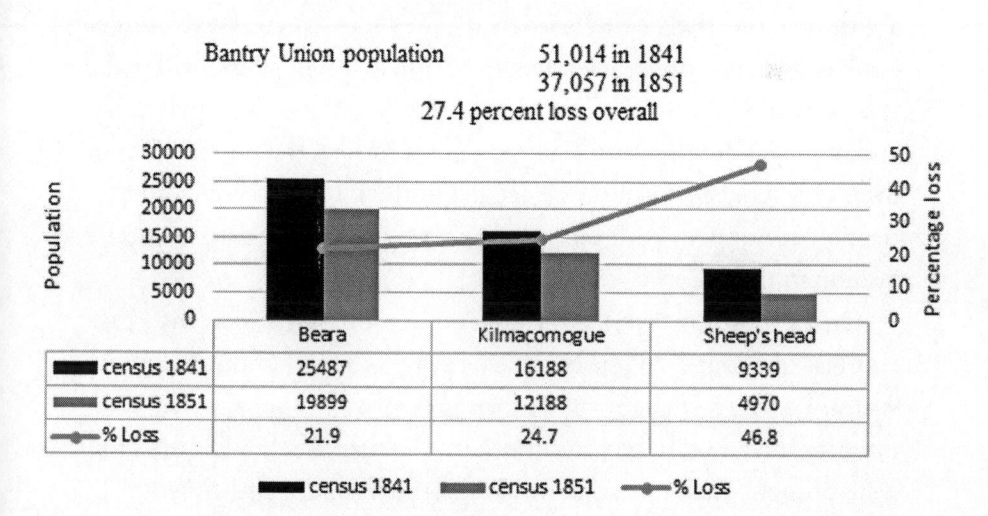

Bantry Union population
51,014 in 1841
37,057 in 1851
27.4 percent loss overall

	Beara	Kilmacomogue	Sheep's head
census 1841	25487	16188	9339
census 1851	19899	12188	4970
% Loss	21.9	24.7	46.8

Fig. 32. Losses from 1841 to 1851 in the Bantry Union. Note that the 1851 census number includes Castletown Union and does not report the two new union totals separately. (Appendix XII contains more detail.)

WORKHOUSE AND OUTDOOR RELIEF NUMBERS

When the elected board of the newly-separated Bantry Union took over in November 1849, the workhouse contained 1,299 inmates, including those from Castletown, where the workhouse would not be ready until 1851. Boys and girls still occupied two auxiliary rented houses in Bantry town. The workhouse infirmary held ninety-five inmates, and the fever hospital housed thirty-seven. The week before the hand-over, one person had died and sixty-one people were on outdoor relief. The amount of rate outstanding was £3,839 2s 5½d.[493] The union finances were on a better footing than when the 'old board' had been dissolved, but the long-term prospects for the poor and gentry alike were grim. The union needed competent leadership just as much in November 1849 as at any time in the previous four years. What they got was essentially the 'old board' from 1847 with a few new members.[494] Whether they were 'older and wiser' and had learned anything from their exile is unclear. The fact that the next minute book is missing (only a few notes survive in a 'rough' book) will make this more difficult for the curious to assess. What is clear is that at the end of 1849, although the blight had not returned, the misery was not over. Outdoor relief again was needed in the following year, and destitution continued, with blight reappearing here and there in patchy fashion in the union.

On 28 February 1850 the number on outdoor relief was only 330, a contrast to about 8,500 in February 1849.[495] The workhouse, though, was still overcrowded. Some of the older girls were sent to stay temporarily in an auxiliary workhouse in Durrus for a few months but were brought back to the main workhouse in mid-August 1850.[496] In October 1850, a letter to John Windele reads, 'The Bantry and Schull Unions are badly off, the potato crop particularly in Bantry is bad and diseased.'[497] In December 1850, Michael Murphy offered the use of a store at Donemark to house the boys, showing that overcrowding continued. Even for the half-year ending 25 March 1851, the average daily number of workhouse inmates was 1,250, evidence of continuing poverty in the union at the beginning of the second half of the nineteenth century.[498]

CONCLUSION

This ten-year account (1839–1849) records a natural disaster that evolved into a calamity where local infighting rivalled and magnified the lapses and iniquity of the government. Despite, or more probably because of, the devastation, the story of the famine in Bantry, with its acts of heroism and wrongdoing (sometimes in the same person), has been erased from public memory.

In 1851 a census was taken of all the townlands in the original Bantry Union. It showed 14,000 less people than in the census taken in 1841. Over 27 per cent of the inhabitants had died or moved away. During the decade of the 1840s, the face of the disaster continually changed. In the famine's early stages, confused crowds of the starving and sick swamped Bantry town, whereas in later famine years the streets became quiet, business was paralysed, shops were closed and the weakened population suffered 'complete prostration of mental and physical exertion'.[499] Writing about Bantry town after the famine, Professor Kevin Hourihan states:

> The depopulation was reflected in Bantry's physical fabric [...] 158 fewer mud huts in the town in 1851 than ten years previously and 256 fewer families in these cabins [...] Second-class houses increased by only twenty-four, and there were only four more first-class houses than in 1841.[500]

Bantry Union was shattered by the disaster. The situation in the union had always been untenable, as there simply was not an adequate base of ratepayers to support the numbers of destitute. In 1849, the 3s in the pound rate in Bantry Union compared with the rate in Cork city of 1s 9d emphasises the unequal burden carried by Bantry Union. Landlords with mortgaged properties could not afford the rates and many had to sell off their property from the 1850s onwards. In 1852, there were forced sales through the Encumbered Estates Court of many parcels of land formerly controlled by the deceased Richard White of Inchiclough.[501] In 1853, larger properties owned by the second Earl of Bantry were sold.

Although intensive farming and reclamation of wasteland began during the 1850s, the collapsed coral sand industry and the moribund fishing industry took longer to recover. The linen industry was never re-established. More important was the demoralisation in the whole area caused by suffering, emigration and death, which led to the loss of small farms and the clustered hamlets known as clachans, particularly numerous in Bantry Union. An entire way of life and traditional culture was damaged irretrievably in less than one decade. Ruins still exist of 'famine houses' throughout Bantry Union where whole families perished or from which they emigrated, one of the few present-day reminders of the famine.

Fig. 33. The cross erected in 1889 over the famine pits in the Abbey cemetery. Photograph by author.

Fig. 34. Famine house in Faranamanagh townland on Sheep's Head peninsula. Photograph by author.

David Lloyd quotes Dr William Wilde, who in 1851, although not speaking specifically of Bantry, blamed the famine for the loss of 'some of the most vital agents of cultural reproduction – fiddlers and pipers, singers and storytellers, hedge-schoolmasters, herbalists, wise women [...] and above all, the Famine had reaped a swathe of the elderly, the great interpreters and adapters of tradition.'[502]

Dr John Forbes, a Scottish medical writer and distinguished physician who travelled in Ireland in 1852, was told that in Bantry the number of teetotallers had shrunk from 500 to 30.[503] He did not enquire if some of the missing had died or emigrated, but he did seem convinced that alcohol was once again a significant problem.

STUDY ON WORKHOUSES

Professor Cormac Ó Gráda, an Irish economic historian, compared union workhouses during the famine on a nationwide basis. He identified five markers of poor management: delay in opening the workhouse, poor attendance of guardians at board meetings, dissolution of the board, high numbers of infectious disease deaths in the workhouse and degree of union indebtedness. All of these were present in Bantry Union. Ó Gráda does not identify the Bantry workhouse as having a delayed opening, but it deserves that designation. In Bantry workhouse, out of 2,896 total deaths between 1845 and 1851, 80.6 per cent of deaths were attributed to infectious disease,[504] placing Bantry workhouse high on the 'worst workhouse' list.[505]

NOTES ON GROUPS AND INDIVIDUALS

THE CLERGY

Despite some bigotry, the clergy were a positive force in the union. The Protestant ministers were diligent in correspondence requesting aid from the government and in securing contributions from their contacts in England. They shared with the Catholic priests and many others a mistaken belief that the government would be motivated to feed people before they starved to death

In Kilcaskan (Adrigole), Revs Wright and Sheahan toiled to keep their flocks alive. Rev. Sheahan died in September 1849. In Bantry, Rev. Alexander Hallowell, the Protestant curate, was noted for his practical care of the destitute throughout the entire famine. He survived an episode of severe illness and returned to the work. He was willing to speak out at a manslaughter trial at the request of the Catholic leader John Shea Lawlor, supporting Lawlor's contention that the victim died of starvation indirectly caused by John Warren Payne's negligence. However, the court refused to hear him. His rector, Rev. John Murphy, took visitors on tours of the area and chaired one relief committee meeting, but he was not reported as writing letters or being intimately involved with the poor. He comes across as concerned but small-minded in the few recorded interactions concerning him.

The respected parish priest of Bantry, Rev. Thomas Barry, was a strong and outspoken advocate for the poor until, much to the union's disadvantage, he was moved abruptly to Cork city in 1847. No information was discovered that explained its suddenness. The remaining curates and his eventual replacement, a Rev. James Barry, worked hard but were not as forceful as Rev. Barry had been.

SECTARIAN SQUABBLING

Outright sectarian squabbling adversely affected famine relief in the Castletown area on Beara, particularly with respect to the effective running of the soup kitchen there. In Bantry the clergy showed mutual respect for each other. On Sheep's Head peninsula sectarian unpleasantness was muted until near the end of the famine. The main offender there was Rev. Crossthwaite in Durrus, who was publicly referred to as 'a noted proselytiser'[506] and who, over the famine's course, seemed to become less rational. He had a contradictory famine history. Initially he was the first to write letters for help to raise relief funds and feed children. In November 1847, he developed a bizarre fantasy that some of the relief money had been embezzled. The fund was eventually found to be one half-penny short and he was found to be in error. One wonders if he had been suffering from mental health problems.[507]

BANTRY TRADERS

Many Bantry traders of both denominations went into debt to keep the workhouse supplied, Thomas Vickery being the most publicised. However, the workhouse minutes in 1847 record some others not directly involved in trade as being paid late or not at all by the first Board of Guardians.

JOHN WARREN PAYNE

This man, who had a finger in every pie in Bantry Union, did not take on the mantel of moral leadership so badly needed. It was to the detriment of the starving and sick that so much power was vested in him.

Other individuals attempted at different points to counterbalance his authority, but their influence was relatively short-term or, as in the case of the clergy, their efforts had limited effect.

After the famine, John Payne was again elected a guardian and continued to amass property. He became a director of the Great Southern and Western Railway and of the Munster and Leinster bank. In 1890, to further his political career, he took on the additional name of Sheares, the surname of his famous great-uncles. He moved to Monkstown in East Cork, from where he unsuccessfully contested a parliamentary seat in 1892. The winner, ironically, was Maurice Healy (1859–1923), the third son of the young Bantry Poor Law clerk of the same name. There is no doubt Payne was an immensely competent and hard-working man. If he had acted in the interests of the poor in Bantry Union, he could have made a significant difference to the outcome. Instead, he focused on personal ambition and lost his chance to ease the suffering in the union.

JEREMIAH O'CALLAGHAN

A *Cork Examiner* reporter, he recorded the horrors of the famine in Bantry Union, as well as the miscarriage of justice and the chicanery of some court proceedings. His accounts were invaluable then to his readers, and they are now indispensable for those seeking eyewitness accounts of the time.

MICHAEL AND JANE MURPHY OF NEWTOWN HOUSE

Michael Murphy, the brother of the rector, was a prominent Protestant in the community, the owner of corn and flour mills, and a former agent of Lord Kenmare; he was probably first elected as a guardian in 1840. He was one of the most consistent guardians in attending the board meetings. He went to England at the beginning of the famine to buy food for the people living around him and lent money to the vice-guardians. He and his letter-writing wife Jane felt an obligation to feed the poor. They were almost certainly involved in setting up the soup kitchen at 'Soup-house Field' near Newtown House, where the old soup pots and the cauldron for holding the coals are still in existence. After the famine he offered one of his stores to house the workhouse boys, and he was elected to the new Bantry Board of Guardians in 1849. He seems to have been a conscientious man, but not a leader of others. No direct quotes attributable to him were found.

It was initially exciting to find that some of his wife's letters had survived and then disappointing to discover her limited perspective. She continually bemoans the absence of her daughter and rarely strays from descriptions of clothes and minor domestic matters. If she had only written more of what was happening around her, she could have added immensely to our understanding. Her daughter died in the early 1850s. The letters do not mention anything of this, and they stop around that point.

Today, almost no folk memory remains of the people described above and the many others who, like John O'Connell, John Shea Lawlor, the vice-guardians and the Poor Law inspectors, were vital to the survival of many in Bantry Union.

QUESTIONS THAT AROSE IN THE COURSE OF THE NARRATIVE

ABSENCE OF VIOLENCE

Why was there not more agitation when food became unavailable? The only aggression recorded was a couple of easily suppressed hunger riots, the gathering around Lord Bantry's lodge in Glengarriff in 1846 and the reports of rate collector intimidation. The explanation may be that people were too physically weak to resist and fight back. Nonetheless, there is some evidence that passivity was typical of the entire area over the preceding twenty years. Despite a history of past tithe agitation, the poor population was consistently described as peaceful. As far as can be understood from the minimal surviving commentary, they did not contribute to their own misfortunes. This seems understandable to some extent in the more oppressive conditions on Beara, but it is not so easily explained elsewhere. This may not be a relevant question from the perspective of the twenty-first century. Perhaps the better question is how did anyone manage to rebel at all?

BURIAL SITE

Another puzzling matter is that the burial place for cholera victims, adjacent to the workhouse, apparently later became a site for the burial of unbaptised babies. It is not clear when this happened. One imagines that the site would have been regarded with some horror for a long time after the famine. Quite possibly, many years intervened before its use changed.

HIGH LOSSES ON SHEEP'S HEAD PENINSULA

The apparently disproportionate losses on Sheep's Head peninsula between 1841 and 1851 raise questions. While Beara and Kilmacomogue lost around one-quarter of their population, Sheep's Head Peninsula lost almost half. No contemporary source reported unusually high losses on the Sheep's Head. Explanations are varied and not particularly satisfactory. Reports did originate from there of farmers abandoning their land. This raises the possibility that more people may have emigrated from Sheep's Head than from the rest of the union. Maybe they were better off financially and thus more able to afford the fare to Canada or Britain than those in the rest of

CONCLUSION

the union? Evidence to support this assumption is lacking. Part of the explanation may be that the inhabitants of Sheep's Head (as the vice-guardians reported) occupied a larger share of the workhouse population than those from other areas. What proportion of the census loss on Sheep's Head was due to emigration, starvation, disease or incarceration in the workhouse is not known.

REMEMBERING THE FAMINE

Bantry has not embraced commemoration of the famine as much as Skibbereen has done. There is no heritage centre and there are few plaques. The Celtic cross commemorating the famine that stands in the Abbey cemetery was erected by Tim Healy MP (born in 1855). He was the second son of Maurice Healy (who at 20 years of age, in 1848, became clerk to the Bantry Union). Tim Healy obtained permission for the cross in 1887 from the contemporary Lord Bantry,[508] and it was erected without ceremony in 1889. The cross stands facing Bantry town, marking the pits dug in 1847 where the remains of thousands of victims were deposited.

> A splendid memorial cross is about being erected in Bantry to the memory of those who died of famine during the memorable period of 1846-8. It is composed of Galway limestone, and consists of two monoliths, the cross itself standing about twelve feet in height upon a base about three feet square, upon which is inscribed the following in lead imperishable lettering :—"To mark the Famine Pit of 1846-8. May God give rest to the souls of the faithful departed." It is the gift of Mr. T. M. Healy, M.P., and it has been ably executed by Mr. Wm. P. O'Neill, sculptor, Great Brunswick-street, Dublin. There will not be any public ceremonial at the unveiling.

Fig. 35. Newspaper notice of the Abbey famine cross erected in 1889. *Dublin Weekly Nation* (28 September 1889).

A WANT OF INHABITANTS: THE FAMINE IN BANTRY UNION

The psychological impact of the devastation was so pervasive that in Bantry, almost 170 years later, the community still professes to know little or nothing about it. Like the gap in the literature, there is a void in present-day Bantry inhabitants' knowledge of the famine years. This may have arisen because the losses were too great to process and thus no 'story' could be passed down to younger generations. One elderly man apologised for not being able to recall any discussion of the famine when he was a youngster. However, he did remember something that always occurred in his grandmother's house near Durrus: when the meal was finished and the crumbs were brushed from the table, he was not allowed to throw them into the fire. Even one crumb had to be put carefully in the pig's bucket. As a child he found this strange, but he recognised that to his grandmother it was of the utmost importance that no food was wasted. The story may not have been passed down in current lore, but as a non-verbal expression of the death and starvation of the 1840s, it has its place with others in the historical record.[509]

APPENDICES

APPENDIX I

BANTRY BOARD OF GUARDIANS
AUGUST 1846 TO OCTOBER 1847

Chairman — Lord Bantry ⎤ Thom's
Vice-Chairman — Viscount Berehaven ⎬ 1845
Deputy Vice-Chairman — Timothy O'Donovan Esq. ⎦ Directory

The following people (noted in the Bantry workhouse minute books) were Bantry guardians for varying amounts of time between August 1846 and October 1847:

- Chairman Lord Bantry (represented on the board by John Warren Payne)
- Vice-chairman Viscount Berehaven (did not attend during the above-mentioned time period)
- Deputy Vice-chairman Timothy O'Donovan (of O'Donovan's Cove)
- Arthur Hutchinson, JP Cooney
- Arthur Hutchins, Esq. Ballylickey
- Samuel Hutchins, JP Ardnagashel
- Emmanuel Hutchins
- George Bird (lawyer, land agent)
- Robert Warner
- Richard O'Donoghue

- Richard Blair (Blair's Cove)
- James Downing
- Florence McCarthy
- David Kirby (on Richard White's death)
- Timothy Sullivan (attended one meeting)
- William Vickery
- Patrick O'Sullivan
- Michael Murphy (Donemark, miller)
- Richard White of Inchaclough
- Richard Evanson (Friendly Cove)
- William Pearson
- John Orpen
- Richard O'Donovan Sr
- Richard O'Donovan Jr

Seamus Crowley notes two additional guardians: a Timothy Pearson and a Timothy O'Leary. He gives no source but may have had access to an earlier minute book that is now missing.[510]

In 1991, Donal FitzGerald submitted an unsourced list of guardians in his article in the *Bantry Historical and Archaeological Society Journal*,[511] and in 1996 Carroll gave another list, again without sources.[512]

APPENDIX II

HOUSE CLASSIFICATION

TABLE A1. TYPES OF HOUSES BY CLASS IN BANTRY UNION

Electoral Division	First class	Second class	Third class	Fourth class	Inhabited	Un-inhabited	Being built	Total houses	Fourth class (%)
Kilmacomogue	20	88	382	1,337	1,827	86	0	1,838	73.1
Bantry town	36	116	360	101	702	11	3	702	14.4
Durrus	6	101	115	487	709	0	0	709	68.6
Kilcrohane	2	8	29	762	801	0	0	801	95.1
Kilcaskan	4	16	259	641	920	4	0	924	69.6
Kilcatherine	0	20	233	974	1,227	9	1	1,237	79.4
Kilaconenagh	4	27	107	946	1,084	12	0	1,096	87.3
Castletown	19	73	13	18	123	2	0	125	14.6
Kilnamanagh	2	32	45	915	1,004	41	2	1,047	91.1

Source: HC, *Report comms. census of Ireland 1841*, p. 172–7.

Note: Drawn from the 1841 census, with an additional column, calculated by the author, showing percentage of fourth-class housing in each electoral division.

APPENDIX III

OCCUPATIONS

TABLE A2. OCCUPATIONAL GROUPINGS FROM THE 1841 CENSUS

	Agriculture	Trade/manufacturing
Bantry Town	240	435
Castletown Berehaven	12	96
Kilmacomogue	1,632	137
Beara peninsula	3,653	701
Durrus and Kilcrohane	1,357	118

Source: HC, *Report comms. census of Ireland 1841*, p. 172–7.

Note: The data refer to the main occupations in 8,381 families in Bantry Union in 1841 out of a total of 8,999. The relatively large number for manufacturing on Beara is probably accounted for by employment at the Allihies mines.

APPENDIX IV

DR STEPHENS' MEASUREMENTS OF BANTRY WORKHOUSE

20 FEBRUARY 1847

BANTRY WORKHOUSE.

	Measurement.	Inmates.	Cubic Feet.		Measurement.	Inmates.	Cubic Feet.
Old Women's Day Room:				**Old Men's Day Room:**			
Height	12			Height	12		
Length	38	90	—	Length	38	48	—
Breadth	16½			Breadth	16½		
Girls' School:				**Boys' School:**			
Height	12			Height	12		
Length	46	78	—	Length	46	60	—
Breadth	16			Breadth	16		
Old Women's Ward, No. 1:				**Old Men's Ward, No. 1:**			
Height	12			Height	12		
Length	36	18	—	Length	36	14	—
Breadth	16			Breadth	16		

Fig. A1. Dr Stephens' measurements of Bantry workhouse, 20 February 1847.

Source: 'Reports to Board of Health in Dublin by Medical Officers on State of Workhouses in Cork, Bantry and Lurgan', *19th Century House of Commons Sessional Papers* (1847).

BANTRY WORKHOUSE—continued.   Bantry Union.

	Measurement.	Inmates.	Cubic Feet.		Measurement.	Inmates.	Cubic Feet.
Old Women's Ward, No. 2:				Old Men's Ward, No. 2:			
Height	11			Height	11		
Length	36½	22	—	Length	36½	14	—
Breadth	16¾			Breadth	16¾		
Ditto Ward, No. 3:				Ditto Ward, No. 3:			
Height	11			Height	11		
Length	38½	24	—	Length	38	14	—
Breadth	16½			Breadth	16½		
Ditto Ward, No. 4:				Ditto Ward, No. 4:			
Height	11			Height	11		
Length	36¼	26	—	Length	36½	6	—
Breadth	16½			Breadth	16½		
		60				48	

WORKHOUSE SLEEPING WARDS.

	Feet.	Inmates.	Cubic Feet.		Feet.	Inmates.	Cubic Feet.
Front Dormitory:				Back Dormitory:			
Height	11			Height	11		
Length	73	48	—	Length	55	20	—
Breadth	17			Breadth	16½		
No. 1, Girls' Ward:				No. 1, Boys' Ward:			
Height	11			Height	11		
Length	40	39	—	Length	46	20	—
Breadth	16¾			Breadth	16¾		
No. 2, Girls' Ward:				No. 2, Boys' Ward:			
Height	11			Height	11		
Length	46	48	—	Length	46	20	—
Breadth	16¾			Breadth	16¾		
Female Dormitory, No. 5:				Male Dormitory, No. 5:			
Height	11			Height	11		
Length	38	18	—	Length	38	17	—
Breadth	16¾			Breadth	16½		
		153				77	

Bantry Workhouse Infirmary.

—	Feet.	Inmates in each.	Cubic Feet to each.	—	Feet.	Inmates in each.	Cubic Feet to each.
Male Side, Ground Floor:				**Upstairs:**			
Height - -	11 3/4	25	160	Height - -	10 1/2	17	217
Length - -	21 1/2			Length - -	21 1/2		
Breadth - -	16 3/4			Breadth - -	16 3/4		
Small ditto:							
Height - -	11 3/4	3	672	Height - -	10 1/4	23	87 3/4
Length - -	10 1/2			Length - -	11 1/2		
Breadth - -	12 3/4			Breadth - -	16 1/2		
Female Side, Ground Floor:							
Height - -	11 3/4	20	211 1/2	Height - -	10 1/4	25	147 3/4
Length - -	21 1/2			Length - -	21 1/2		
Breadth - -	16 3/4			Breadth - -	16 1/4		
				Small ditto:			
				Height - -	10 1/4	15	134
				Length - -	11 3/4		
				Breadth - -	16 3/4		
				Lobby:			
				Height - -	- -	5	—
				Length - -	- -		
				Breadth - -	- -		
		48				85	
						48	
					Total - -	133 in Infirmary.	

Fever Hospital.

—	Feet.	Inmates.	Cubic Feet.	—	Feet.	Inmates.	Cubic Feet.
				Upstairs:			
Height - -	11	25	—	Height - -	12	33	—
Length - -	24 1/2			Length - -	24 1/2		
Breadth - -	17			Breadth - -	17		
Female Side:							
Height - -	11	37	—	Height - -	12	25	—
Length - -	24 1/2			Length - -	24 1/2		
Breadth - -	17			Breadth - -	17		
		62				58	

APPENDIX V

RATEPAYERS IN BANTRY UNION
1846

TABLE A3. RATEPAYERS IN BANTRY UNION, 1846

Electoral Division	Number of occupiers paying rate	Total number of occupiers (families)	Ratepayers as percentage of families (%)
Bantry	580	881	65.8
Kilmacomogue	235	1935	12.1
Durrus East	153	728	49.8
Durrus West	210		
Kilcrohane	44	801	56.7
Kilcaskan	187	945	19.8
Kilcatherine	193	1295	14.9
Kilaconenagh	352	1281	27.5
Kilnamanagh	213	1123	19

Source: HC, *Poor Law Unions (Ireland). Abstract return from the Poor Law Commissioners, showing the name of each union in Ireland, the name of the county in which situated, and of each electoral division; the extent of statute acres, bog or waste, &c.1846*, Volume Page: XXXVI.469, Volume: 36, Paper Number: 262, p. 6. ProQuest: U.K. Parliamentary Papers.

Note: Percentages calculated by author. Table of ratepayers redrawn from a PLC return published in January 1846 showing two additional columns: the total number of families in each electoral division, obtained from the 1841 census, and a calculated column showing the percentage of families who paid rates in the different electoral districts.

APPENDIX VI

DR STEPHENS' REPORT AND DEATH STATISTICS

BANTRY UNION.

REPORT from Dr. *Stephens* to the BOARD OF HEALTH on the BANTRY WORKHOUSE.

Sir,   Bantry, 20 February 1847.

I HAVE the honour to state for the information of the Central Board of Health, that pursuant to their orders I visited the Bantry Workhouse yesterday, and made inquiry into the character of the sickness prevalent in it, also as to the ages of patients who died within the week ended the 6th instant, the duration of their stay in the workhouse previous to death, the state of the house as to ventilation and the diet and drink for the sick, together with the number of cubic feet allowed to each inmate in the sick and healthy wards.

With reference to the workhouse, I find it clean and orderly; the wards are spacious, and not having the number of beds they are capable of accommodating without inconvenience; the air of the house generally good, with the exception of the male infirm ward, in which the air was most impure from want of ventilation, as also the male dormitories for boys from six to ten years of age, whose habits are filthy; the same to be said of the female day-room, which is also a nursery for children and their mothers; the air of this room was most impure, the women being very inattentive to the habits of decency, which the matron, who is herself most orderly, finds it very difficult to make them observe.

The enclosed paper contains the ages of patients, their stay in the house, and the number of cubic feet allowed to each lunatic.

Language would fail to give an adequate idea of the state of the Fever Hospital; such an appalling, awful, and heart-sickening condition as it presented I never witnessed, or could think possible to exist in a civilised or Christian community. As I entered the house, the stench that proceeded from it, and prevailed through it, was most dreadful and noisome; but oh, what scenes presented themselves to my view as I proceeded through the wards and passages: patients lying on straw, naked, and in their excrements, a slight covering thrown over them; in two beds, living beings beside the dead in the same bed with them, and dead since the night before. I saw a woman who had been delivered but four days, almost expiring, with her wretched infant nearly suffocated; I administered at once wine, and had warmth applied, as there had been no medical attendant appointed during the illness of Dr. Tisdall, one of the medical men of the town, I was told had been there two days before; no medicine, no drink, in dirt, no fire, the unhappy beings who were able to express their wants crying out for drink; water, water, asked for, but no one to give it to them; others crying out for something to eat, as they said they were starved; many imploring to be taken out of it as they were not sick, but weak; thirty soon were found fit to be removed. The prevailing disease is dysentery, rendered highly contagious from the fetid state of the several wards. The wards are saturated with wet and ordure, the walls marked with the same. No nurses in the house except one of the paupers, totally unfit for the duties, every person being afraid to enter what was considered a pest-house; it is useless to enlarge or dwell further upon this revolting subject. I directed the clerk of the union to bring to the board room any guardian or guardians he could find; three came, and in the presence of the chaplains of the house, and the master and matron, I laid before them the state of things I had just witnessed, with feelings I will not attempt to describe, and stated to them what should be done to arrest the frightful evil so widely spreading. In the yard, filthy beds and bedding were heaped up and allowed to remain there; the same state of things in the infirmary, where dysentery was almost universal.

The supply of water for the workhouse is by means of being carried by women; the want of it at present was great, from the great increase of washing. It is said to be not good; it is impregnated with iron, and much disliked.

Having done all that was possible for me to do here, I purpose to proceed to Cork, to attend the meeting of the Board of Guardians there on Monday, after which I shall proceed to Mitchelstown, where I hope to be on Tuesday to comply with the wishes of the Central Board of Health.

I have, &c.

A. Moore, Esq.   (signed)   *R. Stephens.*

Bantry Union.

Fig. A2. Dr Stephens' report and death statistics.

Source: 'Reports to Board of Health in Dublin by Medical Officers on State of Workhouses in Cork, Bantry and Lurgan', *19th Century House of Commons Sessional Papers* (1847).

APPENDIX VII

DR KIDD'S PATIENTS IN BANTRY

IRISH MISSION.

Report from Mr. Kidd of Cases treated at Bantry, in Ireland, from the 9th of April to 15th of June, 1847.

Name.	Age.	Period & Nature of Disease	Duration of Treatment.		Result.
			Date.	No. of Days	
William Willis	19	2nd day of fever	April 9 to 13	5	....a
Margaret Rodgers	8	2nd do.	,, 12 to 21	10	Cured.
Anne Harrington	8	14th do.	,, 12 to 21	10	do.
Mary Hutchinson	34	3rd do.	,, 12 to 22	11	do.
Mary Holland	27	4th do.	,, 15 to 23	9	do.
John Collins	15	7th do.	,, 14 to 22	9	do.
Jerry Sullivan	16	14th do.	,, 14 to 21	8	do. } b
Thaddeus Sullivan	10	16th do.	,, 14 to 21	8	do. }
Ellen Sullivan	10	10th do.	,, 15 to 22	8	do.
Mary Rogers	40	3rd do.	,, 12 to May 3	22	do.
Dolly Roohan	43	3rd do.	,, 12 to 26	15	do.
Daniel Murphy	12	2nd do.	,, 22 to May 3	12	do.
Pat. Downey	34	10th do.	,, 13 to 26	14	do.
Joseph Leary	30	5th do.	,, 13 to 30	18	do.
Mary Sullivan	33	5th do.	,, 12 to 26	15	do.
Jerry Sullivan	5	2nd do.	,, 22 to 27	6	do.
John Downey	18	2nd day relapse of fever	,, 18 to May 1	14	do.
Kate Regan	39	5th day of fever	,, 21 to ,, 1	11	do.
Con Carty	14	5th do.	,, 28 to ,, 3	11	do.
Pat. Sullivan	28	3rd do.	,, 23 to ,, 3	11	do.
Pat. Flynn	40	14th day relapse of fever.	,, 23 to 30	8	do.
Dennis Flynn	16	12th day of fever	,, 15 to 29	15	do.
John Downey	32	7th do.	,, 23 to 50	8	do.
Mary Rogers	13	3rd do.	,, 28 to May11	14	do.
Johanna Sullivan	56	14th do.	,, 17 to ,, 7	21	do.
Mary Cronin	16	6th do.	,, 27 to ,, 8	12	do.
Mary Creemeen	50	8th do.	,, 14 to ,, 2	19	do. }
Kitty Creemeen	16	6th do.	,, 14 to ,, 2	19	do. } c
Pat. Creemeen	15	6th do.	,, 14 to ,, 2	19	do. }
Francis M'Evoy	13	7th do.	,, 17 to ,, 4	18	do.d
John Downey	32	7th do.	,, 23 to ,, 1	9	do.
Margaret Patterson	30	2nd do.	,, 28 to ,, 10	13	do.e
Tim. Cronin	24	12th do.	,, 27 to ,, 10	14	do.
Mary Harrington	30	2nd do.	,, 29 to ,, 10	12	do.
Johanna Collins	16	4th do.	,, 21 to ,, 10	20	do.
Patrick Nagle	35	3rd do.	,, 16 to 24	9	do.f
Mary Hutchinson	34	12th do.	,, 16 to May 3	18	Died.g
Roger Humphrey	16	2nd do.	May 1 to 16	16	Cured.
Richard Hutchinson	35	3rd do.	April 28 to May14	17	do.h
Con Roohan	10	2nd do.	,, 24 to ,, 10	17	do.i

a Treatment discontinued, owing to disobedience to directions.
b These two were brothers, six of whose family were seized with fever about the same time. The day of my first visit, the father and one son were buried; and the week before, the mother and daughter died. Of the two survivors, I did not expect the youngest would live another day, and both were so far advanced in fever, that the prognosis was most unfavourable, in addition to which they were reduced to the lowest degree of depression by mental suffering, caused by the loss of the rest of their family and by their great destitution; notwithstanding these circumstances, however, they both recovered.
c These three lay on the same bed in very bad typhus, so bad that they were almost abandoned to their fate by their relatives.
d A case of cerebral typhus.
e A case of low typhoid fever in a phthisical subject.
f Relapsed on April 26th; was again under treatment to May 6th. Cured.
g She was almost convalescent April 26th; on the 28th, relapse ensued, with pleuritis, which proved fatal.
h Was almost convalescent May 6th, when a sad accident occurred to him. During a dreadful night's rain, he lay actually flooded in his bed from the rain pouring in on him from a chasm in the thatch of his cabin. He was so very weak as to be unable to move himself from the bed, and could derive no assistance from the rest of his family (4), who lay in fever at the other end of the wretched cabin, so that he was obliged to remain thus exposed for eight or ten hours till morning, when some charitable neighbour rescued him from the bed that had nearly proved a watery grave. As might have been expected, the fever returned more severely, and his convalescence proved tedious.
i Cured also of an attack of diarrhœa after the fever.

Fig. A3. Dr Kidd's patients in Bantry.

Source: Joseph Kidd, *Homeopathy in acute diseases: narrative of a mission to Ireland during the famine and pestilence of 1847* (London: British Homeopathic Society, 1847).

IRISH MISSION.

Name.	Age.	Period & Nature of Disease	Duration of Treatment.		Result.
			Date.	No. of Days	
Judith Downey	7	3rd day of fever	April 30 to May 7	8	Cured.
Mary Neal	14	12th day relapse of fever	May 8 to 14	7	do.
Jerry Harrington	30	6th day of fever	,, 10 to 14	5	do.
Kate Collins	16	7th do.	,, 1 to 8	8	do.
Pat. Collins	28	3rd do.	,, 4 to 13	10	do.
Mary Leary	13	5th do.	,, 1 to 8	8	do.
Pat. Leary	12	2nd do.	,, 5 to 14	10	do.
Mary Healy	8	2nd do.	April 28 to May 8	11	do. ⎫
Norah Healy	34	3rd do.	,, 26 to ,, 12	17	do. ⎬ j
Joan Healy	12	6th do.	,, 28 to ,, 8	11	do. ⎭
Edward Healy	13	3rd do.	,, 28 to ,, 17	20	do.
Cornelius Sullivan	35	10th do.	,, 26 to ,, 4	9	do.
Pat. Flynn	40	14th day relapse of fever	,, 23 to ,, 4	12	do. k
John Harrington	22	14th day of fever	,, 28 to ,, 12	15	do.
Dan. Harrington	21	21st do.	,, 28 to ,, 8	11	do.
Kate Harrington	45	4th do.	May 1 to 12	12	do.
Judy M'Carthy	46	2nd wk. edema after fever	April 24 to 30	7	do.
Pat. O'Brien	35	2nd d. fever wh. pleuritis	May 6 to 24	19	do.
Daniel O'Brien	29	2nd day of fever	,, 7 to 22	16	do.
Pat. M'Carthy	46	7th do.	,, 12 to 21	10	do.
Rebecca Willis	23	3rd do.	,, 6 to 19	14	do.
Florence Rogers	13	2nd do.	,, 11 to 19	9	do.
Callaghan M'Carthy	21	5th do.	,, 10 to 26	17	do. l
Fanny Hutchinson	22	2nd do.	,, 4 to 20	17	do.
Susan Hutchinson	60	2nd do.	,, 6 to 21	16	do.
Jerry Rohan	48	3rd do.	,, 6 to 21	16	do.
Mary Hussey	34	6th do.	,, 10 to 24	15	do.
Cornelius Cotter	42	12th do.	,, 14 to 24	11	do.
Ellen M'Carthy	16	3rd do.	,, 16 to 25	10	do.
John Kiely	10	4th do.	,, 17 to 24	8	do.
Eugene M'Carthy	12	14th do.	,, 1 to 6	6	do.
Widow Downey	35	5th do.	,, 21 to 29	9	do.
Ellen Connolly	2	4th do.	,, 18 to 24	7	do.
John Connolly	35	4th do.	,, 17 to 24	8	do. m
Jerry Leary	14	3rd do.	,, 17 to 29	13	do.
Mary Driscoll	5	3rd do.	,, 16 to 24	9	do.
Jerry Driscoll	40	8th do.	,, 16 to 29	14	do. n
John Ford	30	6th do.	,, 14 to 28	15	do.
Norry Ford	23	2nd do.	,, 16 to 26	11	do. o
George Sullivan	21	3rd do.	,, 14 to 24	11	do.
Mary Sullivan	10	2nd do.	,, 21 to 26	6	do.
Widow Shea	45	3rd do.	,, 15 to 24	10	do.
Mary Sullivan	60	3rd do.	,, 21 to 28	8	do.
John Mahony	36	3rd do.	,, 22 to 28	7	do.
Pat. Mahony	12	4th do.	,, 23 to 28	6	do.
Pat. Harrington	4	2nd do.	,, 20 to 26	7	do.
Cornelius Regan	5	5th do.	,, 15 to 25	11	do.
Joseph Regan	14	3rd do.	,, 11 to 30	20	do.
John Regan	19	1st do.	,, 11 to 24	14	do.
Mary Connor	5	6th do.	,, 8 to 16	9	do.
Pat. Hussey	32	6th day of fever, with pleuro-pneumonia	,, 10 to 18	9	Died p
John Leary	18	3rd day of fever	,, 19 to June 1	14	Cured.
Judith Cronin	22	3rd do.	,, 21 to ,, 3	14	do.
Kate Cronin	12	5th do.	,, 21 to ,, 9	20	do.
Ellen Downey	21	4th do.	,, 14 to 21	8	do. q.
Kate Downey	68	2nd do.	,, 23 to June 3	12	do. r.
Johanna Sullivan	28	6th do.	,, 24 to ,, 2	10	do.

j These four patients were members of the same family, the entire of whom I had under my care, and all (7) with favourable results.
k Relapsed again on May 7th, under treatment from that day to May 15th. Cured.
l This was a case of cerebral typhus attended for several days with furious delirium.
m This case was complicated with pleuritis.
n This was a most melancholy case of utter destitution, with his entire family (4) in fever, without straw to lie upon or clothes to cover him, without food, drink, or fire, till I directed the attention of the Rev. Mr. Hallowell to his case. After his convalescence, he was confined to bed (the earth floor) for a fortnight, for want of clothes to dress himself with.
o A case of low typhus, occurring soon after her accouchement.
p Along with the pulmonic complication, this person had to contend with extreme mental and physical depression, the effect of his sad destitution.
q Relapsed on May 24th, and was again under my care to June 2nd. Cured.
r This old woman was the fifth of one family under my care, all of whom recovered.

IRISH MISSION.

Name.	Age.	Period & Nature of Disease	Duration of Treatment.		Result.
			Date.	No. of Days	
John Cronin	22	5th day of fever	May 26 to June 2	8	Cured.
Giles Harrington	40	2nd do.	,, 28 to ,, 7	11	do.
Margaret Ford	32	6th do.	,, 19 to ,, 5	18	do.s
Daniel Sullivan	32	2nd do.	,, 27 to ,, 14	19	do.
Patrick Butler	12	2nd do.	June 3 to 10	8	do.
Mary Butler	40	5th do.	May 23 to June 15	24	do.t
Mary Connor	36	2nd do.	,, 27 to ,, 2	7	do.
Dennis Harrington	35	1st do.	,, 26 to ,, 10	16	do.
John Harrington	3	1st do.	,, 27 to ,, 4	9	do.
Mary Carty	12	5th do.	,, 24 to ,, 2	10	do. ⎫
Mary Carty	45	5th do.	,, 26 to ,, 10	16	do. ⎪
Peggy Carty	6	3rd do.	,, 24 to ,, 2	10	do. ⎬ u
John Carty	26	3rd do.	,, 24 to ,, 3	11	do. ⎪
Dennis Carty	21	2nd do.	,, 25 to ,, 2	9	do. ⎭

s Relapsed on June 7th, was again under treatment to June 14th. Cured.
t A case of low typhus, with extreme nervous depression.
u Six members of this family recovered from fever under my care. Dennis Carty relapsed on June 4th, was again under my treatment to June 10th. Cured.

APPENDIX VIII

RECORDS OF DEATHS OF A FEW BANTRY EMIGRANTS TO NEW BRUNSWICK

Recently, some information has become available of people from Bantry who died after the voyage. The following are those passengers on the *Brothers*, from Bantry to St John, who arrived on 11 May 1846, hospital name not given:

Julia Connel, 18 years old, RC [Roman Catholic], admitted 16 June, died 5 October 1846.

Ellen McArty, 23 years old, RC, admitted 17 June, died 20 July 1846.

Mrs Norrie Collins, 32 years old, RC, admitted 13 July, died 29 September 1846.

Mary Collins, 1 year and 3 months old, RC, admitted 13 July, died 8 September 1846.

John Collins, 3 years and 6 months old, RC, admitted 13 July, died 31 August 1846.

Margaret Conner/Cronin, 22 years old, RC, admitted 26 April, died 13 May 1847 (maybe an error in the date).

These are the passengers on the *Themis*, from Bantry to St John, who arrived on 21 June 1846 and died shortly thereafter, hospital unknown:

Margaret McArty, 20 years old, RC, from Kerry, admitted 25 July, died 20 August 1846.

Peter O'Brien, 28 years old, RC, admitted 19 August, died 26 September 1846.

These are the passengers on the *Dealy*, from Bantry to St John, who arrived in May 1847 and died between 7 May and July 1847 in the hospital on Partridge Island, as reported in the *New Brunswick Courier*:

Bridget Conny, 10 years old.

Catherine Collins, 17 years old.

Ellen Haley, 17 years old.

Rachel Kingston, 33 years old.

Source: Daniel F. Johnson, *Irish emigration to New England through the port of Saint John, New Brunswick, Canada, 1841 to 1849*, Baltimore, Md 1997.

APPENDIX IX

HIGHEST RATEPAYERS, KILCROHANE

NOVEMBER 1848

November 23, 1848.

The Names of the highest Ratepayers in Kilcrohane are as follows:—
From Rate-Book.

Township.	Names.	Amount. £. s. d.	Remarks.
Gartoolassa	Wm. O'Sullivan, Esq.	16 2 2½	This is a good mark. Promises to pay.
Ardahill	Dan. O'Donovan, Esq.	22 8 10½	Lands waste. Tenants ran away. No distress.
Ditto	Alex. O'Donovan, Esq.	35 15 10½	Ditto ditto.
Tuellig	Rich. O'Donovan, Esq.	16 19 3	Tenants paupers. No distress.
Gurteeniash	Rev. Wm. Evanson	7 18 4⅖	Tenants ran away. Lands waste.
Diotto	Mr. Chas. Evanson	6 7 6½	Ditto ditto.
Rea	Patrick Tobin	13 15 6$\frac{3}{16}$	Promises to pay.
Knuckeen	Patrick Brien	6 7 11½	No distress.
Rossnacahana	Daniel Dawly	5 17 11$\frac{3}{16}$	Pauper. No distress on the said holding.
Knuckeen	John Sheehan	1 15 4	Nearly waste.
Tariammarra	Michael Murphy	4 11 11	Promises to pay.
Reemmore	William Barry	2 18 8	Very poor, but promises to pay by instalments.

Fig. A4. The highest ratepayers in Kilcrohane listed by the vice-guardians in their correspondence to the Poor Law commissioners on 25 November 1848.

APPENDIX X

NAMES OF BANTRY PAID VICE-GUARDIANS

RETURN showing the Names of Unions in which Paid Guardians were appointed, the Names of the Paid Guardians, and the Dates of Appointment.

NAMES OF UNIONS.	NAMES OF PAID GUARDIANS.	DATES OF APPOINTMENT.
Bantry	Denis Clarke and Augustus Gallwey	19 Oct. 1847.
	Thomas Willis, to succeed Mr. Gallwey	13 Dec. –
	*Captain Lang, *pro tem.* for Mr. Willis	28 Dec. 1848.
	*Captain Lang, to succeed Mr. Willis	2 Feb. 1849.
	John Peard, junior, to succeed Captain Lang	17 – –
	Richard F. Lodge, *pro tem.* for Mr. Peard	19 Mar. –
	*Captain Haymes, to succeed Mr. Lodge	21 April –
	Stephen O'Halloran, to act during the absence of Mr. Clarke.	24 May –
	*Captain Haymes, to succeed Mr. Peard	29 Aug. –
	William Geraghty, to succeed Captain Haymes	11 Oct. –

Fig. A5. Names of Bantry paid vice-guardians.

Source: HC, Poor Law Unions (Ireland). *Return showing the financial state of each union in Ireland, where paid guardians were appointed, at the time of their appointment, comparing it with the financial state of the same unions when they were removed;--also, copies of all reports and resolutions made by boards of guardians in those unions where paid guardians have acted, &c.* Volume Page: L.109 Volume: 50 Paper Number : 251, 1850. https://parlipapers.proquest.com/parlipapers/docview/t70.d75.1850-027012

APPENDIX XI

LOSSES IN THE NINE ELECTORAL DIVISIONS OF BANTRY UNION 1841–51

Fig. A6. A more detailed graph, taken from census data, showing losses in each electoral division between 1841 and 1851.

Source: 'Census of Ireland 1851: Part I., Area, Population, and Number of Houses, by Townlands and Electoral Divisions, County of Cork (W. Riding)', *19th Century House of Commons Sessional Papers* (1853).

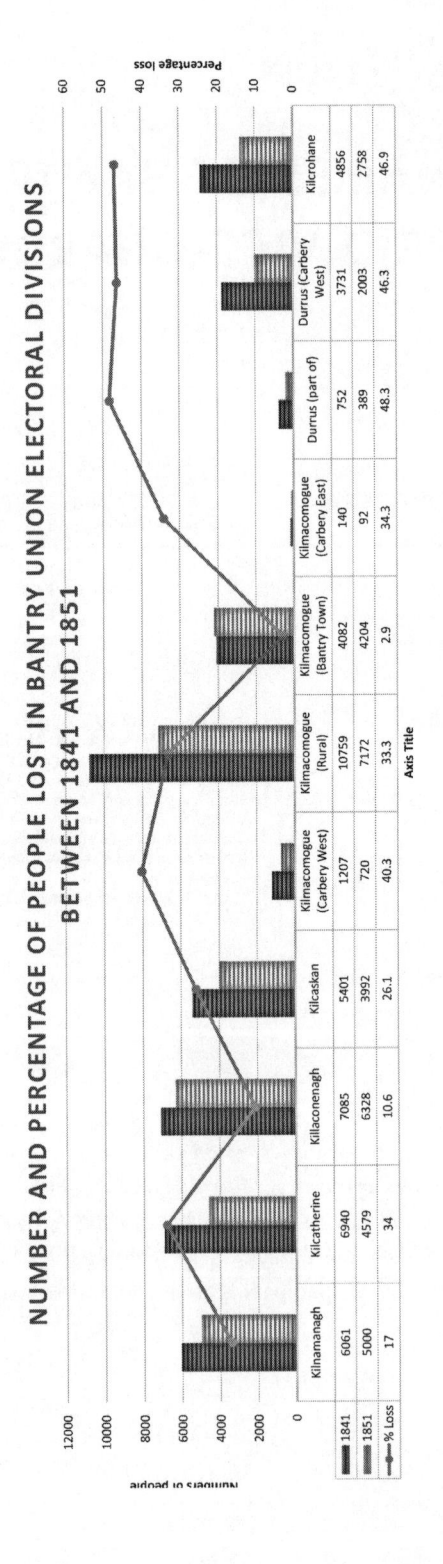

	Kilnamanagh	Kilcatherine	Killaconenagh	Kilcaskan	Kilmacomogue (Carbery West)	Kilmacomogue (Rural)	Kilmacomogue (Bantry Town)	Kilmacomogue (Carbery East)	Durrus (part of)	Durrus (Carbery West)	Kilcrohane
1841	6061	6940	7085	5401	1207	10759	4082	140	752	3731	4856
1851	5000	4579	6328	3992	720	7172	4204	92	389	2003	2758
% Loss	17	34	10.6	26.1	40.3	33.3	2.9	34.3	48.3	46.3	46.9

BIBLIOGRAPHY

PRIMARY SOURCES

CORK CITY AND COUNTY ARCHIVES

BANTRY BOARD OF GUARDIANS MINUTE BOOKS

BG/43, vol. A2	20 October 1846 to 19 October 1847
BG/43, vol. A1	Missing
BG/43, vol. A3	25 January 1848 to 21 November 1848
BG/43, vol. A4	28 November 1848 to 11 September 1849
BG/43, vol. A5	Missing
BG/43, vol. A6	24 July 1850 to 12 March 1851

BANTRY BOARD OF GUARDIANS ROUGH MINUTE BOOKS

BG/43, vol. AA1	4 August 1846 to 10 August 1847
BG/43, vol. AA2	26 December 1848 to 30 October 1849
BG/43, vol. AA3	16 November 1849 to 4 June 1851

NATIONAL ARCHIVES OF IRELAND

FAMINE RELIEF COMMISSION PAPERS, 1845–47

RLFC2	Distress Reports, Z series t from the Chief Secretary's Office.
RLFC2/717166,	24 November 1845
RLFC2/717166,	25 November 1845
RLFC3/1	Series of incoming letters received by the Relief Commission
RLFC 3/7/943,	23 March 1846
RLFC 3/7/945,	24 March 1846
RLFC 3/1/1376,	9–14 April 1846
RLFC 3/1/2077,	NAI, 5 May 1846
RLFC 3/1/3172,	NAI, 10 June 1846

RLFC 3/1/2669,   NAI, 27 May 1846
RLFC 3/1/3024,   NAI, 11 June 1846
RLFC 3/2/6/4,   5 September 1846
RLFC 3/2/6/28,   5 September 1846
RLFC 3/2/6/26,   16 October 1846
RLFC 3/2/6/26,   23 October 1846
RLFC 3/2/6/28,   November 1846–February 1847
RLFC 3/2/6 28,   29 October 1846
RLFC 3/2/6/5,   25 October 1846
RLFC 3/2/6/23,   14 December 1846
RLFC 3/2/6/8,   20 January 1847
RLFC 3/2/6/5,   February 1847

Replies to Inspector General of Constabulary circular questionnaire
RLFC 5/6/13, 28 August 1846

County inspecting officers report
RLFC 7/6/24, 16 January 1847

CHIEF SECRETARY'S OFFICE REGISTERED PAPERS

1820s papers
CSO/RP/1822/1890
CSO/RP/1822/442
CSO/RP/1822/442,1822

1847 paper
CSO/RP 79931/2, 30 September 1847
1847 distress papers
CSO/RP D213, 2 January 1847
CSO/RP D5844, 18 May 1847
CSO/RP D7946, 3 September 1847
CSO/RP D7988, 23 September 1847
CSO/RP D79901/2, 7 October 1847

NATIONAL LIBRARY OF IRELAND

Tisdall Hutchins papers, Pratt correspondence, 1838–1853, NLI MS 8685
The Lawrence Photographic collection: catalogue.nli.ie/Record/vtls000320929

BIBLIOGRAPHY

ROYAL IRISH ACADEMY

Manuscripts
RIA 4/B/9/31 (1), 8 September 1849
RIA 4/B/10/55, 17 October 1850

BRITISH PARLIAMENTARY PAPERS

Appendices A to C to the Tenth Annual Report of the Poor Law Commissioners, Volume Page: XIX.57 Volume: 19 Paper Number: 589, 1844.

Appendices B to F to the Eighth Annual Report of the Poor Law Commissioners, Volume Page: XIX.119, Volume: 19, Paper Number: 399, 1842.

Appendices to the Eleventh Annual Report of the Poor Law Commissioners, Volume Page: XXVII.279 Volume: 27 Paper Number: 660, 1845.

Appendices to the Twelfth Annual Report of the Poor Law Commissioners, Volume Page: XIX.33 Volume: 19 Paper Number: 745, Appendix B, 1846.

Appendix to the Report of the Commissioner Appointed to Inquire into the Execution of the Contracts for Certain Union Workhouses in Ireland, Volume Page: XXX.551 Volume: 30 Paper Number: 568, 1844.

The Census of Ireland for the Year 1851. Part I. Showing the Area, Population, and Number of Houses by Townlands and Electoral Divisions. County of Cork. (West Riding.), Volume Page: XCI.499 Volume: 91 Paper Number: 1551 (1853).

The Census of Ireland for the Year 1851. Part V. Tables of Deaths. Vol. II. Containing the Tables and Index, Volume Page: XXIX.261, XXX.1 Volume: 29;30 Paper Number: 2087-I 2087-II, 1856.

Commons Sitting of Monday, February 8, 1841, Title: Third Series, Volume 56.

Copies or Extracts of Correspondence Relating to the State of Union Workhouses in Ireland, Volume Page: LV.27, 141, 231 Volume: 55;141;231 Paper Number: 766 790 863, 1847.

Correspondence Explanatory of the Measures Adopted by Her Majesty's Government for the Relief of Distress Arising from the Failure of the Potato Crop in Ireland, Volume Page: XXXVII.41 Volume: 37 Paper Number: 735, 1846.

Correspondence from January to March 1847, Relating to the Measures Adopted for the Relief of the Distress in Ireland. Board of Works Series. [Second Part.], Volume Page: LII.1 Volume: 52 Paper Number: 797 (1847).

Correspondence from July 1846, to January 1847, Relating to the Measures Adopted for the Relief of the Distress in Ireland. Board of Works Series. 1847, 764 L.1 vol. 50.

Correspondence from July, 1846, to January, 1847, Relating to the Measures Adopted for the Relief of the Distress in Ireland. Commissariat Series, Page: LI.1 Volume: 51 Paper Number: 761, 1847.

Courtenay, William the E. Devon, 'Royal Com. Of Inquiry into State of Law and Practice in Respect to Occupation of Land in Ireland, Appendix to Minutes of Evidence, Part Iv.; Index to Minutes of Evidence, Part V', in *19th Century House of Commons Sessional Papers* (1845).

Crampton, Philip, *Report of the Commissioners of Health, Ireland, on the Epidemics of 1846 to 1850*, Volume Page: XLI.239 Volume: 41 Paper Number: 1562, 1853 (1853).

Destitute Persons (Ireland). A Bill for the Temporary Relief of Destitute Persons in Ireland, Volume Page: I.243 Volume: 1 Paper Number: 19, 1847.

Distress (Ireland). Fourth Report of the Relief Commissioners, Constituted under the Act 10th Vic., Cap. 7, Volume Page: XVII.143 Volume: 17 Paper Number: 859, 1847.

Distress (Ireland.) Supplementary Appendix to the Seventh, and Last, Report of the Relief Commissioners, Constituted under the Act 10th Vic., Cap. 7, Volume Page: XXIX.121 Volume: 29 Paper Number: 956, 1848.

Evidence Taken before Her Majesty's Commissioners of Inquiry into the State of the Law and Practice in Respect to the Occupation of Land in Ireland. Part II, Volume Page: XX.1 Volume: 20 Paper Number: 616 (Dublin 1845).

Fifth Annual Report of the Commissioners for Administering the Laws for Relief of the Poor in Ireland: With Appendices, Volume Page: XXIII.155 Volume: 23 Paper Number: 1530, 1852.

Fifth Annual Report of the Poor Law Commissioners: With Appendices.', in *Volume Page: XX.1 Volume: 20 Paper Number: 239, 1839, Plan B.*

First Annual Report of the Commissioners for Administering the Laws for Relief of the Poor in Ireland, with Appendices, Volume Page: XXXIII.377 Volume: 33 Paper Number: 963, 1848.

First Report from His Majesty's Commissioners for Inquiring into the Condition of the Poorer Classes in Ireland, with Appendix (A.) and Supplement.Appendix B, 1835, Volume Page: XXXII Pt.I.1, XXXII Pt.II.1 Paper Number: 369.

First Report of the Commissioners of Inquiry into the State of the Irish Fisheries; with the Minutes of Evidence, and Appendix. 1837, Volume Page: XXII.1 Volume: 22 Paper Number: 77.

Fourteenth Report from the Select Committee on Poor Laws (Ireland); Together with the Proceedings of the Committee, Minutes of Evidence, Appendix, and Index, Paper Number: 572, 28 December 1848 (1849).

BIBLIOGRAPHY

Fourth Report from the Select Committee of the House of Lords Appointed to Inquire into the Operation of the Irish Poor Law, and the Expediency of Making Any Amendment in Its Enactments; and to Report Thereon to the House; Together with the Minutes of Evidence, Volume Page: XVI.543 Volume: 16 Paper Number: 365, 1849.

Landed Estates Court Rentals 1850–1885. Findmypast.

The Mirror of Parliament for the First Session of the Thirteenth Parliament of Great Britain and Ireland: Session 1837–1838 (London: 1838).

Papers Relating to Proceedings for Relief of Distress, and State of Unions and Workhouses in Ireland, 1848, Volume Page: LIV.313, LV.1, LVI.1 Volume: 54;55;56 Paper Number: 919 955 999 (1848).

Papers Relating to Proceedings for the Relief of the Distress, and State of the Unions and Workhouses, in Ireland. Fourth Series, 1847, Volume Page: LIV.29 Volume: 54 Paper Number: 896 (1847–48).

Papers Relating to Proceedings for the Relief of the Distress, and State of Unions and Workhouses, in Ireland. Eighth Series, 1849, Volume Page: XLVIII.221 Volume: 48 Paper Number: 1042, December 1848 (1849).

Papers Relating to the Aid Afforded to the Distressed Unions in the West of Ireland, Volume Page: XLVIII.7, 77, 87, 121, 171 Volume: 48;77;87;121;171 Paper Number: 1010 1019 1023 1060 1077, 1849.

Poor Employment (Ireland). A Bill [as Amended by Committee and on Report] to Facilitate the Employment of the Labouring Poor for a Limited Period in Distressed Districts in Ireland, Volume Page: III.143 Volume: 3 Paper Number: 672, 1846.

Poor Law (Ireland). Returns of the Days on Which Each Assistant Poor-Law Commissioner, in Ireland, Attended Meetings of Boards of Guardians, in the Years 1844 and 1845, and up to the 31st Day of March 1846; &C., Volume Page: XXXVI.451 Volume: 36 Paper Number: 453, 1846.

Poor Law Commission Office Dublin (ed.) *Exemption of £4 Tenements from Rates Made Prior to the Passing of the Irish Poor Law Amendment Act: Circular Addressed to Boards of Guardians in Ireland*, No. 13, 22 April, 1844.

Poor Law Unions (Ireland). Abstract Return from the Poor Law Commissioners, Showing the Name of Each Union in Ireland, the Name of the County in Which Situated, and of Each Electoral Division; the Extent of Statute Acres, Bog or Waste, &C. &C.1846, Volume Page: XXXVI.469 Volume: 36 Paper Number: 262.

Poor Law Unions (Ireland). Return Relative to Poor Law Unions, and of Persons Holding Land, &C. In Ireland, Volume Page: XXXVIII.209 Volume: 38 Paper Number: 593 (1845).

A WANT OF INHABITANTS: THE FAMINE IN BANTRY UNION

Poor Law Unions (Ireland). Return Showing the Financial State of Each Union in Ireland, Where Paid Guardians Were Appointed, at the Time of Their Appointment, Comparing It with the Financial State of the Same Unions When They Were Removed;–Also, Copies of All Reports and Resolutions Made by Boards of Guardian Have Acted, &C., Volume Page: L.109 Volume: 50 Paper Number: 251, (1850).

Poor Relief (Ireland). A Bill [as Amended by the Lords] Intititled, an Act to Make Further Provision for the Relief of the Destitute Poor in Ireland, Volume Page: III.213 Volume: 3 Paper Number: 417, (1847).

Poor Relief (Ireland). A Bill [as Amended in Committee and on Re-Commitment] for the More Effectual Relief of the Destitute Poor in Ireland, Volume Page: V.345 Volume: 5 Paper Number: 238 (1838).

Poor Relief (Ireland). Returns of the Number of Persons Who Were Receiving Relief on the Last Day of February 1850, in Each Union in Ireland;–and of the Number of Persons, Distinguishing the Males from the Females, on in-Door Relief, on the Same Day, between the Ages of Fifteen and Forty, Who Have Been Inmates of the Workhouse for More Than a Year, Volume Page: L.181 Volume: 50 Paper Number: 377, (1850).

Public Works (Ireland). Returns of All Sums of Money Voted or Applied, Either by Way of Grant or Loan, in Aid of Public Works in Ireland, since the Union, &C., Volume Page: XLIV.493 Volume: 44 Paper Number: 540, 1839.

Rate in Aid (Ireland.) Account Showing the Total Sum Assessed as Rate in Aid on Each Union in Ireland, under the Act 12 Vict. C. 24, &C.–Also, Account Showing the Total Sum Appropriated to Each Union out of the General Rate in Aid Fund, Down to the 31st December 1851., Volume Page: XLVI.125 Volume: 46 Paper Number: 871852, (1852).

Relief Coms., Fifth, Sixth and Seventh Reports, Correspondence, Volume Page: XXIX.27 Volume: 29 Paper Number: 876, 1848.

Relief Districts (Ireland). Instructions to Committees of Relief Districts, Extracted from Minutes of the Proceedings of the Commissioners Appointed in Reference to the Apprehended Scarcity, Volume Page: XXXVII.473 Volume: 37 Paper Number: 171, 1846.

Report of the Commissioners Appointed to Take the Census of Ireland, for the Year 1841.Appendix, Volume Page: XXIV.1 Volume: 24 Paper Number: 504 (Dublin 1843).

Scarcity Commission. The Weekly Reports of the Scarcity Commission, Showing the Progress of Disease in the Potatoes, the Complaints Which Have Been Made, and the Applications for Relief, in the Course of the Month of March 1846, Volume Page: XXXVII.429 Volume: 37 Paper Number: 201, 1846.

Third Report of the Commissioners for Inquiring into the Condition of the Poorer Classes in Ireland, Volume Page: XXX.1 Volume: 30, Paper Number: 43 (London 1836).

Workhouses (Ireland). Abstract Copy of the Reports Made to the Board of Health in Dublin, by the Medical Officers Sent to Inquire into the State of the Workhouses in Cork, Bantry, and Lurgan, Volume Page: LV.11 Volume: 55 Paper Number: 257, 15 March, 1847.

NEWSPAPERS

Cork Examiner
Cork Constitution
Southern Reporter
Clare Journal
Dublin Evening Mail
Tipperary Vindicator
Warder and Dublin Weekly Mail
Dublin Evening Post
Freeman's Journal
Kerry Evening Post
Pilot
Nation
Wexford Independent
Downpatrick Recorder
Newry Cork Examiner
Tuam Herald
Limerick Chronicle
Leeds Intelligencer
Times
Shipping and Merchantile Gazette
Salisbury and Winchester Journal
London Evening Standard
Globe
Morning Post
Illustrated London News
Morning Chronicle
Bath Chronicle
London Evening Standard
Derbyshire Advertiser and Journal
Balls Weekly Messenger
Standard
Daily News
Morning Advertiser
Hereford Journal
London Daily News
Gloucester Journal 2

A WANT OF INHABITANTS: THE FAMINE IN BANTRY UNION

CONTEMPORARY TEXTS

Aldwell, Alexander, *The County and City of Cork Post-Office General Directory, 1844–45* (Cork: F. Jackson, 1844).

Bennett, William, *Narrative of a Recent Journey of Six Weeks in Ireland: In Connexion with the Subject of Supplying Small Seed to Some of the Remoter Districts* (London: Charles Gilpin, 1847).

Bunbury, Sir Charles James Fox, *1836 Memorials* (Cambridge: Cambridge University Press, 2011).

Carlyle, Thomas, and James Anthony Froude, *Reminiscences of My Irish Journey in 1849* (London: S. Low, Marston, Searle, & Rivington, 1882).

Chatterton, Georgiana Lady, *Rambles in the South of Ireland During the Year 1838* (London: Saunders and Otley, 1839).

Corrigan, Dominic Sir, *On Famine and Fever as Cause and Effect in Ireland; with Observations on Hospital Location, and the Dispensation in Outdoor Relief of Food and Medicine* (Dublin: J. Fannin and Co, 1846).

East, Rev. John, *Glimpses of Ireland in 1847* (Dublin: J. M'Glashan, 1847).

Foster, Thomas Campbell, *Letters on the Condition of the People of Ireland* (London: 1846).

Inglis, Henry D., *Ireland in 1834: A Journey Throughout Ireland, During the Spring, Summer, and Autumn of 1834.* (London: Whittaker, 1835).

Irish Relief Association, *Report of the Proceedings of the Irish Relief Association for the Destitute Peasantry; Being a Re-Organization of the Association Formed During the Period of Famine in the West of Ireland in 1831* (Dublin: Irish Relief Association, 1848).

Johnson, James, *A Tour in Ireland: With Meditations and Reflections* (London: S. Highley, 1844).

Kidd, Joseph, *Homeopathy in Acute Diseases: Narrative of a Mission to Ireland During the Famine and Pestilence of 1847* (London: British Homeopathic Society, 1847).

——, *Homeopathy in Acute Disease: Narrative of a Mission to Ireland During the Famine and Pestilence of 1847* (London: 1849).

Kohl, J.G., *Travels in Ireland* (London: Bruce and Wyld, 1844).

Leigh, Samuel, *Leigh's New Pocket Road-Book of Ireland* (London: Leigh and Son, 1835).

Lewis, Samuel, and R. Creighton, *A Topographical Dictionary of Ireland: Comprising the Several Counties, Cities, Boroughs, Corporate, Market and Post Towns, Parishes, and Villages, with Historical and Statistical Descriptions* (London: S. Lewis & Co, 1837).

Luckombe, Philip, *Tour through Ireland* (Dublin: 1780).

Maguire, John Francis, *Father Mathe: A Biography* (London: 1863).

Nicholson, Asenath, *Annals of the Famine in Ireland in 1847, 1848, and 1849* (New York: 1851).

———, *Welcome to the Stranger* (New York: 1847).

O'Byrne, William R., *A Naval Biographical Dictionary, Vol. One* (London: John Murray, 1849).

O'Rourke, John, *The History of the Great Irish Famine of 1847* (Dublin: 1902).

Prendergast, John Patrick, 'Letter to the Earl of Bantry or, a Warning to English Purchasers of the Perils of the Irish Incumbered Estates Court; Exemplified in the Purchase by Lord Charles Pelham Clinton, M.P., of Two Estates in the Barony of Bere, County of Cork' (Dublin: 1854).

Pim, Jonathan, *The Conditions and Prospects of Ireland* (Dublin: 1848).

Hussey, S.M., *The Reminiscences of an Irish Land Agent* (London: 1904).

Society of Friends, *Transactions of the Central Relief Committee of the Society of Friends During the Famine in Ireland, in 1846 and 1847* (Dublin: 1852).

Slater, I., *Slater's National Commercial Directory of Ireland: Including, in Addition to the Trades' Lists, Alphabetical Directories of Dublin, Belfast, Cork and Limerick* (Manchester: I. Slater, 1846).

Stark, Archibald, *The South of Ireland in 1850: The Journal of a Tour in Leinster and Munster* (Dublin: James Duffy, 1850).

Sullivan, A.M., *New Ireland: Political Sketches and Personal Reminiscences of Thirty Years of Irish Public Life* (London, Glasgow: 1877).

Sullivan, T.D., *Bantry, Berehaven and the O'Sullivan Sept* (Dublin: 1908).

Thackeray, William Makepeace, *The Irish Sketch Book of 1842* (London: 1878).

Goodlake, Francis, and Francis J. O'Kelley, *The Great Irish Famine of 1845–1846. A Collection of Leading Articles, Letters, and Parliamentary and Other Public Statements, Reprinted from the Times* (London: Francis Goodlake at The Times, 1880).

Thom's, *Thom's Irish Almanac and Official Directory* (Dublin: 1845).

Townsend, Horatio, *Statistical Survey of the County of Cork: With Observations on the Means of Improvement; Drawn up for the Consideration, and by the Direction of the Dublin Society* (Dublin: Graisberry and Campbell, 1810).

Trevelyan, Charles E., *The Irish Crisis: Being a Narrative of the Measures for the Relief of the Distress Caused by the Great Irish Famine of 1846–7* (London: 1880).

Windele, John, *Historical and Descriptive Notices of the City of Cork, and Its Vicinity: Gougaun Barra, Glengariff, and Killarney* (Cork: Messrs. Bolster, 1840).

SECONDARY SOURCES

Aalen, F.H.A., Kevin Whelan and Matthew Stout, *Atlas of the Irish Rural Landscape* (Cork: Cork University Press, 2011).

Anon., 'Carrigboy National School, 1915-2015' (Cork: 2015).

Belchem, John, 'Priests, Publicans and the Irish Poor: Ethnic Enterprise and Migrant Networks in Mid-Nineteenth-Century Liverpool', *Immigrants & Minorities*, 23 (2005).

Bielenberg, Andy, *Cork's Industrial Revolution, 1780–1880: Development or Decline?* (Cork: Cork University Press, 1991).

Bourke, Freddie, *The Famine Decade in Clonlara, County Clare 1840–1850* (Clare: Yardfield Books, 1998).

Brown, Thomas N., 'Nationalism and the Irish Peasant, 1800–1848', *The Review of Politics*, 15 (1953).

Burke, Helen, *The People and the Poor Law in 19th Century Ireland* (West Sussex: WEB, The Women's Education Bureau, 1987).

Callan Heritage Society, *The Famine in the Kilkenny/Tipperary Region* (Kilkenny: Callan Heritage Society, 1998).

Carroll, Michael J., *A History of Bantry and Bantry Bay* (Cork: M.J. Carroll, 2008).

Cassidy, Crona, *The Great Famine in Stranorlar, County Donegal* (Kildare: Chris Shea Lawlor, 2012).

Comerford, Patrick, *The Great Famine: A Church of Ireland Perspective* (Dublin: APCK, 1996).

Conaghan, Pat, *The Great Famine in South-West Donegal* (Donegal: Bygones Enterprise, 1997).

Costello, Michael (ed.), *The Famine in Kerry* (Kerry: Kerry Archaeological and Historical Society, 1997).

Cousens, S.H., 'The Regional Pattern of Emigration During the Great Irish Famine, 1846–51', *Transactions and Papers (Institute of British Geographers)* (1960).

———, 'The Regional Variation in Mortality During the Great Irish Famine', *Proceedings of the Royal Irish Academy. Section C: Archaeology, Celtic Studies, History, Linguistics, Literature*, 63 (1962).

Crossman, Virginia, *Politics, Law and Order in Nineteenth-Century Ireland* (Dublin: Gill & Macmillan, 1996).

———, *Politics, Pauperism and Power in Late Nineteenth Century Ireland* (Manchester: Manchester University Press, 2006).

———, 'Poverty and the Poor Law in Ireland, 1850–1914', *The English Historical Review*, 130 (2013).

———, *The Poor Law in Ireland 1838–1948*. Vol. 10. (Dublin: Economic and Social History Society of Ireland, 2006).

Crossman, Virginia, and Peter Gray, *Poverty and Welfare in Ireland 1838–1948* (Dublin: Irish Academic Press, 2011).

Crowley, John, William J. Smyth, Michael Murphy, Charlie Roche and Tomás Kelly, *Atlas of the Great Irish Famine: 1845–52* (Cork: Cork University Press, 2012).

Cusack, George, and Sarah Judith Goss, *Hungry Words: Images of Famine in the Irish Canon* (Dublin: Irish Academic Press, 2006).

Dickson, David, 'In Search of the Old Irish Poor Law', in Rosalind Mitchison and Peter Roebuck (eds), *Economy and Society in Scotland and Ireland 1500–1939* (Edinburgh: John Donald, 1988).

Donnelly, James S., 'The Administration of Relief', in W.E. Vaughan (ed.), *A New History of Ireland* (Oxford: OUP, 1989).

———, 'Famine and Government Response, 1845–6', in W.E. Vaughan (ed.), *A New History of Ireland* (Oxford: OUP, 1989).

———, 'Production, Prices and Exports, 1846–51', in W.E. Vaughan (ed.), *A New History of Ireland* (Oxford: OUP, 1989).

———, *The Land and the People of Nineteenth-Century Cork* (1975).

———, 'Irish Property Must Pay for Irish Poverty', in Richard Hayes and Chris Morash (ed.), *Fearful Realities* (Dublin: Irish Academic Press, 1996).

Dooley, Terence W.M., 'Estate ownership and management in nineteenth and early twentieth century Ireland', in *Sources for the History of Landed Estates in Ireland* (Dublin: Irish Academic Press, 2000).

Edwards, R. Dudley, T. Desmond Williams, ed., *The Great Famine: Studies in Irish History, 1845–52* (Dublin: Lilliput Press, 1956).

Eiríksson, Andrés, and Cormac Ó Gráda, *Irish Landlords and the Great Irish Famine*. Vol. WP96/13 (Dublin: University College Dublin, Department of Economics, 1996).

Everett, Nigel, *Wild Gardens: The Lost Demesnes of Bantry Bay* (Cork: Hafod Press, 2001).

Finnane, Mark, *Insanity and the Insane in Post-Famine Ireland* (London: Croom Helm, 1981).

FitzGerald, Garret, Gillian O'Brien, Cormac Ó Gráda, Michael Murphy and James Kelly, *Irish Primary Education in the Early Nineteenth Century: An Analysis of the First and Second Reports of the Commissioners of Irish Education Inquiry, 1825–6.* Vol. 2 (Dublin: Royal Irish Academy, 2013).

Foynes, Peter, *The Great Famine in Skibbereen* (Cork: Irish Famine Commemoration Skibbereen Ltd., 2004).

Galvin, Michael, *Black Blight: The Great Famine, 1845–1852: A Four Parish Study* (Cork: Litho Press, 1995).

Geary, Laurence, 'The Great Famine in County Cork: A Socio-Medical Analysis', in Sean Farrell and Michael De Nie (eds), *Power and Popular Culture in Modern Ireland: Essays in Honour of James Donnelly, Jr* (Dublin: Irish Academic Press, 2010).

Geary, Laurence M., 'The Best Relief the Poor Can Receive Is from Themselves', in Laurence M. Geary and Oonagh Walsh (eds), *Philanthropy in Nineteenth-Century Ireland* (Dublin: Four Courts Press, 2015).

——, *Medicine and Charity in Ireland, 1718–1851* (Dublin: University College Dublin Press, 2004).

Geary, Laurence M., and Margaret Kelleher, *Nineteenth-Century Ireland: A Guide to Recent Research* (Dublin: University College Dublin Press, 2005).

Goodbody, Rob, 'Quakers & the Famine', *History Ireland*, 6 (1998).

Grace, Daniel, *The Great Famine in Nenagh* (Tipperary: Relay Books, 2000).

Gráda, Cormac Ó, 'Yardsticks for Irish Workhouses During the Great Famine', in *Poverty and Welfare in Ireland, 1838–1948* (Dublin: Irish Academic Press, 2011).

Gray, Peter, 'Conceiving and Constructing the Irish Workhouse, 1836–45', *Irish Historical Studies*, 38 (2012).

——, *Famine, Land, and Politics: British Government and Irish Society, 1843–1850* (Dublin: Irish Academic Press, 1999).

——, *The Making of the Irish Poor Law, 1815–43* (Manchester: Manchester University Press, 2009).

Gregory, Fewer Thomas, 'The Archaeology of the Great Famine: Time for a Beginning', *Irish Historic Settlement Newsletter*, 8 (1997), pp. 8–13.

Hamrock, Ivor (ed.), *The Famine in Mayo, 1845–1850* (Mayo: Mayo County Council, 1998).

Harrington, Gerard, *In the Path of Heroes* (Cork: Beara Historical Society, 2000).

Harrison, Richard S., *Béara and Bantry Bay* (Cork: Rossmacowen Historical Society, 1990).

Hatton, Helen E., *The Largest Amount of Good: Quaker Relief in Ireland, 1654–1921* (Kingston: McGill-Queen's University Press, 1993).

Healy, Shirley, 'Tralee Poor Law Union during the Famine', submitted for MA degree, UCC, Cork, 1998.

Hickey, Patrick, 'A Coffin-Cross from Bantry, 1847', *The Furrow*, 39, 5 (May 1988), pp. 333–4.

Hickey, Patrick, *Famine in West Cork: The Mizen Peninsula Land and People, 1800–1852* (Cork: Mercier Press, 2002).

Hollett, D., *Passage to the New World: Packet Ships and Irish Famine Emigrants, 1845–1851* (Gwent: P.M. Heaton, 1995).

Humphries, Francis, 'St. James, Durrus: A Parish History' (Forum Publications, 1992).

Ian Gregory, Niall Cunningham and C.D. Lloyd, *Troubled Geographies: A Spatial History of Religion and Society in Ireland* (Bloomington: Indiana University Press, 2013).

James, Kevin J., 'Tourism, Landscape, and the Irish Character: British Travel Writers in Pre-Famine Ireland. By William H. A. Williams. Pp Xi, 267. Madison: University of Wisconsin Press. 2008. $65', *Irish Historical Studies*, 36 (2009).

Donnelly, James S., *The Great Irish Potato Famine* (Dublin: Sutton Publishing, 2001).

Jordan, Margaret, 'The Life and Times of John Shea Lawlor', *Irish Family History Society*, 24 (2008).

Kelly, John, *The Graves Are Walking* (Kirkus Media LLC, 2012).

Kennedy, Liam, Paul S. Ell, E. Margaret Crawford and Leslie A. Clarkson, *Mapping the Great Irish Famine: A Survey of the Famine Decades* (Dublin: Four Courts Press, 1999).

Kerr, Donal A., *The Catholic Church and the Famine* (Dublin: Columba Press, 1996).

Kierse, Sean, *The Famine Years in the Parish of Killaloe, County Clare* (Clare: Boru Books, 1984).

Killen, John, *The Famine Decade: Contemporary Accounts, 1841–1851* (Belfast: Blackstaff Press, 1995).

Kinealy, Christine, 'The British Relief Association and the Great Famine in Ireland', *French Journal of British Studies* (2014)

———, *Repeal and Revolution: 1848 in Ireland* (Manchester: Manchester University Press, 2009).

Kinealy, Christine, Jason King and Ciarán Reilly, *Women and the Great Hunger* (Hamden, CT: Quinnipiac University Press, 2016).

Kinsella, Anna, *County Wexford in the Famine Years, 1845–1849* (Wexford: Duffry Press, 1995).

Lee, Joseph, *The Modernisation of Irish Society* (Dublin: 1989).

Lengel, Edward G., 'The Irish through British Eyes: Perceptions of Ireland in the Famine Era.', *Albion*, 35 (2003).

Lucas, A.T., *Nettles and Charlock as Famine Food* (O'Kelly Archaeology Offprints, 1955).

Lynch, Linda G., 'Death and Burial in the Poor Law Union Workhouses in Ireland', *The Journal of Irish Archaeology*, 23 (2014).

MacKay, D., *Flight from Famine: The Coming of the Irish to Canada* (Toronto: McClelland and Stewart, 1990).

Mac Suibhne, Maire, *Famine in Muskerry* (Cork: Cuilin Greine Press, 1997).

Mary O'Sullivan, 'Herbs and Cures', in *The Schools' Collection, Volume 0290, Page 187* (Dublin: National Folklore Collection, UCD, 1930s).

McCall, Dorothy, *When That I Was* (London: Faber and Faber, 1952).

Merry, Andrew, *The Hunger: Being Realities of the Famine Years in Ireland, 1845 to 1848* (London: 1910).

Miller, I., 'The Chemistry of Famine: Nutritional Controversies and the Irish Famine, C.1845–7', *Med Hist.*, 56 (2012).

Mokyr, Joel, 'The Deadly Fungus: An Econometric Investigation into the Short-Term Demographic Impact of the Irish Famine, 1846–1851', *The Journal of Economic History*, 40, 1 (1978).

———, 'Malthusian Models and Irish History', *The Journal of Economic History*, 40 (1980).

Mokyr, Joel, and Cormac Ó Gráda, 'What Do People Die of During Famines: The Great Irish Famine in Comparative Perspective', *European Review of Economic History*, 6 (2002).

Morash, Chris, *Writing the Irish Famine* (Oxford: Clarendon Press, 1995).

Murchadha, Ciarán Ó, *The Great Famine: Ireland's Agony, 1845–1852* (Dublin: Bloomsbury, 2011).

Murphy, Maria, 'The Famine in Dunmanway 1845–1848', submitted for MA degree, UCC, Cork, 2010.

Murphy, Peter, *Poor, Ignorant Children: Irish Famine Orphans in Saint John, New Brunswick* (Halifax: D'Arcy McGee Chair or Irish Studies, Saint Mary's University, 1999).

Murphy, Sean, *The Comeraghs 'Famine, Eviction and Revolution': The Great Famine in Waterford 1845/49* (Waterford: Comeragh Publications, 1996).

Newman, Eileen, 'The Great Famine in the Poor Law Union of Mallow', submitted for MA degree, UCC, Cork, 1998.

Notter, Isaac Nash, *Bantry, County Cork: Past and Present* (unknown, nd, Bantry library).

Ó Cathaoir, Brendan, *Famine Diary* (Dublin: Irish Academic Press, 1999).

Ó Gráda, Cormac, *Black '47 and Beyond: The Great Irish Famine in History, Economy, and Memory* (Princeton: Princeton University Press, 1999).

——, *Health, Work, and Nutritional Status in Pre-Famine Ireland* (Dublin: UCD Centre for Economic Research, 1992).

——, *Ireland before and after the Famine: Explorations in Economic History, 1800–1925* (Manchester: Manchester University Press, 1994).

Ó Gráda, Cormac, and Andrés Eiríksson, *Ireland's Great Famine: Interdisciplinary Perspectives* (Dublin: University College Dublin Press, 2006).

Ó Gráda, Cormac, and John Keating, *Famine 150: Commemorative Lecture Series* (Dublin: Teagasc, 1997).

Ó Súilleabháin, Seán, Johnny Bat and Patsy Leary, *An Account of the Irish Famine (1845–1852) in the Area of Kenmare, Co. Kerry* (Dublin: Irish Folklore Commission, UCD, 1945).

Ó Tuathaigh, Gearóid, *Ireland before the Famine, 1798–1848* (Dublin: Gill & Macmillan, 2007).

O'Brien, Daniel M., *Beara: A Journey through History* (Cork: Beara Historical Society, 1991).

O'Brien, George, *The Economic History of Ireland from the Union to the Famine* (London: Longmans, Green, 1921).

O'Connor, John, *The Workhouses of Ireland: The Fate of Ireland's Poor* (Dublin: Anvil Books, 1995).

Ó Duigneain, Proinnsios, *North Leitrim in Famine Times 1840–50* (Leitrim: P. Ó Duigneain, 1987).

O'Flaherty, Liam, *Famine* (New York: The Literary Guild, 1937).

Ó Flanagan, Patrick, and Cornelius G. Buttimer, *Cork: History & Society: Interdisciplinary Essays on the History of an Irish County*. Vol. 6. (Dublin: Geography Publications, 1993).

O Mahony, Colman, *Cork's Poor Law Palace. Workhouse Life 1838–90* (Cork: Rosmathún Press, 2005).

O'Riordan, Edmund, *Famine in the Valley* (1997).

Patriquin, Larry, 'Why Was There No "Old Poor Law" in Scotland and Ireland?', *The Journal of Peasant Studies*, 33 (2006), 219–47.

Póirtéir, Cathal, *The Great Irish Famine* (Cork: 1995).

Purdon, Edward, *The Irish Famine, 1845–52* (Cork: Mercier Press, 2000).

Read, Charles, 'The Repeal Year in Ireland: An Economic Reassessment', *The Historical Journal*, 58 (2015), 111–35.

Reilly, Ciaran, *John Plunket Joly and the Great Famine in King's County* (Dublin: Four Courts Press, 2012).

———, *Strokestown and the Great Irish Famine* (Dublin: Four Courts Press, 2014).

Robins, Joseph, *The Miasma: Epidemic and Panic in Nineteenth-Century Ireland*. Vol. 72 (Dublin: 1995).

Scoble, Robert, *Raven: The Turbulent World of Baron Corvo* (London: 2013).

Sheehan, Sean, *Jack's World: Farming on the Sheep's Head Peninsula, 1920–2003* (Cork: Atrium, 2007).

Society of Friends, *Transactions of the Central Relief Committee of the Society of Friends During the Famine in Ireland, in 1846 and 1847: With an Index by Rob Goodbody* (Dublin: E. Burke, 1996).

Thackeray, William Makepeace, *The Irish Sketch Book of 1842* (London: 1878).

Timothy W. Guinnane, Cormac Ó Gráda, *The Workhouse and Irish Famine Mortality* (Dublin: 2000).

Vaughan, W.E., ed., *Ireland under the Union 1801–70* (Oxford: OUP, 1989).

Walker, Brian, 'Missed opportunities and political failures: The great famine general election of 1847', *History Ireland*, 17 (2009).

Went, Arthur E.J., 'Ancient Times: The Irish Pilchard Fishery', in *Proceedings of the Royal Irish Academy. Section B: Biological, Geological, and Chemical Science* (JSTOR, 1945).

Williams, R. Alan, *The Berehaven Copper Mines: Allihies, Co. Cork, S.W. Ireland* (Sheffield: Northern Mine Research Society, 1991).

Winstanley, Michael J., *Ireland and the Land Question, 1800–1922* (London: Methuen, 1984).

Woodham-Smith, Cecil, *The Great Hunger, Ireland 1845–1849* (New York: 1962).

WEBSITES/BLOGS

Crowley, Pat, West Cork History/ Durrus History, Wordpress (2017), https://durrushistory.com/, accessed 18 Oct. 2020.

Bantry genealogy & history (2017), http://www.corkgen.org/publicgenealogy/cork/, accessed 18 Oct. 2020.

Irish seaweed research group, Ryan Institute NUI Galway, http://www.seaweed.ie/irish_seaweed_contacts/doc/FactSheets.pdf, accessed 18 Oct. 2020.

Meghen, P.J., Building the Workhouses, http://www.limerickcity.ie/media/Media,3942,en.pdf, accessed 18 Oct. 2020.

Oughterard Heritage, 'The Famine Part 1', Oughterard Heritage: A Community History of Oughterard, County Galway (26 Nov. 2015), http://www.oughterardheritage.org/content/topics/murt-molloy-killannin-and-oughterard-local-history/the-famine-barony-of-moycullen-co-galway-1845-1850, accessed 28 Feb. 2017.

STUDENT PAPERS, THESES, ADDITIONAL DATABASES

Cotter, Catherine, 'From Prosperity to Pauperism: The Poor Law Union of Midleton during the Great Famine', submitted for MPhil degree, UCC, Cork, 1999.

Crowley, John, 'Representing Ireland's Great Famine (1845–1852): A Cultural Geographic Perspective', 2003.

Derby, Lisa, 'The Great Irish Famine: A Further Understanding of Its Complexities through the Use of Human Communication Theory', submitted for PhD, 2000.

Flanagan, Catherine, 'The Great Famine in Kinsale', submitted for MA degree, UCC, Cork, 2016.

Henderson, Lori, 'The Irish Famine: A Historiographical Review', 2005.

Martin, James Gerard, 'The Society of St Vincent De Paul as an Emerging Social Phenomenon in Mid-Nineteenth Century Ireland', submitted for MA, 1993.

O Mahony, Colman, 'Workhouse Relief in Cork: 1838–1888', 2003.

Crowley, Seamus, 'Famine in Bantry', unpublished, 1971.

Landed Estates Court Rentals 1850–1885, Findmypast, https://search.findmypast.ie/record?id=ire%2flec%2f4506856%2f00167&parentid=ire%2flec%2f4506856%2f00166%2f001, accessed 18 Oct. 2020.

Famine orphan girl data base, Irish Famine memorial Sydney, https://irishfaminememorial.org/orphans/database/, accessed 18 Oct. 2020.

ENDNOTES

1. For an illuminating article on this topic see: Aleida Assman, 'Transformations between history and memory', *Social Research*, 75, 1 (Spring 2008), pp. 49–72.

2. Personal communication, Jeremiah O'Mahony, Ahakista, 2017.

3. *Illustrated London News* (20 February 1847).

4. Kevin J. Hourihan, 'Town growth in West Cork: 1600–1960', *Cork Historical and Archaeological Society*, 82 (1977), pp. 89–92; Richard S. Harrison, *Bantry in Olden Days* (Cork: R.S. Harrison, 1992), pp. 24–9; Donal Fitzgerald, 'The Famine in Bantry', *Bantry Historical and Archaeological Society*, 1 (June 1991), pp. 83–91; Seamus Crowley, 'Famine in Bantry' (unpublished paper: Cork County Library, 1971), pp. 1–5; Michael J. Carroll, *A History of Bantry and Bantry Bay* (M.J. Carroll, 2008), pp. 145–9.

5. CCCA (Cork City and County Archives), Rental [Durrus] U137/RL/A/026, 1853–1859.

6. Christopher Morash, *Writing the Irish Famine* (New York, Oxford: Clarendon Press, 1995), pp. 2–3.

7. Leo Tolstoy, writing about happy and unhappy families in Anna Karenina (1878).

8. See David Dickson, who described aid through parish vestries of the Established Church in 'In search of the old Irish poor law' in Peter Roebuck and Rosamund Mitchinson (eds), *Economy and Society in Ireland and Scotland, 1500–1839* (Edinburgh: John Donald, 1988), pp. 149–59.

9. HC (British Parliamentary Papers), *Third report of the commissioners for inquiring into the condition of the poorer classes in Ireland*, Volume Page: XXX.1, Volume: 30, Paper Number: 43 (London: 1836), pp. 3–9, 18–24. ProQuest: U.K. Parliamentary Papers.

10. George Nicholls, *Report of G. Nicholls on Poor Laws, Ireland*, Volume Page: LI.201, Volume: 51 Paper Number: 69 (1837), p. 21. ProQuest: U.K. Parliamentary Papers.

11. *The Mirror of Parliament for the first session of the Thirteenth Parliament of Great Britain and Ireland: Session 1837–1838* (London: 1838), p. 1579.

12. Peter Gray, *The Making of the Irish Poor Law, 1815–43.* (Manchester: Manchester University Press, 2009), p. 197.

13 Peter Gray, 'Conceiving and constructing the Irish workhouse, 1836–45', *Irish Historical Studies*, 38 (2012), p. 8.

14 Virginia Crossman, *The Poor Law in Ireland, 1838–1948* (The Economic and Social History Society of Ireland, 2006), p. 10. Professor Crossman says that while the government was 'concerned about Irish poverty they were not concerned enough to commit to paying for its relief'.

15 HC, *Poor relief (Ireland). A bill [as amended in committee and on re-committment] for the more effectual relief of the destitute poor in Ireland*, Volume Page: V.345, Volume: 5, Paper Number: 238 (1838). https://parlipapers.proquest.com/parlipapers/docview/t70.d75.1837-17425?accountid=14504 (accessed 28 September 2020)

16 HC, *Evidence taken before Her Majesty's Commissioners of Inquiry into the state of the law and practice in respect to the occupation of land in Ireland*. Part II, Volume Page: XX.1, Volume: 20, Paper Number: 616 (Dublin: 1845), pp. 923–47.

https://parlipapers.proquest.com/parlipapers/docview/t70.d75.1845-022467?accountid+14504 (accessed 28 September 2020)

HC, William E. Devon Courtenay, 'Royal Com. of Inquiry into State of Law and Practice in respect to Occupation of Land in Ireland, Appendix to Minutes of Evidence, Part IV.; Index to Minutes of Evidence, Part V', in *19th Century House of Commons Sessional Papers* (1845), Appendix B 1031, pp. 735–43.

17 *Southern Reporter* (12 September 1839).

18 *Southern Reporter* (29 December 1840).

19 *Southern Reporter* (10 October 1840).

20 HC, *Commons Sitting of Monday, February 8, 1841, Title: Third Series*, Volume 56, pp. 375–453. *ProQuest: U.K. Parliamentary Papers.*

21 *Thom's Irish Almanac and Official Directory* (Dublin: 1845).

22 *Southern Reporter* (17 October 1835).

23 Poor Law Commissioners, Index of orders 2005/57/1, Bantry Union (NAI [National Archives of Ireland], 1838–1855).

24 Donal Fitzgerald, 'The Famine in Bantry', p. 87; Michael J. Carroll, *Bay of Destiny* (Cork: Bantry Design Studios, 1996), p. 263; Seamus Crowley, 'Famine in Bantry', p. 3.

25 *Southern Reporter* (12 December 1840).

26 *Thom's Irish Almanac and Official Directory* (Dublin: 1845).

27 Irish Archive resources, Bantry Board of Guardians, IE CCCA/BG/43 (Bantry Board of Guardians minute books) 2017.

28 Personal communication, Tomas Ó Súilleabháin, Bantry, 2018.

29 *The Parliamentary Gazetteer of Ireland* (Dublin: Fullerton, 1846), p. 221.

30 Geraldine Powell, 'Life in a West Cork clachan', *Journal of the Cork Historical & Archaeological Society*, 123 (2018), p. 32.

31 HC, *Report of the commissioners appointed to take the census of Ireland, for the year 1841. Appendix*, Volume Page: XXIV.1, Volume: 24, Paper Number: 504 (Dublin, 1843) pp. 172–4. *ProQuest: U.K. Parliamentary Papers.*

ENDNOTES

32 James S. Donnelly, *The Land and People of Nineteenth-Century Cork* (London: 1975), p. 126.

33 Samuel Lewis and R. Creighton, *A topographical dictionary of Ireland: comprising the several counties, cities, boroughs, corporate, market and post towns, parishes, and villages, with historical and statistical descriptions*, (London: S. Lewis & Co, 1837), pp. 16, 27, 41, 129–30, 157, 185–7, 206, 307–8, 590–1, 665. Lewis appears to rate arability in Bantry Union at an average of 20 per cent, while in the Skibbereen Union it was estimated to be about 33 per cent. The same relationship seems roughly confirmed by looking at the tables for 'land under cultivation' in the 1841 census and at physical maps, but this would need further study to arrive at a secure conclusion.

34 John Forbes, *Memorandums made in Ireland in the autumn of 1852* (London: 1853), p. 100.

35 *Cork Examiner* (14 July 1847). William O'Sullivan Jr of Carriganass challenged Shea Lawlor.

36 BL/E/B/321-329, The Bantry Estate Collection, Special Collections & Archives, UCC Library, University College Cork, Ireland.

37 Terence Dooley, 'Estate ownership and management in nineteenth and early twentieth century Ireland', *Sources for the History of Landed Estates in Ireland* (Dublin: Irish Academic Press, 2000), p. 2.

38 Daphne Du Maurier, *Hungry Hill* (London: Victor Gollancz, 1943).

39 Patrick J. Prendergast, *Letter to the Earl of Bantry or, A warning to English purchasers of the perils of the Irish Incumbered estates court; exemplified in the purchase by Lord Charles Pelham Clinton, M.P., of two estates in the Barony of Bere, county of Cork* (Dublin: 1854) pp. 1–22.

40 Robert Scoble, *Raven: The Turbulent World of Baron Corvo* (London: Strange Attractor, 2013). A collection of essays on Frederick Rolfe.

41 Not related to Daniel O'Connell according to T.C. Foster. He testified to the Devon Commission in 1844.

42 HC, *Evidence taken before Her Majesty's Commissioners of Inquiry into the state of the law and practice in respect to the occupation of land in Ireland. Part II.*, Volume Page: XX.1, Volume: 20, Paper Number: 616 (Dublin 1845), p. 938. ProQuest: U.K. Parliamentary Papers.

43 'O'Donovan estates, Muintervara', West Cork History – History of Durrus/Muintervara (9 October 2011) https://durrushistory.com/2011/10/09/odonovan-estates-muintervara/ (accessed 28 September 2020).

44 HC, *Evidence taken before Her Majesty's Commissioners of Inquiry into the state of the law and practice in respect to the occupation of land in Ireland. Part II.*, p. 944.

45 Ibid, p. 924.

46 Ibid, p. 940.

47 Ibid, p. 924.

48 1st Earl of Bantry, Notes from First Earl of Bantry concerning relief for the poor, CSO/RP/1822/442, NAI, 1822; 1st Earl of Bantry, Application of Lord Bantry for post on Linen Board, CSO/RP/1822/1890, NAI 1822; 1st Earl of Bantry, Letter requesting advance for construction of a bridewell and market house in Bantry, CSO/RP/1822/442, NAI 1822.

49 Sir Charles James Fox Bunbury, *1836 Memorials* (Cambridge: Cambridge University Press, 2011), p. 201.

50 HC, *Evidence taken before Her Majesty's Commissioners of Inquiry into the state of the law and practice in respect to the occupation of land in Ireland.* Part II., p. 940.

51 Harrison, *Bantry in Olden Days*, p. 22.

52 Lewis and Creighton, *A topographical dictionary*, p. 186.

53 Harrison, *Bantry in Olden Days*, p. 21.

54 Ibid, p. 21.

55 Obtainable online from the UCD historic map digital archive. http://geohive.maps.arcgis.com/apps/webappviewer/index.html?id=9def-898f708b47f19a8d8b7088a100c4 (accessed 28 September 2020)

56 I. Slater, *Slater's National Commercial Directory of Ireland: including, in addition to the trades' lists, alphabetical directories of Dublin, Belfast, Cork and Limerick* (Manchester: I. Slater, 1846).

57 Andy Bielenberg, *Cork's Industrial Revolution, 1780–1880: Development or Decline?* (Cork: Cork University Press, 1991), p. 12.

58 *The Parliamentary Gazetteer of Ireland* (1846), p. 222.

59 NAI CSO/RP/1826/1641 1826.

60 Windele, *Historical and descriptive notices of the city of Cork* (Cork: Messrs. Bolster, 1840), p. 262. Windele was an antiquarian and a historian.

61 Lewis and Creighton, *A topographical dictionary*, p. 186.

62 Ibid, p. 186.

63 Windele, *Historical and descriptive notices of the city of Cork,* p. 262.

64 *London Evening Standard* (8 January 1849).

65 *The Parliamentary Gazetteer of Ireland* (1846), p. 222.

66 HC, *First report of the Commissioners of Inquiry into the State of the Irish Fisheries; with the minutes of evidence, and appendix. 1837*, Volume Page: XXII.1, Volume: 22, Paper Number: 77 pp. 129–42. https://parlipapers.proquest.com/parlipapers/docview/t70.d75.1837-16938?accountid=14504 (accessed 28 September 2020)

67 James Johnson, *A tour in Ireland: with meditations and reflections* (London: S. Highley, 1844), p. 129.

68 *The Parliamentary Gazetteer of Ireland* (1846), p. 251.

69 HC, *First report of the Commissioners of Inquiry into the State of the Irish Fisheries*, p. 139.

70 Pat Crowley, West Cork history/Durrus history, WordPress. 2017 https://durrushistory.com//?s=weavers&search=Go (accessed 28 September 2020)

ENDNOTES

71 William E. Hogg, *Old Mills of Ireland: A Listing of the Old Mills of Ireland taken from Mid-19th Century Valuation Office Documents* (Dublin: William E. Hogg, 2015), p. 319.

72 Crowley, West Cork history/Durrus history. https://durrushistory.com//?s=weavers&search=Go (accessed 28 September 2020)

73 I. Slater, *Slater's National Commercial Directory of Ireland*, p. 157.

74 HC, *Report comms. census of Ireland 1841*, p. 172–7.

75 Joel Mokyr, 'The deadly fungus: an econometric investigation into the short-term demographic impact of the Irish famine, 1846–1851', *The Journal of Economic History*, 40, 1 (Cambridge: Cambridge University Press, 1978), p. 29. Joel Mokyr is an economic historian who has written extensively on the Irish famine.

76 Thomas Campbell Foster, *Letters on the condition of the people of Ireland* (London: 1846), p. 402.

77 This range is calculated from the table of occupations (Appendix III).

78 Foster, *Letters on the condition of the people of Ireland*, pp. 401–5.

79 Cormac Ó Grada, 'Ireland's great famine: an overview', *Centre for Economic Research, working Paper series* (2004), p. 2.

80 HC, *Report comms. census of Ireland 1841*, p. 172–7.

81 Thomas E. Jordan, *Ireland's children quality of life, stress and child development in the famine era* (London: Greenwood Press, 1998), p. 44.

82 William Wilde, *Report of the Commissioners: the census of Ireland for the year 1841* (Dublin: 1843), p. 74.

83 HC, *First report from His Majesty's commissioners for inquiring into the condition of the poorer classes in Ireland, with appendix (A.) and supplement. appendix B, 1835*, Volume Page: XXXII Pt.I.1, XXXII Pt.II.1, Paper Number: 369, p. 112. ProQuest: U.K. Parliamentary Papers.

84 *The Parliamentary Gazetteer of Ireland* (1846), pp. 222, 375.

85 Mary O'Sullivan, Herbs and Cures, The Schools' Collection, Volume 0290, National Folklore Collection, UCD, 1930s, p. 187.

86 William Makepeace Thackeray, *The Irish sketch book of 1842* (London: 1878) pp. 340–1.

87 *Southern Reporter* (12 December 1840).

88 CCCA BG/43/AA2, April 1849, *passim*.

89 *Wexford Independent* (21 January 1843).

90 Poor Law Commission Office Dublin, Exemption of £4 tenements from rates made prior to the passing of the Irish Poor Law Amendment Act: circular addressed to Boards of Guardians in Ireland, No. 13, 22 April, 1844.

91 HC, *Seventh annual report of the Poor Law Commissioners, with appendices*, Volume Page: XI.291, Volume: 11, Paper Number: 327 (1841), pp. 192-209. *ProQuest: U.K. Parliamentary Papers*.

92 HC, *Appendices B to F to the eighth annual report of the Poor Law Commissioners*, Volume Page: XIX.119, Volume: 19, Paper Number: 399 (1842), pp. 382–400. *ProQuest: U.K. Parliamentary Papers*.

93 Ibid, p. 378.

94 HC, *Appendices A to C to the tenth annual report of the Poor Law Commissioners*, Volume Page: XIX.57, Volume: 19, Paper Number: 589 (1844), pp. 518–19. *ProQuest: U.K. Parliamentary Papers*.

95 HC, *Appendix to the report of the commissioner appointed to inquire into the execution of the contracts for certain union workhouses in Ireland*, Volume Page: XXX.551, Volume: 30, Paper Number: 568 (1844), p. 91. *ProQuest: U.K. Parliamentary Papers*.

96 HC, *Public works (Ireland). Returns of all sums of money voted or applied, either by way of grant or loan, in aid of public works in Ireland, since the union, &c.*, Volume Page: XLIV.493, Volume: 44, Paper Number: 540 (1839), p. 18. *ProQuest: U.K. Parliamentary Papers*.

97 HC, *First annual report of the Commissioners for Administering the Laws for Relief of the Poor in Ireland, with appendices*, Volume Page: XXXIII.377, Volume: 33, Paper Number: 963 (1848), p. 112. *ProQuest: U.K. Parliamentary Papers*.

98 Personal communication Tom Spillane, builder, Bantry Hospital, 27 January 2017.

99 'Return of Number of Union Workhouses in Ireland, with Insufficient Supply of Water and Sewage', *19th Century House of Commons Sessional Papers* (1843).

100 *Southern Reporter* (24 January 1843).

101 Ibid.

102 *Warder and Dublin Weekly Mail* (4 March 1843).

103 William E. Devon Courtenay, 'Royal Com. of Inquiry into State of Law and Practice in respect to Occupation of Land in Ireland, Appendix to Minutes of Evidence, Part IV.; Index to Minutes of Evidence, Part V', *19th Century House of Commons Sessional Papers* (1845), Appendix B 1031, p. 738.

104 Thomas Carlyle and James Anthony Froude, *Reminiscences of my Irish journey in 1849* (London: S. Low, Marston, Searle, & Rivington, 1882). p. 118.

105 HC, *Poor law (Ireland). Returns of the days on which each Assistant Poor-Law Commissioner, in Ireland, attended meetings of Boards of Guardians, in the years 1844 and 1845, and up to the 31st day of March 1846; &c.*, Volume Page: XXXVI.451, Volume: 36, Paper Number: 453 (1846), pp. 7, 8, 12. *ProQuest: U.K. Parliamentary Papers*.

106 HC, *Appendices to the eleventh annual report of the Poor Law Commissioners. 1845*, p. 237.

107 Asenath Nicholson, *Welcome to the Stranger* (New York: 1847), p. 275.

108 Ibid, p. 277.

109 Ibid, pp. 284, 300.

110 Nicholson, *Welcome to the Stranger*, pp. 294–5.

111 *Cork Examiner* (9 May 1845).

112 *Cork Examiner* (1 July 1846).

113 HC, *Appendices to the eleventh annual report of the Poor Law Commissioners, 1845*, p. 238.

114 John O'Connor, *The workhouses of Ireland: the fate of Ireland's poor* (Dublin: Anvil Books, 1995), pp. 120–54; P.J. Meghen, 'Building the workhouses'. http://www.limerickcity.ie/media/Media,3942,en.pdf (accessed 7 December 2017); Linda G. Lynch, 'Death and Burial in the Poor Law Union Workhouses in Ireland', *The Journal of Irish Archaeology*, 23 (2014), pp. 189–203.

115 A.M. Sullivan, *New Ireland: political sketches and personal reminiscences of thirty years of Irish public life* (London, Glasgow: 1877), p. 62.

116 Roberts had been a schoolteacher at the Kinsale workhouse.

117 HC, *Copies or extracts of correspondence relating to the state of union workhouses in Ireland*, Volume Page: LV.27, 141, 231, Volume: 55;141;231, Paper Number: 766 790 863 (1847), pp. 66, 71, 78, 83, 87, 104. ProQuest: U.K. Parliamentary Papers.

118 HC, *Appendices to the twelfth annual report of the Poor Law Commissioners*, Volume Page: XIX.33, Volume: 19, Paper Number: 745, appendix B (1846), pp. 203–89. *ProQuest: U.K. Parliamentary Papers.*

119 HC, *Appendices to the eleventh annual report of the Poor Law Commissioners. 1845*, Volume Page: XXVII.279, Volume: 27, Paper Number: 660, p. 6. *ProQuest: U.K. Parliamentary Papers.*

120 HC, *Report comms. census of Ireland 1841*, pp. 172–7.

121 CCCA BG/43/AA2 April 1849, *passim*.

122 HC, *Report comms. census of Ireland, 1841*, pp. 174–7. (Numbers of ratepayers calculated by author.)

123 James S. Donnelly, *The Great Irish Potato Famine* (Gloucestershire: Sutton Publishing, 2001), p. 41.

124 *Cork Examiner* (10 September 1845).

125 *Cork Examiner* (12 November 1845).

126 *Southern Reporter* (11 December 1845).

127 NAI RLFC2/717166 (Famine Relief Commission Papers), 24 November 1845.

128 NAI RLFC2/717166, 25 November 1845.

129 *Southern Reporter* (25 October 1845).

130 *Supplement to Southern Reporter* (16 October 1845).

131 *Cork Examiner* (9 May 1845).

132 *Cork Examiner* (22 December 1845).

133 Christine Kinealy, *This Great Calamity: The Irish Famine 1845–1852* (Roberts Rinehart, 1995), p. 38.

134 Helen Burke, *The people and the poor law in 19th century Ireland* (West Sussex: WEB, The Women's Education Bureau, 1987). p. 107.

135 HC, *Relief districts (Ireland). Instructions to committees of relief districts, extracted from minutes of the proceedings of the commissioners appointed in reference to the apprehended scarcity*, Volume Page: XXXVII.473, Volume: 37, Paper Number: 171 (1846), pp. 1–3. *ProQuest: U.K. Parliamentary Papers.*

136 *Southern Reporter* (26 March 1846).
137 *Southern Reporter* (12 March 1846).
138 *Leeds Intelligencer* (14 March 1846).
139 HC, *Scarcity Commission. The weekly reports of the Scarcity Commission, showing the progress of disease in the potatoes, the complaints which have been made, and the applications for relief, in the course of March 1846*, Volume Page: XXXVII.429, Volume: 37, Paper Number: 201 (1846), p. 9. ProQuest: U.K. Parliamentary Papers.
140 NAI RLFC 3/7/943, 23 March 1846.
141 NAI RLFC 3/7/945, 24 March 1846.
142 *Hereford Journal* (18 March 1846).
143 *Cork Examiner* (2 March 1849).
144 *Cork Examiner* (8 September 1910).
145 HC, *Correspondence explanatory of the measures adopted by Her Majesty's government for the relief of distress arising from the failure of the potato crop in Ireland*, Volume Page: XXXVII.41, Volume: 37, Paper Number: 735 (1846), pp. 114–16. ProQuest: U.K. Parliamentary Papers.
146 NAI RLFC 3/1/1376, 9–14 April 1846.
147 *Southern Reporter* (23 June 1846).
148 NAI RLFC 3/1/2077, 5 May 1846.
149 NAI RLFC 3/1/3172, 10 June 1846.
150 NAI RLFC 3/1/2669, 27 May 1846.
151 NAI RLFC 3/1/3024, 11 June 1846.
152 *Cork Examiner* (15 May 1846).
153 HC, *Poor employment (Ireland). A bill [as amended by committee and on report] to facilitate the employment of the labouring poor for a limited period in distressed districts in Ireland*, Volume Page: III.143, Volume: 3, Paper Number: 672 (1846), pp. 1–10. ProQuest: U.K. Parliamentary Papers.
154 James S. Donnelly, 'The administration of relief', in W. E. Vaughan (ed.), *A New History of Ireland* (Oxord: Oxford University Press, 1989), pp. 299–305.
155 *Cork Examiner* (17 August 1846).
156 NAI RLFC 5/6/13, 28 August 1846.
157 Jane Murphy, Tisdall Hutchins papers, Pratt correspondence, NLI (National Library of Ireland) MS 8685, 1838–1853.
158 *Cork Examiner* (4 September 1846).
159 NAI RLFC 3/2/6/4, 5 September 1846.
160 NAI RLFC 3/2/6/28, 5 September 1846.
161 *Constitution* (15 September 1846); *Cork Examiner* (14 September 1846).
162 *Cork Examiner* (24 September 1846).
163 *Cork Examiner* (21 September 1846); *Constitution* (22 September 1846); *The Nation* (26 September 1846).
164 O'Sullivan family of Carriganass near Kealkil. The son, a JP, was charged with battering tenants in Scart. *Cork Examiner* (23 February 1848).
165 *Constitution* (19 November 1846).
166 NAI RLFC 3/2/6/26, 16 October 1846.
167 NAI RLFC 3/2/6/26, 23 October 1846.
168 NAI RLFC 3/2/6/28, November 1846–February 1847.
169 NAI RLFC 3/2/6 28, 29 October 1846.
170 NAI RLFC 3/2/6/5, 25 October 1846.
171 *Tablet* (19 December 1846)
172 *Times* (17 November 1846).

ENDNOTES

173 *Cork Examiner* (23 November 1846).
174 HC, *Correspondence from July, 1846, to January, 1847, relating to the measures adopted for the relief of the distress in Ireland. Commissariat series*, Page: LI.1, Volume: 51, Paper Number: 761 (1847), p. 197. *ProQuest: U.K. Parliamentary Papers*.
175 HC, *Correspondence from July, 1846, to January, 1847, relating to the measures adopted for the relief of the distress in Ireland. Commissariat series*, p. 197. *ProQuest: U.K. Parliamentary Papers*.
176 *The Warder* (5 December 1846).
177 CCCA BG/43/AA1, August 1846, *passim*.
178 Ibid, September 1846.
179 Ibid, October and November 1846.
180 *Cork Examiner* (21 December 1846).
181 HC, *Correspondence from July, 1846, to January, 1847, relating to the measures adopted for the relief of the distress in Ireland. Board of Works series. 1847,* 764 L.1, Volume 50, p. 385. *ProQuest: U.K. Parliamentary Papers*.
182 A Captain Reid.
183 NAI RLFC 3/2/6/23, 14 December 1846; *The Morning Chronicle* (16 December 1846).
184 *Cork Examiner* (21 December 1846).
185 Ibid.
186 Ibid.
187 *Tablet* (26 December 1846).
188 HC, *Correspondence from July, 1846, to January, 1847, relating to the measures adopted for the relief of the distress in Ireland. Board of Works series. 1847,* p. 457. *ProQuest: U.K. Parliamentary Papers*.
189 *Constitution* (29 December 1846).
190 *Freeman's Journal* (30 December 1846).
191 *Bath Chronicle* (31 December 1846).
192 HC, *Copies or extracts of correspondence relating to the state of union workhouses in Ireland*, Volume Page: LV.27, 141, 231, Volume: 55;141;231, Paper Number: 766 790 863 (1847), p. 25. *ProQuest: U.K. Parliamentary Papers*.
193 HC, *Correspondence from July, 1846, to January, 1847, relating to the measures adopted for the relief of the distress in Ireland. Commissariat series*, Volume Page: LI.1, Volume: 51, Paper Number: 761 (1846), p. 427. *ProQuest: U.K. Parliamentary Papers*.
194 HC, *Destitute persons (Ireland). A bill for the temporary relief of destitute persons in Ireland*, Volume Page: I.243, Volume: 1, Paper Number: 19 (1847). *ProQuest: U.K. Parliamentary Papers*.
195 *Cork Examiner* (4 January 1847).
196 NAI CSORP (Chief Secretary's Office Registered Papers) D213, 2 January 1847.
197 *Constitution* (19 January 1847). The petition was signed by four Evansons, three O'Donovans, Rev. Quinn PP Durrus, Rev. Charles McCarthy PP Kilcrohane, Robt Lawton coastguard officer, and Rev. Crossthwaite.
198 Listed in the article as: Daniel Capey of Crooha, Jeremiah Connelly, Daniel Turner, Tim Harrington of Roosk, Mary Sullivan, Edward McCarthy of Derrincurrin and John Shea of Voorslamon.
199 *Cork Examiner* (1 January 1847).
200 *Southern Reporter* (28 January 1847).

201 HC, *Correspondence from July, 1846, to January, 1847, relating to the measures adopted for the relief of the distress in Ireland. Board of Works series, 1847*, p. 152–3. ProQuest: U.K. Parliamentary Papers.

202 HC, *Correspondence from July, 1846, to January, 1847, relating to the measures adopted for the relief of the distress in Ireland. Commissariat series*, p. 502. ProQuest: U.K. Parliamentary Papers.

203 NAI RLFC 3/2/6/8, 20 January 1847.

204 NAI RLFC 3/2/6/5, February 1847.

205 The victims were named as Catherine Sheehan (aged 2), Jeremiah McCarthy, Richard Finn, Michael Linehan, John Driscoll and Michael Sullivan.

206 *Cork Examiner* (8 January 1847); *Constitution* (9 January 1847).

207 *Cork Examiner* (22 January 1847). Victims were Timothy Connell, Mary Hoolihan, Timothy Hoolihan (11 months), Timothy Driscoll, John Wholehan (earlier refused admission), Catherine Connelly, Timothy Coughlan, Jeremiah Shanahan, Harriet Swiney and Cornelius Harrington (aged 16).

208 *Times* (27 January 1847).

209 *Transactions of the Central Relief Committee of the Society of Friends during the Famine in Ireland in 1846 and 1847* (Dublin: Edmund Burke, 1996), p. 187.

210 *Constitution* (26 January 1847).

211 NAI RLFC 7/6/24, 16 January 1847.

212 Hazel Vickery, Personal communication, Bantry 2017.

213 *Southern reporter* (26 January 1847).

214 NAI RLFC 7/6/24, 16 January 1847.

215 *Constitution* (16 January 1847).

216 Pyburn. https://www.duchas.ie/en/cbes/4921585/4882184 (accessed 28 September 2020)

217 *Southern Reporter* (6 February 1847).

218 *Tablet* (30 January 1847).

219 *Freeman's Journal* (11 February 1847).

220 *Dumfries and Galloway Standard* (10 February 1847).

221 *Standard* (13 February 1847).

222 The British Relief Association for the Relief of Distress in Ireland and the Highlands of Scotland raised double the amount of money that was donated to the Quakers.

223 *Report of the British Association for the relief of the extreme distress of Ireland and Scotland* (London: 1849), p. 61.

224 Ibid, p. 64.

225 *Transactions of the Central Relief Committee of the Society of Friends during the Famine in Ireland in 1846 and 1847*, p. 191.

226 HC, *Correspondence from January to March 1847, relating to the measures adopted for the relief of the distress in Ireland. Board of Works series, [Second part.]*, Volume Page: LII.1, Volume: 52, Paper Number: 797, p. 161. ProQuest: U.K. Parliamentary Papers.

227 Ibid, p. 207.

228 *Tablet* (27 February 1847).

229 Ibid, p. 208.

ENDNOTES

230 *Constitution* (16 February 1847); John Mathias (Sean) Ryan reported Hussey was known as the most hated land agent in Ireland ('Deer Forests, Game Shooting and Landed Estates in the South West of Ireland, 1840–1970', submitted for PhD degree, 2001, p. 115); *Times* (12 January 1847).

231 Carroll, *Bay of Destiny* (1996) p. 265, 269.

232 S. Hussey, *The Reminiscences of an Irish Land Agent* (London and Edinburgh: 1904), p. 52.

233 NAI RLFC 3/2/6/28, November 1846–February 1847.

234 BL/EP/B/2316 (1), The Bantry Estate Collection, Special Collections & Archives, UCC Library, University College Cork, Ireland.

235 Three, six and four attendees, respectively.

236 Murphy, Tisdall Hutchins papers, Pratt correspondence, NLI MS 8685, 1838–1853, January 1847.

237 *Constitution* (6 February 1847); CCCA BG/43/A2 February 1847, *passim*.

238 *Constitution* (6 February 1847).

239 HC, *Workhouses (Ireland). Abstract copy of the reports made to the Board of Health in Dublin, by the medical officers sent to inquire into the state of the workhouses in Cork, Bantry, and Lurgan*, Volume Page: LV.11, Volume: 55, Paper Number: 257 (1847). ProQuest: U.K. Parliamentary Papers.

240 *The Warder* (6 March 1847).

241 *Southern Reporter* (15 April 1847).

242 *Salisbury and Winchester Journal* (3 April 1847).

243 *The Warder* (6 March 1847).

244 *The Constitution* (18 March 1847).

245 *Southern Reporter* (17 April 1847).

246 *Southern Reporter* (10 April 1847); *Southern Reporter* (17 April 1847).

247 Major General Burgoyne.

248 *The Nation* (17 April 1847).

249 *The Warder* (17 April 1847).

250 *Southern Reporter* (15 April 1847).

251 *Southern Reporter* (22 April 1847).

252 CCCA BG/43/AA1, April 1847, *passim*.

253 *Newry Telegraph* (3 April 1847).

254 *Dublin Evening Mail* (2 May 1849).

255 *Southern Reporter* (29 April 1847).

256 *Southern Reporter* (27 April 1847). It was distributed as follows: local distributors were Patrick Sullivan, 24 tons all through Beara, Richard Notter, 24 tons Sheep's Head area, Jeremiah O'Connell, 32 tons Bantry, Glengarriff, Kealkill and Durrus.

257 Those of Hutchins, Lawlor and probably Richard White.

258 *Report of the British Association for the relief of extreme distress of Ireland and Scotland*, pp. 67–8.

259 *Cork Examiner* (19 May 1847).

260 NAI CSORP D5844, 18 May 1847.

261 *Cork Examiner* (5 May 1847).

262 Ibid.

263 *Daily News* (18 May 1847); *Gloucester Journal* (22 May 1847).

264 *Freeman's Journal* (3 June 1847).

265 HC, *Distress (Ireland.) Supplementary appendix to the seventh, and last, report of the Relief Commissioners, constituted under the act 10th Vic., cap. 7*, Volume Page: XXIX.121, Volume: 29, Paper Number: 956, 1848, p. 31. *ProQuest: U.K. Parliamentary Papers*

266 *Cork Examiner* (24 May 1847).

267 *Southern Reporter* (13 May 1847). (Also reported by *Cork Examiner* on 19 May and *Freeman's Journal* on 18 May).

268 Sullivan, *New Ireland: political sketches and personal reminiscences of thirty years of Irish public life*, p. 63.

269 *Tablet* (22 May 1847).

270 John East, *Glimpses of Ireland in 1847* (Thomson Press, 2010), pp. 33–60.

271 *Times* (6 May 1847).

272 Joseph Kidd, *Homeopathy in acute diseases: narrative of a mission to Ireland during the famine and pestilence of 1847* (London: British Homeopathic Society, 1847), p. 45–7.

273 Ibid, p. 24.

274 Joseph Kidd, 'Of the Fever and dysentery of Ireland in 1847', *British Journal of Homeopathy*, 26 (January 1848), p. 87.

275 *Cork Mercantile Chronicle* (6 January 1823).

276 Dorothy McCall, *When That I Was* (London: Faber and Faber, 1952), p. 202.

277 Joseph Kidd, *Homeopathy in acute diseases: narrative of a mission to Ireland during the famine and pestilence of 1847*, p. 50.

278 *Cork Examiner* (9 June 1847).

279 *Southern Reporter* (10 June 1847).

280 *Southern Reporter* (22 June 1847).

281 *Cork Examiner* (8 September 1910).

282 BL/E/B/400-406, The Bantry Estate Collection, Special Collections & Archives, UCC Library, University College Cork, Ireland.

283 *Saunders News-Letter* (13 September 1784).

284 Nigel Everett, *Wild gardens: the lost demesnes of Bantry Bay* (Cork: Hafod Press, 2001), pp. 46–7, 59–64, 146–7.

285 BL/E/B/2280, The Bantry Estate Collection, Special Collections & Archives, UCC Library, University College Cork, Ireland;BL/B/2283, The Bantry Estate Collection, Special Collections & Archives, UCC Library, University College Cork, Ireland; BL/E/B/2282, The Bantry Estate Collection, Special Collections & Archives, UCC Library, University College Cork, Ireland.

286 *Nenagh Guardian* (18 November 1868).

287 *Morning Post* (1 June 1847).

288 CCCA BG/43/AA2 (letter dated 23 June 1849).

289 CCC BG/43/AA2 (letter from PLC dated 18 July 1849).

290 CCCA BG/43/Vol. A6, 18 December 1850.

291 HC, *Relief Coms., Fifth, Sixth and Seventh Reports, Correspondence*, Volume Page: XXIX.27, Volume: 29, Paper Number: 876, 1848, p. 10. *ProQuest: U.K. Parliamentary Papers*.

292 HC, *Distress (Ireland). Fourth report of the Relief Commissioners, constituted under the act 10th Vic., cap. 7*, Volume Page: XVII.143, Volume: 17, Paper Number: 859 (1847), p. 16. *ProQuest: U.K. Parliamentary Papers.*

293 Sullivan, *New Ireland: political sketches and personal reminiscences of thirty years of Irish public life*, p. 62.

294 Ibid, p. 65.

295 J. Mahony, Personal communication, 2017. Jeremiah O'Mahoney said his great-grandfather was a 'bodyman' in Kilcrohane during the famine.

296 John O'Rourke, *The History of the Great Irish Famine of 1847: with notices of earlier irish famines* (Dublin, London: McGlashan and Gill, 1875), pp. 394–5.

297 *Dublin Weekly Nation* (24 July 1847).

298 Brian Walker, 'Politicians, Elections and Catastrophe: The General Election of 1847', *Irish Political Studies*, 22, 1 (2007), p. 2.

299 *Cork Examiner* (9 August 1847).

300 *Belfast Protestant Journal* (24 July 1847).

301 *Constitution* (22 July 1847).

302 HC, *Distress (Ireland). Fourth report of the Relief Commissioners, constituted under the act 10th Vic., cap. 7*, p. 6. *ProQuest: U.K. Parliamentary Papers.*

303 HC, *Distress (Ireland). Supplementary appendix to the seventh, and last, report of the Relief Commissioners, constituted under the act 10th Vic., cap. 7*, p. 18. *ProQuest: U.K. Parliamentary Papers.*

304 *Cork Examiner* (12 July 1847).

305 George L. Bernstein, 'Liberals, the Irish Famine and the Role of the State', *Irish Historical Studies*, 29, 116 (1995), p. 523. https://www.jstor.org/stable/30006773 (accessed 30 April 2019)

306 HC Deb 10 July 1847 vol 94 cc153-67153

307 *Derbyshire Advertiser and Journal* (3 September 1847).

308 Charles E. Trevelyan, 'The Irish crisis: being a narrative of the measures for the relief of the distress caused by the great Irish famine of 1846-7', *Edinburgh Review*, 175 (1848).

309 HC, *Poor relief (Ireland). A bill [as amended by the Lords] intituled, an act to make further provision for the relief of the destitute poor in Ireland*, Volume Page: III.213, Volume: 3, Paper Number: 417 (1847). *ProQuest: U.K. Parliamentary Papers.*

310 Ibid, p. 4.

311 *Cork Examiner* (20 September 1847).

312 *Tablet* (7 August 1847).

313 *Constitution* (15 July 1847).

314 *Constitution* (2 July 1847).

315 CCCA BG/43/Vol AA1, June 1847, *passim*.

316 In private ownership a few miles west of the village of Kilcrohane.

317 *Cork Examiner* (9 August 1847).

318 *Cork Examiner* (26 August 1847).

319 *Cork Examiner* (24 September 1847).

320 *Cork Examiner* (8 September 1847).

321 *Cork Examiner* (30 August 1847).

322 *Southern Reporter* (31 August 1847).

323 *Cork Examiner* (23 August 1847).

324 *Cork Examiner* (30 August 1847).

325 Chief Poor Law Commissioner Edward Twistleton and Count Strzelecki, a noted philanthropist, initially an agent of the British Relief Association and later its sole agent.

326 HC, *Papers relating to proceedings for the relief of the distress, and state of the unions and workhouses, in Ireland. Fourth series – 1847*, Volume Page: LIV.29, Volume: 54, Paper Number: 896, p. 2. *ProQuest: U.K. Parliamentary Papers*.

327 NAI CSORP D7946, 3 September 1847.

328 *Cork Examiner* (20 September 1847).

329 NAI CSORP D7988, 23 September 1847.

330 NAI CSORP 79931/2, 30 September 1847.

331 NAI CSORP D79901/2, 7 October 1847.

332 CCCA BG/43/Vol A2, September 1847, *passim*.

333 *Cork Examiner* (10 September 1847).

334 *Cork Examiner* (20 September 1847).

335 *Cork Examiner* (24 September 1847).

336 CCCA BG/43/Vol A2, 28 September 1847.

337 *Cork Examiner* (1 October 1847).

338 *Southern Reporter* (2 October 1847).

339 *Cork Examiner* (6 October 1847).

340 *Southern Reporter* (9 October 1847).

341 *Cork Examiner* (11 October 1847).

342 *Cork Examiner* (11 October 1847); CCCA BG/43/Vol A2, 5 October 1847.

343 CCCA BG/43/Vol A2, October 1847, *passim*.

344 Denis Clarke appears to have been from Larch Hill in Co. Galway. He married Barbara St Leger. He died aged 70 in Dublin in 1887. https://civilrecords.irishgenealogy.ie/churchrecords/images/deaths_returns/deaths_1887/06198/4772496.pdf (accessed 28 September 2020)

345 HC, *Papers relating to proceedings for the relief of the distress, and state of the unions and workhouses, in Ireland. Fourth series – 1847*, Volume Page: LIV.29, Volume: 54, Paper Number: 896, p. 204–5. *ProQuest: U.K. Parliamentary Papers*.

346 Ibid, p. 206.

347 *Kerry Evening Post* (12 January 1848).

348 HC, *Papers relating to proceedings for the relief of the distress, and state of the unions and workhouses, in Ireland. Fourth series – 1847*, p. 208. *ProQuest: U.K. Parliamentary Papers*.

349 Ibid, p. 207.

350 This anomaly may have arisen due to Guardian Timothy O'Donovan's attempt to enfranchise Kilcrohane occupants so they could vote in county elections.

351 HC, *Papers relating to proceedings for the relief of the distress, and state of the unions and workhouses, in Ireland. Fourth series – 1847*, p. 207; HC, *Papers relating to proceedings for relief of distress, and state of unions and workhouses in Ireland, 1848*, Volume Page: LIV.313, LV.1, LVI.1, Paper Number: 919 955 999, pp. 206–11. *ProQuest: U.K. Parliamentary Papers*.

352 Ibid, pp. 249–52.

353 Willis had written a pamphlet comparing Dublin and London parishes in terms of sanitary and housing conditions: Thomas Willis, *Facts Connected with the Social and Sanitary Conditions of the Working Classes in the City of Dublin* (Dublin: 1845). He was an apothecary who later registered as a doctor and was a co-founder of the St Vincent de Paul Society in Ireland (see James Gerard Martin, 'The Society of St Vincent De Paul as an Emerging Social Phenomenon in Mid-Nineteenth Century Ireland', thesis, National Colleges of Ireland, 1993.)

354 BL/EP/B/2317, The Bantry Estate Collection, Special Collections & Archives, UCC Library, University College Cork, Ireland.

355 HC, *Papers relating to proceedings for relief of distress, and state of unions and workhouses in Ireland* (1848), p. 950. ProQuest: U.K. Parliamentary Papers.

356 Ibid, p. 15.

357 HC, *Papers relating to proceedings for relief of distress, and state of unions and workhouses in Ireland* (1848), Volume Page: LIV.313, LV.1, LVI.1, Paper Number: 919 955 999. *ProQuest: U.K. Parliamentary Papers*.

358 *Cork Examiner* (16 February 1848).

359 *Southern Reporter* (3 February 1848).

360 *Cork Examiner* (16 February 1848).

361 *Cork Examiner* (6 March 1848).

362 Daphne du Maurier's novel *Hungry Hill* was based on the Puxley family's story.

363 CCCA BG/43/Vol A3, Februry 1848, *passim*.

364 CCCA BG/43/Vol A3, March 1848, *passim*.

365 Denis O'Sullivan, E. Power, R. Orpen, Nathaniel Evanson, William Murphy, Anthony Nicholson, Richard Nicholson and James O'Sullivan.

366 HC, *First annual report of the Commissioners for Administering the Laws for Relief of the Poor in Ireland, with appendices*, Volume Page: XXXIII.377, Volume: 33, Paper Number: 963 (1848), p. 113. *ProQuest: U.K. Parliamentary Papers*.

367 HC, *Papers relating to proceedings for relief of distress, and state of unions and workhouses in Ireland* (1848), Volume Page: LIV.313, LV.1, LVI.1, Volume: 54;55;56, Paper Number: 919 955 999, pp. 951–7. *ProQuest: U.K. Parliamentary Papers*.

368 HC, *First annual report of the Commissioners for Administering the Laws for Relief of the Poor in Ireland, with appendices*, p. 121. *ProQuest: U.K. Parliamentary Papers*.

369 Viz.: Kilmocamogue 4s 7d, East Durrus 2s 11d, West Durrus 4s 2d, Kilcrohane 4s 7d, Kilcaskan 4s 7d, Kilcatherine 2s 11d, Killaconenagh 2s 11d, Kilnamanagh 2s 11d, Bantry 4s 2d (Bantry rate struck in July).

370 Paddy O'Keefe, a Bantry historian, spent years (unsuccessfully) attempting to track the passenger lists. His papers are in the Paddy O'Keefe collection in the Cork City and County Archives.

371 Paddy O'Keefe, CCCA letter, April 1960.

372 Paddy O'Keefe, CCCA, extracts from Lloyds records 1958.
373 *The Girl's Own Paper*, 4, 148 (1882), p. 53. Slightly adapted by author.
374 Emigration to British North America 1847–48, British Parliamentary Papers, 1847–48, XLVII (986), pp. 468–71, 473–9, CMSIED 9802558.
375 Irish Famine memorial Sydney, Famine orphan girl database. http://www.irishfaminememorial.org/en/orphans/database/ (accessed 21 July 2018).
376 Tisdall and Hutchins (Pratt correspondence 1838–1852), NLI MS 8685.
377 *Freeman's Journal* (11 May 1848). He married the eldest daughter of the Rector of Inchigeela.
378 *Constitution* (16 May 1848).
379 *Cork Examiner* (24 May 1848).
380 Christine Kinealy, *Repeal and Revolution 1848 in Ireland* (Manchester: Manchester University Press, 2009), p. 3.
381 *Cork Examiner* (7 June 1848); *Cork Examiner* (14 June 1848); *Examiner* (26 June 1848).
382 *Examiner* (11 February 1848).
383 *Morning Advertiser* (17 June 1848).
384 *Cork Examiner* (26 May 1848).
385 *Limerick Chronicle* (10 May 1848).
386 CCCA BG/43/Vol AA2, 19 October 1849.
387 *Constitution* (15 July 1848).
388 *Cork Examiner* (10 July 1848); *Dublin Weekly Nation* (15 July 1848).
389 *Evening Mail* (31 July 1848).
390 *Kerry Evening Post* (2 August 1848).
391 *The Pilot* (4 August 1848).
392 *Constitution* (3 August 1848).
393 HC, *Papers relating to proceedings for relief of distress, and state of unions and workhouses in Ireland, 1848*, p. 22. ProQuest: U.K. Parliamentary Papers.
394 CCCA BG/43/Vol A3, 29 August 1848.
395 HC, *Papers relating to proceedings for relief of distress, and state of unions and workhouses in Ireland, 1848*, p. 1. ProQuest: U.K. Parliamentary Papers. Relief to schoolchildren was closed on 20 August 1848.
396 Christine Kinealy, 'The British Relief Association and the Great Famine in Ireland', *French Journal of British Studies* (2014), p. 21.
397 *Southern Reporter* (17 August 1848).
398 *Bristol Times and Mirror* (19 August 1848).
399 *Weekly Chronicle (London)* (19 August 1848).
400 *Dublin Evening Post* (5 September 1848).
401 *Cork Examiner* (2 March 1849).
402 *Cork Examiner* (2 February 1849).
403 CCCA BG/43/A3 (September 1848)
404 CCCA BG/43/A3 (September–21 November 1848)
405 HC, *Papers relating to the aid afforded to the distressed unions in the west of Ireland*, Volume Page: XLVIII.7, 77, 87, 121, 171, Volume: 48;77;87;121;171, Paper Number: 1010 1019 1023 1060 1077, p. 21. ProQuest: U.K. Parliamentary Papers.
406 Ibid.

407 Ibid, p. 22.
408 *Cork Examiner* (6 November 1848); HC, *First annual report of the Commissioners for Administering the Laws for Relief of the Poor in Ireland, with appendices*, pp. 162–4. *ProQuest: U.K. Parliamentary Papers.*
409 *Freeman's Journal* (27 October 1848); *Ballyshannon Herald* (2 July 1847).
410 HC, *Papers relating to the aid afforded to the distressed unions in the west of Ireland*, p. 23. *ProQuest: U.K. Parliamentary Papers.*
411 Ibid, p. 25.
412 HC, *Fourteenth report from the Select Committee on Poor Laws (Ireland); together with the proceedings of the committee, minutes of evidence, appendix, and index*, Paper Number: 572, 28 December 1848, p. 114. *ProQuest: U.K. Parliamentary Papers.*
413 HC, *Papers relating to proceedings for the relief of the distress, and state of unions and workhouses, in Ireland. Eighth series – 1849*, Volume Page: XLVIII.221, Volume: 48, Paper Number: 1042, December 1848, p. 101. *ProQuest: U.K. Parliamentary Papers.*
414 CCCA, BG 43 A4 (November 1848–January 1849)
415 *Constitution* (16 January 1849). The depots were in Kilcrohane, Carrigboy, Bantry, Glengarriff, Adrigole, Eyeries, Castletown. It seems likely that relief would have been distributed in those places as well.
416 Jeremiah O'Mahony, Ahakista, personal communication.
417 *Cork Examiner* (1 January 1849).
418 HC, *Fourteenth report from the Select Committee on Poor Laws (Ireland); together with the proceedings of the committee, minutes of evidence, appendix, and index*, p. 114. *ProQuest: U.K. Parliamentary Papers.*
419 HC, *Papers relating to proceedings for the relief of the distress, and state of unions and workhouses, in Ireland. Eighth series, 1849*, pp. 102–3. *ProQuest: U.K. Parliamentary Papers.*
420 *Cork Examiner* (1 January 1849).
421 *Times* (4 January 1849).
422 *Shipping and Mercantile Gazette* (25 January 1849).
423 *Limerick Chronicle* (28 February 1849).
424 Patrick Hickey, 'A Coffin-Cross from Bantry, 1847', *The Furrow*, 39, 5 (May 1988), pp. 333–4.
425 Ibid.
426 *Southern Reporter* (10 Februrary 1849).
427 *Cork Examiner* (12 Februrary 1849).
428 *Cork Examiner* (16 February 1849).
429 CCCA, BG 43 A4, February 1849.
430 *Cork Examiner* (19 February 1849).
431 *Southern Reporter* (24 February 1849).
432 *Tipperary Vindicator* (7 March 1849).
433 *Freeman's Journal* (8 February 1849).
434 *Dublin Evening Post* (3 March 1849).
435 *Southern Reporter* (1 March 1849).
436 *Cork Examiner* (16 February 1849).
437 *London Daily News* (27 March 1849).
438 *Cork Examiner* (30 March 1848).

439 *Wexford Independent* (14 April 1849). Somers Payne was John W. Payne's father. John Payne did not attend, almost certainly because his infant son and wife had just died.

440 *Dublin Evening Mail* (16 April 1849).

441 HC, *Rate in aid (Ireland.) Account showing the total sum assessed as rate in aid on each union in Ireland, under the act 12 Vict. c. 24, &c. – also, account showing the total sum appropriated to each union out of the general rate in aid fund, down to the 31st December 1851*, Volume Page: XLVI.125, Volume: 46, Paper Number: 87 (1852) p. 3. ProQuest: U.K. Parliamentary Papers. Statistics published in 1852 show that the Bantry Union contribution to the Rate-in-Aid fund was £560 19s 1d, of which £411 10s 3d was paid by December 1851. By 1851 the union had received £7,808 10s, of which £7,305 10s was applied to 'destitution' and £518 to workhouse clothing, bedding and accommodation.

442 *London Standard* (1 May 1849).

443 *Downpatrick Recorder* (28 April 1849).

444 *Cork Examiner* (13 April 1849)

445 *Morning Post* (15 May 1849).

446 *Southern Reporter* (12 May 1849). These amounts contradict an earlier reference. Possibly the amount was reduced without a notation in the minutes.

447 *Southern Reporter* (12 May 1849).

448 He was previously posted to Tipperary Union.

449 HC, *Papers relating to the aid afforded to the distressed unions in the west of Ireland*, p. 32. ProQuest: U.K. Parliamentary Papers.

450 Ibid, p. 43. (The total rate amount was £8,465, of which £6,255 was collected.)

451 *Cork Examiner* (25 May 1849).

452 *Newry Cork Examiner* (26 May 1849); *London Evening Standard* (28 May 1849).

453 *Southern Reporter* (29 May 1849).

454 *Dublin Evening Mail* (25 May 1849); *Southern Reporter* (26 May 1849).

455 CCCA BG/43/Vol. AA2, June 1849, passim.

456 *Cork Examiner* (21 February 1849).

457 *Cork Examiner* (1 June 1849).

458 *Freeman's Journal* (9 June 1849).

459 *Essex Standard* (22 June 1849).

460 CCCA BG/43/Vol. A4, May 1849, passim.

461 CCCA, BG/43/Vol. A4, 3 July 1849.

462 HC, *Report of the Commissioners of Health, Ireland, on the epidemics of 1846 to 1850*, Volume Page: XLI.239, Volume: 41, Paper Number: 1562 (1853), p. 36. ProQuest: U.K. Parliamentary Papers.

463 *Dublin Evening Post* (7 July 1849).

464 *Southern Reporter* (14 July 1849).

465 CCCA BG/43/Vol. AA2 July 1849 passim.

466 CCCA BG/43/Vol. AA2 (note dated 18 July 1849).

467 *Freeman's Journal* (23 July 1849).

468 *Illustrated London News* (4 August 1849).

469 *Dublin Evening Mail* (27 July 1849).

470 *Balls Weekly Messenger* (10 September 1849).
471 CCCA BG/43/Vol. AA2, 20 July 1849.
472 *Southern Reporter* (6 October 1849).
473 CCCA BG/43/Vol. AA2, 17 September 1849.
474 *Southern Reporter* (20 September 1849).
475 *Freeman's Journal* (8 August 1849).
476 *Illustrated London News* (7 July 1849). Total fare from London via a steamer from Bristol to Killarney amounted to £3 2s.
477 *Southern Reporter* (8 July 1849).
478 *Morning Advertiser* (28 August 1849).
479 RIA (Royal Academy of Ireland) 4/B/9/32, 9 September 1849; RIA 4/B/9/31 (1), 8 September 1849.
480 *Morning Post* (24 September 1849).
481 *Illustrated London News* (29 September 1849).
482 *Freeman's Journal* (27 August 1849).
483 Donnelly, *The Land and the People*, p. 122. This statistic is from 1851.
484 *Tuam Herald* (1 September 1849).
485 HC, *First report of the commissioners for inquiring into the number and boundaries of Poor-Law Unions and electoral divisions in Ireland*, Volume Page: XXIII.369, 393, Volume: 23;393, Paper Number: 1015 1015-II, 1849, *passim*. *ProQuest: U.K. Parliamentary Papers*.
486 *Southern Reporter* (6 October 1849).
487 Jeremiah Sullivan, Alexander Sullivan, Daniel Donovan in Bantry Union, and William Murphy, Timothy Harrington and Timothy Donovan in Castletown Union.
488 *Dublin Evening Mail* (15 February 1850).
489 *Clare Journal* (13 September 1849). He and his wife had a second daughter born in Bantry.
490 http://www.willcalendars.nationalarchives.ie/search/cwa/details.jsp?id=1639525737 (accessed 18 June 2019)
491 HC, *Fourth report from the Select Committee of the House of Lords appointed to inquire into the operation of the Irish Poor Law, and the expediency of making any amendment in its enactments; and to report thereon to the House; together with the minutes of evidence*, Volume Page: XVI.543, Volume: 16, Paper Number: 365 (1849), p. 807. *ProQuest: U.K. Parliamentary Papers*. The census figures do not contain the inaccuracy of the PLC and Boundary Commission figures, which had let an extra 6,000 inhabitants slip into the numbers for Kilcatherine in the early 1840s.
492 HC, *The census of Ireland for the year 1851. Part I. Showing the area, population, and number of houses by townlands and electoral divisions. County of Cork. (West Riding.)*, Volume Page: XCI.499, Volume: 91, Paper Number: 1551, pp. 3–23. *ProQuest: U.K. Parliamentary Papers*.
493 *Southern Reporter* (3 October 1849).
494 At the first board meeting on 6 November 1849, Richard O'Donovan was in the chair. Also present were John W. Payne, Richard Evanson, Michael Murphy, John Bird, Richard Tobin and Robert Warren.

495 HC, *Poor relief (Ireland). Returns of the number of persons who were receiving relief on the last day of February 1850, in each union in Ireland; – and of the number of persons, distinguishing the males from the females, on in-door relief, on the same day, between the ages of fifteen and forty, who have been inmates of the workhouse for more than a year*, Volume Page: L.181, Volume: 50, Paper Number: 377 (1850), p. 1. *ProQuest: U.K. Parliamentary Papers*.

496 CCCA BG/43/Vol. A6, August 1850, passim.

497 Thomas Swanton, RIA 4/B/10/55, 17 October 1850.

498 HC, *Fifth annual report of the Commissioners for Administering the Laws for Relief of the Poor in Ireland: with appendices*, Volume Page: XXIII.155, Volume: 23, Paper Number: 1530 (1852), p. 170. *ProQuest: U.K. Parliamentary Papers*.

499 *Cork Examiner* (13 April 1849).

500 Kevin Hourihan, 'Town growth in West Cork: Bantry 1600–1960', *Cork Historical and Archaeological Society*, LXXXII (1977), pp. 89–92.

501 Landed Estates Court Rentals, 1850–1885, Findmypast. https://search.findmypast.ie/record?id=ire%2flec%2f4506856%2f00167&parentid=ire%2flec%2f4506856%2f00166%2f001 (accessed 28 September 2020)

502 David Lloyd, *Irish Culture and Colonial Modernity, 1800–2000: The Transformation of Oral Space* (California: University of California, 2011), p. 71.

503 John Forbes, *Memorandums made in Ireland in the autumn of 1852* (1853), p. 104.

504 HC, *The census of Ireland for the year 1851. Part V. Tables of deaths. Vol. II. Containing the tables and index*, Volume Page: XXIX.261, XXX.1, Volume: 29;30, Paper Number: 2087-I 2087-II (1856), p. 90–5. *ProQuest: U.K. Parliamentary Papers*.

505 Cormac Ó Gráda, 'Yardsticks for Irish Workhouses during the Great Famine', in Virginia Crossman and Peter Gray (eds), *Poverty and Welfare in Ireland, 1838–1948* (Dublin: Irish Academic Press, 2011), p. 31.

506 *Cork Examiner* (19 November 1849).

507 *Kerry Evening Post* (12 January 1848).

508 *Constitution* (8 June 1887).

509 Anonymous elderly man in de Barras café, Bantry, 2018.

510 Seamus Crowley, 'Famine in Bantry' (unpublished paper: Cork County Library, 1971).

511 Donal Fitzgerald, 'The Famine in Bantry', *Bantry Historical and Archaeological Society*, 1 (June 1991), p. 87.

512 Michael J. Carroll, *Bay of Destiny* (Cork: Bantry Design Studios, 1996), p. 263.

Geraldine Powell grew up in Dublin in a family that emphasised scholarship. The nursery walls were covered with peeling maps of eighteenth-century Europe. Her earliest memories include running around ancient ruins during weekend outings of the Royal Antiquarian Society. Summers in the Ballingeary Gaeltacht provided a nationalist influence, while an education by English nuns did somewhat the opposite.

After qualifying in medicine, Geraldine moved to the United States. She worked as a pathologist, then as a psychiatrist with Vietnam veterans, and later with prisoners and in the community health system. In addition to her medical career, she studied creative writing at the University of California, San Diego. A few of her short stories were broadcast in the United States and on RTÉ.

During the 1980s and 1990s, Geraldine, her husband and three children visited West Cork frequently and bought a holiday home there, a cottage in an old clachan near Bantry. Over twenty-four years of visits, rehabbing, exploring and reading about the area, she became fascinated by the extreme contrasts and complexity of society in nineteenth-century Munster. When, in 2016, she returned to live in Ireland, she continued researching and received an MA in local history from UCC.

Geraldine Powell now lives with her husband in Dungarvan, Co. Cork.